Instructor's Resource Manual

for

Frey, Botan, and Kreps
Investigating Communication
An Introdction to Research Methods
Second Edition

Prepared by

Jim L. Query, Jr.
Loyola University Chicago

Allyn and Bacon
Boston   London   Toronto   Sydney   Tokyo   Singapore

Copyright © 2000 by Allyn & Bacon
A Pearson Education Company
160 Gould Street
Needham Heights, Massachusetts 02494

Internet: www.abacon.com

All rights reserved. The contents, or parts thereof, may be reproduced for use with *Investigating Communication:* An Introduction to Research Methods, Second Edition, by Lawrence R. Frey, Carl H. Botan, and Gary L. Kreps, provided such reproductions bear copyright notice, but may not be reproduced in any form for any other purpose without written permission from the copyright owner.

ISBN 0-205-31377-9

Printed in the United States of America

10 9 8 7 6 5 4 3 2 1   03 02 01 00

PREFACE

On behalf of the text's authors---Professors Lawrence Frey, Carl Botan, and Gary Kreps—it is my pleasure to welcome each of you to the second edition of the Instructor's Resource Manual (IRM). Working diligently over several months and guided by the tireless editing of Professor Larry Frey, it is my firm belief that you will find this manual to be a significant ally in the classroom. As much as possible, Larry and I have attempted to create a manual that will appeal to a variety of communication courses and areas of expertise spanning several methodological boundaries. We have also diligently strived to reach out to instructors just beginning to teach a methods course as well as the more experienced professionals.

I would be remiss if I did not indicate that this was my first IRM; however, I have been teaching quantitative research methods since 1990, and qualitative research methods for one year. I was able, then, to draw from my past experience as well as what has worked effectively in my current research method courses.

While you will find several new features present in this edition of the IRM, from my perspective, one in particular stands out and it may not be as readily visible as others: My underlying teaching philosophy [www.homestead.com/profjims/teachingphilosophy.html]. Briefly, it is drawn from three primary sources including my undergraduate and graduate student learning experiences; my teaching experiences predominately with undergraduate students; and the writings of Professors Dewey, Kreps, Mill, Rogers, Walzer, and Whitehead. In general, these scholars reinforce the values of a liberal arts education, encourage teachers to develop instructional strategies tailored to a variety of learning styles, and champion the adoption of a "win-win" mentality between teachers and students. Subsequently, the bulk of my teaching rests on at least five major premises: students must be able to demonstrate their understanding of key communication principles and concepts across contexts; a strong theoretical grounding/ preparation should enhance students' critical thinking, writing, and application skills; students should be challenged to learn and excel; students should have a voice concerning many aspects of the course; and teachers should help students meet high performance standards.

Admittedly, the preceding are lofty goals and no one piece of scholarship could hope to achieve all of those. To a great extent, however, my teaching philosophy shaped many of the exercises, assignments, student study tips, and questions contained in this IRM. Larry and I also made some "tough" choices in what to include in this edition of the IRM. You will, for example, find somewhat fewer exercises than in the first edition. You will, however, now find detailed, complete sentence outlines for each chapter which you may also disseminate to your students. There are several other NEW features as well and some of these include:

- Hollywood Squares' Learning Simulation
- Scientific Method Exercise
- Current Event Article Analysis Exercise
- Multiple Choice and Essay Exam Study Tips For Students

- Multiple Choice Question Challenge Procedure
- Detailed Handouts for a Quantitative Research Project
- Sample Informed Consent Form
- Potential Net Sites Facilitating Plagiarism
- Film Lists for Understanding Quantitative and Qualitative Research Methods
- Handout for a Qualitative Research Project
- New Multiple Choice Questions
- New True and False Questions
- New Essay/Short Answer Questions

Regarding the exam questions, you should be able to discern that a significant number of the items are drawn from extant research and current events that help "drive home" the saliency of the material. The multiple choice (MC) challenge procedure is also designed to provide you and your students with a "safety net" to address questions that could be interpreted in another way than what I or Larry originally intended. We would also encourage each of you to subject the MC questions to an item analysis and then share your results with us. This type of analysis enables test writers to discern the discriminating power of individual questions, the degree of difficulty posed to the upper and lower sections of the class, and to identify "problematic" question stems and/or choices. Most universities offer this type of service as long as opscan sheets are used to record student responses. One final note here, we strongly encourage that you use a variety of testing methods to help recognize varying student writing and analytical skills.

Regarding citations, note that the majority of sources used in the IRM appears in the text's bibliography; thus, only a few full citations appear in this manual.

ACKNOWLEDGMENTS

This manual would not have been possible without the help of several talented and caring individuals. I would like to first profoundly thank Larry Frey, Carl Botan, and Gary Kreps for providing me with this wonderful and most challenging opportunity. Their confidence and trust meant a great deal to me. I would also like to deeply thank Ms. Karon Bowers of Allyn and Bacon, and her assistant, Ms. Jennifer Becker. I especially appreciated all the understanding and patience so aptly demonstrated by Karon. Allyn and Bacon is lucky to have such a consummate professional on board.

Although this manual bears my name, and I alone should be held accountable for any errors, I owe Larry Frey a great debt. He is without question the most meticulous editor I have ever encountered. The overall caliber of this manual was significantly enhanced due to his diligence and impeccable standards. Thank you so much dude.

This manual also would not have been possible without the unwavering support and writing contributions of many gifted and skilled friends, colleagues, family members, and students. These include: Lyle Flint, Ball State University; Pat Arneson, Duquesne University; Connie Fletcher,

Dan Brower, John Smarrelli, all at Loyola University Chicago; Ms. Nikki Caso, Loyola University Chicago; Ms. Cathy Denise Tapley, State of Florida Corrections Department; Ethel Monroe, Loyola University Chicago, Ellen Walsh Bonaguro, Ithaca College; Patricia Geist, San Diego State University; Sunwolf, Santa Clara University; Patricia Amason, University of Arkansas: and Korrie Klier, Colorado State University. I would like to extend a very special recognition to Nikki and Cathy Denise for their wonderful editorial work and writing contributions. In addition to being outstanding learners, they both have great hearts.

My family has been like a "rock" of support to me during this process and throughout my entire academic career. I would not have accomplished all that I have without their priceless support. I am privileged to have such them in my life and at my side: My mom, Treva; my dad, Jim; my brother Johnny; my sister, Rosie, and my "adopted family" the Boyds---Daryle, Sherry, Norm, and Tommy (deceased). A very special thanks goes to my daughter, Julie, for all her hugs, kisses, and understanding while Dad struggled to finish this manual. I could ask for no greater gift.

I would also like to thank so many of my past and present students who rose to the challenge of the "dreaded" methods' course at Ohio University, the University of Tulsa, and Loyola University Chicago. I appreciate very much all their sharing of "lived experience" that greatly enriched our classroom discussions, and my life as well.

Jim L. Query, Jr., Ph.D.
Associate Professor
Loyola University Chicago
jquery@luc.edu

TABLE OF CONTENTS

Preface

Sample Course Syllabus	1
Possible Multiple Choice Exam Study Tips	4
Student Quiz/Exam Challenge Procedures	5
Possible Essay Exam Study Tips	6
Prospectus and Final Paper Assignment	7
Detailed Information About Writing A Prospectus and Final Research Paper	9
Student Data Preparation and Term Paper Checklist	15
Sample Informed Consent Form	17
Potential Net Paper Sites Facilitating Plagiarism	18
Potential Assignments in a Qualitative Communication Methods Course	23
Student Information About Writing a Qualitative Communication Research Paper	24
Professor Exercise	26
Possible Class Interview Exercise	27
Hollywood Squares Simulation: A Template Possible Responses for Celebrities	28
Research Process Exercise: Using the Scientific Method	34
Current Event Article Analysis Possible Assignment	35

Films for Understanding Research Methods   37

Films for Understanding Qualitative Methods   38

Methods Reference Sources   40

Chapter 1:
Introduction to the Research Culture, Detailed Outline
Multiple Choice, T/F, Short Answer/Essay Questions   46

Chapter 2:
Asking Questions About Communication, Detailed Outline
Multiple Choice, T/F, Short Answer/Essay Questions   59

Chapter 3:
Finding, Reading, and Using Research, Detailed Outline
Multiple Choice, T/F, Short Answer/Essay Questions   75

Chapter 4:
Observing and Measuring Communication Variables, Detailed Outline
Multiple Choice, T/F, Short Answer/Essay Questions   91

Chapter 5:
Designing Valid Communication Research, Detailed Outline
Multiple Choice, T/F, Short Answer/Essay Questions   107

Chapter 6:
Research Ethics and Politics, Detailed Outline
Multiple Choice, T/F, Short Answer/Essay Questions   124

Chapter 7:
Experimental Research, Detailed Outline
Multiple Choice, T/F, Short Answer/Essay Questions   138

Chapter 8:
Survey Research, Detailed Outline
Multiple Choice, T/F, Short Answer/Essay Questions   153

Chapter 9:
Textual Analysis, Detailed Outline
Multiple Choice, T/F, Short Answer/Essay Questions   166

Chapter 10:
Naturalistic Research, Detailed Outline
Multiple Choice, T/F, Short Answer/Essay Questions   176

Chapter 11:
Describing Quantitative Data, Detailed Outline
Multiple Choice, T/F, Short Answer/Essay Questions   188

Chapter 12:
Inferring From Data: Estimation and Significance Testing,
Detailed Outline, Multiple Choice, T/F, Short Answer/Essay Questions   198

Chapter 13:
Analyzing Differences Between Groups, Detailed Outline
Multiple Choice, T/F, Short Answer/Essay Questions   209

Chapter 14:
Analyzing Relationships Between Variables, Detailed Outline
Multiple Choice, T/F, Short Answer/Essay Questions   219

Chapter 15:
Epilogue: Concluding Research, Detailed Outline
Multiple Choice, T/F, Short Answer/Essay Questions   229

Sample Syllabus: Communication Research Methods*
*This template may be modified to accommodate a quarter system as well.

[Insert Professor Information]

Introduction

Along with effective communication skills and a good working knowledge of business principles, understanding communication theory and research methods is one of the most important skills for the communication major in today's marketplace. The goals of this course are to help you become a knowledgeable consumer and a limited producer of communication theory and research.

To accomplish these goals, information will be provided that enables you to:
1) Understand the relationship between philosophy, theory, and research methods in the study of communication
2) Understand major theories, research questions/hypotheses, and variables that are important to the current study of communication
3) Understand four research methodologies used to investigate communication behavior: experimental; survey; textual analysis (rhetorical criticism, content analysis, interaction analysis, and performance studies); and naturalistic inquiry
4) Understand quantitative data analysis procedures within the broader context of the communication inquiry process
5) Critically evaluate communication and other behavioral/scientific research
6) Design and conduct your own communication research project

Required Textbooks

Frey, L. R., Botan, C. H., & Kreps, G. L. (2000). Investigating communication: An introduction to research methods (2nd ed.). Needham Heights, MA: Allyn & Bacon.

Frey, L. R., Botan, C. H., Friedman, P. G., & Kreps, G. L. (1992). Interpreting communication research: A case study approach. Englewood Cliffs, NJ: Prentice Hall. (Labeled CB in syllabus)

Course Calendar

Aug 30-Sept 1   Introduction to the Course

Sept 6-20   Part I: Foundations of Communication Research
    Chapter 1 (TB): Introduction to the Research Culture
    Chapter 1 (CB): Interpreting Communication Research
    Chapter 2 (TB): Asking Questions About Communication
    Chapter 3 (TB): Finding, Reading, and Using Research

Sept 22-Oct 4   Part II: Planning and Designing Communication Research
                Chapter 4 (TB): Observing and Measuring Communication Variables
                Chapter 5 (TB): Designing Valid Communication Research
                Chapter 6 (TB): Research Ethics and Politics
Oct 6-Nov 1   Part III: Methodologies for Conducting Communication Research
                Chapter 7 (TB) & Section I (CB): Experimental Research
                Chapter 8 (TB) & Section II (CB): Survey Research
                Chapter 9 (TB) & Section III (CB): Textual Analysis
                Chapter 10 (TB) & Section IV (CB): Naturalistic Inquiry
Nov 3-Dec 1   Part IV: Analyzing and Interpreting Quantitative Data
                Chapter 11 (TB): Describing Quantitative Data
                Chapter 12 (TB): Inferring From Data: Estimation and Significance Testing
                Chapter 13 (TB): Analyzing Differences Between Groups
                Chapter 14 (TB): Analyzing Relationship Between Variables
Dec 6   Communication Research Methods: A Summary
                Chapter 15 (TB): Epilogue: Concluding Research

Course Evaluation

1. Examinations (15% each): Three examinations are scheduled for October 1, October 29, and Friday, December 18, 10:20am-12:20. The examinations are based on identifications/definitions and short explanations. Failure to take an examination will result in a grade of "F" for that examination. There are no make-up examinations given in this course, except for extreme circumstances (e.g., medical emergency).

2. Final Communication Research Project (30% for written final paper; 15% for prospectus): Each person/dyad/group will complete a final research project about some aspect of communication. Each person/dyad/group must submit a prospectus (which is the first three parts of the final paper: introduction, review of the literature, and research question or hypothesis) on October 8. Two copies of the final paper are due December 1, and a short, non-graded oral summary of the paper will be given during the class periods of December 1-3. (This presentation is factored into the participation grade, explained below, in terms of whether it was given.) Failure to complete the prospectus on time will result in a grade of "F" for both the prospectus and the final paper. Failure to complete the final paper on time will result in a grade of "F" for that assignment. (See handout for other information about this paper.)

    Any communication theory, variable, or context is permissible to study for this final research project. The purpose may be to describe communicative behavior but most projects go beyond this to examine how communication is related to other variables. The following list might give you some ideas for communication research projects (also see the handout of previous high-quality projects done for this course):

A. Study the effects of psychological/personality traits (such as people with high versus

low self- esteem) on communicative behavior.
- B. Examine the persuasive effects of different sources (such as high versus low credible sources), messages, channels, contexts, and receivers.
- C. Categorize/code and/or examine the effects of a particular type of communicative behavior (such as self-disclosure or compliance-gaining strategies) within an interpersonal relationship.
- D. Examine the nature and effects of nonverbal behaviors (such as facial expressions, eye contact, gestures, or the use of space or time).
- E. Examine the relationship between communicative behavior and various outcomes (such as satisfaction or productivity) within a group or organization.
- F. Study communication differences between various populations (such as males and females, African Americans and Caucasians, U.S. Americans and members of other cultures).
- G. Study changes in newspaper coverage of important topics or the content of television shows over the past 10-20 years.
- H. Conduct a media gratifications study that examines the reasons why people use various mass media.
- I. Examine the effects of various mass media use on beliefs, attitudes, values, and/or behavior (such as the effects of televised violence on the development of aggressive tendencies in children).
3. Participation (10%): Participation is evaluated based on attendance at sessions where in-class exercises are used (of which there is almost one daily), verbal participation in class discussions (i.e., sharing your viewpoints, which helps make the discussions more lively, as well as asking questions about the course content, which helps both you and others understand the material better), and your work on any additional assignments required for the course (such as turning in a list of potential topics to study, finding and documenting various communication library sources, critiquing an article in a communication journal, etc.).

Final Notes:

1. Academic dishonesty in the form of cheating and/or plagiarism in all its forms (from using the ideas, organization, supporting sources, and/or words of another [including other students] without giving credit to the original author, to allowing or paying another to write a paper for one's own benefit, to purchasing and using a pre-written paper for course credit, as well as using another's paper available on the Internet), will result in a grade of "F" for the assignment, an "F" for the course, and referral to student judiciaries. Academic misconduct on an examination also results in course failure and referral to student judiciaries.
2. The deadlines for all academic work in this course are "hard" deadlines; no late work will be accepted, except in cases of extreme circumstances (e.g., medical emergency) and/or university-authorized class absences.
3. No data for your final paper may be collected without my expressed approval of the

data-collection methods and sample. Failure to comply will result in a grade of "F" for the final paper.
4. People who get into trouble in this course do so by not keeping in touch with me and/or by not coming to class. Make appointments with me or come in during my office hours and talk with me about your final research project or any other aspects of this course. Please take full advantage of this offer. The more I know about what and how you are doing, the better you are likely to do in this course.

Possible Multiple Choice Exam Study Tips For Your Students

- To prepare for the mutliple choice part part of the exam, you may want to have your students develop and respond to a series of Self-Review Questions (SRQs). Examples are numerous and can be easily created by the students themselves. For instance, one possible SRQ could be: Explain, recognize, and evaluate (ERE) proprietary research. Another could be, describe the implications of nominal data measurements.
- Students should be encouraged to create and work through SRQs on a regular basis. All of us lead busy lives and some "cramming" is unavoidable. Extensive last-minute preparation, however, is highly associated with lower performance and higher test anxiety. I emphasize the preceding points as much as possible.
- Drawing from the modeled multiple choice questions, you can create sample quiz/exam questions for practice purposes. I typically use 8-10 sample questions before every quiz and exam. All professors, in varying degrees, test in unique ways. It has been my experience that the sample questions lower student anxiety and help engender a coaching type of climate in the classroom.
- To help students to organize and recall material, you may encourage them to develop some mnemonic devices or hooks and incorporate some of these into your lectures. For example, you may use acronyms like DAPF to help them remember the descriptive, predictive, assumption-laden, and falsifiable characteristics of a theory. These devices should be used in moderation.
- Encourage your students to vary the order of their study. Most memory experts agree that typically information at the beginning and end is better recalled than the information residing in the middle.
- As much as possible, use current event articles to reinforce the understanding and retention of key concepts and principles. For instance, I have found that few students miss the concept of "representativeness" after reading about a mammogram study that failed to use a representative sample. Local and national newspapers are a wonderful resource (see the current event exercise).
- Encourage students to develop "fun" simulations like Hollywood Squares to better grasp the material. I also encourage them to develop conversations with others and within themselves as they work through the myriad of material. I have found that if a student can explain for example, random sampling, to a friend, then, he or she can explain that same concept well on the exam.
- Students should be advised that rote learning alone will not be sufficient to pass the

course. The exam's questions will test their ability to understand and apply theoretical and research principles and concepts across situations. Although such "applied" items may seem difficult, one can handle most examples if he/she is able to explain, recognize, and evaluate the target concepts and principles.

As the students develop their own research project, encourage them to apply the material to their study. In this way, saliency is enhanced and the "intellectual challenge" of many concepts is lessened.

Student Quiz/Exam Challenge Procedures
For Multiple Choice Items

While we have taken considerable care in constructing the multiple choice questions, it is possible that students may feel their response is "equally as likely" as the keyed choice. The procedure below allows students to voice those concerns and if the instructor retains possession of the quizzes and exams, then, successful challenges can aid the development of additionally effective questions. I have used this procedure successfully for several years and it does foster a "win-win" climate.

Instructions

The purpose of this handout is to identify the necessary steps for successfully challenging a multiple choice item on a quiz or hour exam. Please note, also, that I review the computer-generated item analysis for each question prior to the exam's return. Hence, preliminary adjustments are possible. These procedures only apply to the multiple-choice part of the quizzes and exams. All challenges must be written and legible.

Number of Potential Challenges

6 per each hour exam
3 per each quiz

Step 1

Using 4-5 sentences, explain your response. That is, why did you choose it? Cite evidence or reveal your logic. "It looked good" will not work here.

Step 2

Using 4-5 sentences, explain my keyed response. That is, why did I choose it? Cite evidence or explicate my reasoning. "He's the prof" will not work here.

Step 3

Using 4-5 sentences, demonstrate how your response is equally as likely as my keyed response. Remember, the standard here is not one of "better;" it is one of equal plausibility.

Possible Impact

Depending on the cogency of your challenge, you may receive full, partial, or no credit. Only those students who successfully challenge an item will receive subsequent credit. All challenges are due one week after the quiz/exam.

Possible Essay Exam Study Tips For Your Students

- To prepare for the essay part of the exam, you may want to have your students develop and reproduce an outline. Many former students have used this technique successfully. Please remember, to remind them, however, that they cannot bring the outline into class unless of course, you opt for more of an open book or modified take home exam approach.
- Another key strategy is to urge your students to be sure to demonstrate their understanding of the concepts and principles in question. It also has been helpful for many of them to assume they are writing to another college friend, while still using the academic style of third person. They are also encouraged to avoid mere reproduction of information without sufficient explanation and analysis.
- As most classes are pressed for time, and it may not always be possible to hold an essay exam separate from the objective part of the exams (e.g., classes that meet once weekly), it is often a good idea to have students use only detailed case to "drive home" their understanding of key concepts and principles, Multiple examples, while ideal, may not be practical.
- To save time, I always encourage my students to provide a legend of abbreviations at the top margin of the paper. Additionally, they should use those consistently throughout the essay. Some examples could include: comm= communication; sci. method= scientific method; etc. The caliber of the essay exam should not be unnecessarily lowered due to one's lack of physical hand and finger speed.
- Finally, I recommend to all my students that they "build-in" at least five to eight minutes to review and proof their written essays.

Prospectus and Final Paper Assignment

The purpose of this handout is to ID my expectations and tips for the term paper. To ease your perusal, an outline format is employed. PLEASE PLAN YOUR PREP TIME NOW.

Ideal GroupSize = 3-4 Individuals

While you must coordinate your activities and cooperate with one another, each member writes an individually-authored prospectus. For the final paper, individual sections will be authored by all class members. You may also choose to complete the assignment alone.

Optional risk-free prospectus due date: March 9, 1999.

Final Prospectus Due Date: March 25, 1999.

Paper Due Date: April 20, 1999.

Oral Presentations: April 20, 1999.

Weight: Prospectus @ 18%; Paper @ 27%.

Total Length Parameters:
While I am reluctant to specify a fixed range, most successful completed papers have spanned 25-35 pages (not including data tables, appendices, references). Sections 1-3 below comprise the prospectus.

Required Sources:
At least 15, including your texts. To aid your efforts, you should also draw from the forthcoming bib, "recent publications in Communication journals."

Format:
All papers should adhere to the standards specified in the Writing Standard Guide, follow correct documentation procedures (APA), and must be typed using double-spacing. Assume also, that you are writing to a theory and research neophyte. A "neophyte" is one who is new to an area, and thus, has much to discover.

PRIOR APPROVAL REQUIRED:
NO DATA FOR YOUR STUDY MAY BE COLLECTED UNTIL THE PROFESSOR HAS APPROVED IN WRITING YOUR DATA-COLLECTION METHODS AND SAMPLE. NON-COMPLIANCE WILL RESULT IN A GRADE OF "F." NO AUTHORIZATION WILL BE FORTHCOMING FOR PROSPECTI WHICH RECEIVE AN "F."

Assignment Explication:
1). Select and describe a COMMUNICATION-BASED event or situation which intrigues you and/or the group. Your analysis should describe the nature of the event or situation, explicate its history, and detail key outcomes that are shaped by communication. Some possible events/situations include: relationship development, maintenance, and/or termination among

adolescents, young adults, middle-aged adults, or the elderly; communication between parents and children; communication among siblings; communication with terminally-ill individuals; communication in support groups; communication between students and instructors; communication among health care providers; communication between spouses; communication of health promoting messages via mass media campaigns; communication with battered women; communication with sexually abused individuals; communication with homeless individuals; or communication with disabled individuals. Of course, there are many other possibilities, and you are not limited to the preceding topic areas. <u>The key here is to focus on the communicative patterns of individuals in some context which excites, perplexes, or challenges you and/or the group.</u> [LABEL AS INTRO SECTION] **Be advised, however, that this section is not a brief overview. In the past, most successful authors have used several pages to provide an overview of the selected topic.**

2). Justify your selection of the topic. Describe its prevalence, implications for individuals, families, organizations, and/or society at large. Focus your analysis by indicating why others should study the selected topic. Also, explicate theory-based and pragmatic benefits that may be realized if your study is conducted. [LABEL AS RATIONALE SECTION] **In this section, the author seeks to convince the audience that the topic is worthy of study, and has several potential and pragmatic implications.**

3). Generate an abbreviated communication theory which accounts for the key features and relationships which exist in your context. Review past research to build a sound foundation for your study. Similar to the case study text and class examples, you must describe what is currently known about your topic. In particular, how do past research and existing theories inform the focus of your theory? The lit review thus provides a rationale for the study's hypotheses (hys) and/or Research Questions (RQs). Be sure to explain how your conceptual variables may be operationalized. Your operationalizations must be consistent with the data type of each variable. [LABEL AS LIT REVIEW SECTION] **Assuming you've laid a strong foundation in sections one and two, this section serves as the framework of the "house". It is without question the most revealing section of the piece. You must describe, explain, and evaluate existing research that informs our understanding of your topic. This "literature review" helps justify your theory and/or hys/RQs.**

4). Identify two RQs or two hypotheses (hys) to help test your theory.

*************PROSPECTUS STOPS HERE***

4 (Cont'd.) Collect data using a small sample; that is, if you are using a questionnaire (20 individuals), semi-structured interview (5 individuals), or content analysis (5 different articles, stories, or texts, this number is somewhat dependent on their length). Briefly describe the nature of your sample. For human participants, this includes biological sex, age, education, SES level, occupation, etc. For written material (e.g., you're studying a written story or written speech), this includes date of publication, source type and readership, editorial policy if known, and historical events which may have influenced the writing/delivery of the "stories" or speeches. How are the sample's characteristics important to knowledge advancement and theory-building? Or are they?? MOST OF THIS INFO WILL BE PLACED IN THE METHODS SECTION. THE ACTUAL SAMPLE CHARACTERISTICS ARE PLACED IN THE RESULTS SECTION UNDER DEMOGRAPHICS.

5). Using an appropriate data analytical technique, report what the data reveal. Specifically, were your hys confirmed, rejected, or mixed? [LABEL AS RESULTS SECTION]

6). Speculate on the ramifications of these findings. Briefly describe three key limitations which limit generalizability. Briefly explain directions for future research. [LABEL AS DISCUSSION SECTION]

Detailed Student Information About Writing a Prospectus and Final Research Paper

<u>Advantages</u>
You will gain on-hands experience conducting a small study.

You will see first-hand how many of the concepts and principles discussed in the text work and discover some of their ramifications.

You will be better able to evaluate how research is conducted and understand some of the necessary trade-offs to meet the needs and schedules of "real" individuals.

<u>Disadvantages</u>
You may feel overwhelmed by the jargon that surrounds communication inquiry.

You may feel that your study is too narrow in scope to enhance your understanding.

You may feel that the amount of work essential to the project, and the tight time constraints, are daunting.

<u>The Bottom-Line</u>
It is our firm belief, however, and NOT merely because we are professors, that this experiential learning will serve each of you well. Indeed, we are convinced that whether in pursuit of an advanced degree, while perusing *Consumer Reports*, or helping an employer evaluate a study of some proposed action steps, this project and course should make a major impact in your professional and personal life.

Writing and Conceptual Tips

The following suggestions apply to writing the prospectus as well as the final paper. The prospectus is the first three parts of the final paper: the introduction, review of literature, and research question/hypothesis. Please look at some of the superior final papers done previously for this course to see how these papers should be written.[students can also refer to samples located at www.homestead.com/profjims/directory.html under the CMUN 248 heading].

1. Purpose of the Prospectus/Final Paper: The prospectus/final paper must be concerned with some communication concept/variable. The purpose may be simply to describe a communication concept/variable, but most projects go beyond description to relate a communication concept/variable to other variables of interest. Most papers look either at the effects of a variable (which may or may not be communication-based) on communicative behavior or examine the effects of communicative behavior on another variable (which may or may not be communication-based). You are not limited to two variables, but no more than three independent variables and two dependent variables probably should be studied.

2. Title: Construct a clear title for the prospectus/final paper that captures the essence of your research. Most projects examine either differences between groups (such as "Male and Female Compliance-Gaining Strategies," or "The Effects of Gender on Compliance-Gaining Strategies")or relationships between variables (such as, "The Relationship Between Intelligence and Communication Competence," or "The Effects of Intelligence on Communication Competence"). Think about constructing a creative title by providing a catchy first part, followed by a colon, with the second part specifying the variables of interest (e.g., "Birds of a Feather Flock Together: The Effects of Communicator Style Similarities on Interpersonal Attraction").

3. Introduction: While the length of this section may vary, it is crucial to set the stage here and provide a sound overview of the topic. This section also establishes the purpose of the study. Start with an introduction to the general area of research (but don't make this too general), followed by some content that explains the specific focus of your research (do not phrase the purpose as a formal research question and/or hypothesis; instead, explain the specific purpose of the research in text form). This section concludes by pointing out the significance/importance of your research for communication scholars, practitioners (including educators), and/or the general public.

4. Literature Review: This is the longest and most important part of the research prospectus. Here are some suggestions:

A. The purpose of the literature review section is to summarize what is known about the area of research that interests you. Make sure to provide enough information so that the reader understands what has been studied and what has been found about the topic.

B. The best possible literature to review are empirical studies in scholarly, academic (e.g., edited or original research) books and journals, especially communication journals. (See the textbook or Chapter 1 of the casebook for a list of communication journals.) You may use textbooks, magazines, and newspapers for some general orienting information (perhaps for the introduction to the paper), but the majority of the review should be actual research studies published in journals or scholarly texts.

C. The best possible research to review are empirical studies that link the variables that interest you. If there are a number of these studies (say five or more), you can restrict your review solely to these. If there are only a limited number of these studies, you should provide a more general overview of each of the variables, and then focus on the studies that examine the relationship between them in as much depth as possible. If there are no studies about the relationship between the specific variables you are investigating, review what is known about each of these variables separately and then make the link between them yourself in the research questions and/or hypotheses section. If there are no studies about the specific variables that interest you, review studies that are relevant to the general area of research you are examining.

D. Stay away, for the most part, from reviewing rhetorical and critical work, as these are more appropriate for other types of courses. Concentrate, instead, on quantitative research studies that link the variables of interest.

E. Use some organizing scheme for reviewing the research studies. (See the text for some suggestions about organizing this part of the paper.) An organizing scheme provides helpful transitions between studies and shows the relationship between each study more clearly.

F. If you are going to review a specific study fully (as opposed to discussing general findings from numerous studies), make sure you explain the purpose of the study (including what research questions and/or hypotheses were advanced), the methods, the findings, and the significance/implications of these findings (including how these findings relate to your own research project), in that order.

G. When reviewing studies, write in the past tense, except when discussing the implications of the findings, which is written in the present tense.

5. Research Questions or Hypotheses (Choose one of these as the heading for this section): This is the concluding section of the research prospectus and starts with a transition paragraph from the previous section that summarizes the relevant literature and leads logically to the research questions or hypotheses you have advanced for your study. That is, provide a clear transition from the previous section to this one. If there was plenty of research in the areas of interest, show how your project is an extension of this research. If there was limited prior research available, create a link between the previous findings and your interests. Immediately prior to giving the research question or hypothesis is a statement such as, "Therefore, the following research question is posed:" or "Therefore, the following hypothesis is advanced:" and then the research question

or hypothesis is given. Please see the textbook for how to phrase formal research questions and hypotheses. Here are some additional suggestions:

A. It is preferable to advance a hypothesis as opposed to a research question. If a hypothesis is not appropriate because there is not enough knowledge available about the topic to make a prediction, then advance a research question.

B. Phrase research questions or hypotheses with regard to (1) description (e.g., RQ1: What compliance-gaining strategies do males and females use?), (2) significant differences between groups (e.g., H1: Males use significantly more threats as a compliance-gaining strategy than females), and/or (3) relationships between variables (e.g., RQ1: Is there a relationship between intelligence and communication competence?). The particular phrasing depends on the purpose of the research, the type of variables studied (nominal versus ordered), and whether you are advancing an open-ended or closed-ended research question or a directional or non-directional hypothesis.

C. If there is more than one independent variable, you can put them together in one research question or hypothesis (e.g., RQ1: Is there a relationship between age, intelligence, and communication competence?; or RQ1: Adult males use significantly more compliance-gaining strategies than adult females or male and female children) or pose separate research questions or hypotheses (e.g., H1: Males use significantly more threat and promise compliance-gaining strategies than women. H2: Adults use significantly more threat and promise compliance-gaining strategies than children). The choice will depend on whether you anticipate interaction effects between the independent variables. If you have questions about this particular type of research question/hypothesis, see me.

D. Indent the formal research question(s) and/or hypothesis(es) the same as you would for a new paragraph. Start with RQ or H, followed by a number, followed by a colon, followed by the actual research question or hypothesis. Align the second and third sentences. For example: RQ1: Is there a significant difference between men and women with regard to the use of threats in gaining compliance?

E. The prospectus ends with the research question or hypothesis, followed by a bibliography. You must provide a complete citation for all sources referenced in the essay. [go to www.homestead.com/profjims/jimsclasses.html and click on the "Help with APA" link at the bottom of the page].

Final Paper Tips

Note: You must obtain my approval of the methods you will use to conduct the research. Do not collect any data without my expressed approval. Failure to do so will result in a grade of "F" for this assignment.

6. Methodology: This is a relatively short part of the final paper and includes the following two subsections, which are labeled explicitly (the first letter is capitalized, and the subtitle is placed flush left and underlined) (see the handout featuring examples of methods sections in previous papers): A. Research Participants: These are the people in your sample. Include any information about them you wish, but provide the total number of participants. You might also want to indicate their mean age, type (i.e., university students, married couples, etc.), and any other pertinent information. Don't get too carried away, however, with information of the respondents that is not that important.

    If you are doing a content analysis of texts, then this section would be labeled Texts, and you would describe the nature of these texts (e.g., how many, from where they were obtained, etc.).

B. Procedures: Describe what you did with the research participants in a straightforward manner (i.e., "Respondents filled out a questionnaire that measured .. ."). Ensure that you explain in sufficient depth how the independent and dependent variables were measured. If an existing instrument was used, provide the appropriate citation in the text and in the bibliography, and put a copy of the instrument in the appendix to the paper. If you created an instrument, describe how it was created and how it measured the variable of interest (i.e., interval-level measurement using 5-point Likert scales, ranging from 1 = Strongly Agree to 5 = Strongly Disagree). Put a copy of any instrument(s) employed in the appendix to the paper.

    If you are conducting a content analysis of texts, describe the units of analysis, the categories into which the texts/units were coded, and the people who coded the texts, making sure to provide the percentage of agreement score between/among coders.

7. Results: This section of the paper is a straightforward description of the results for each of the hypotheses or research questions. Don't comment on the results, merely provide them. The following statement is an example: "As the results demonstrate, there was a significant difference between men and women with respect to trust ($t = 5.40$, $d.f. = 34$, $p < .01$). Specifically, women trusted men ($M = 4.50$, $SD = 1.20$) to a significantly greater degree than men trusted women ($M = 3.30$, $SD = 1.10$). Hence, the data from this study support the first hypothesis." Include any relevant tables of results in this section. Put each table on a separate page immediately following the first mention of it, and include a title for the table. (Tables should only be included if you and I have discussed including them.)

8. Discussion: This section is where you comment in some substantive depth about what the results reveal and how to interpret them. This is the most important part of the final paper, for it is your chance to examine the results in some detail. Discuss the following points in this order: A. What were the general findings from this study? Provide a one-paragraph summary of the results. B. What is the significance of the

findings? What do they "mean"? What are the implications of these findings for communication theorists and researchers, practitioners (such as organizational consultants or educators), and/or the general public?
C. What were the apparent "problems" or "deficiencies" with this study, and how might they be corrected in a future study? Try to be specific in discussing these problems. All of the projects suffer from sample selection (i.e., nonrandom samples) and small sample size, so identify unique and specific problems evidenced in your study.
D. Explain one or two specific directions for future research based on the findings from your study. What should researchers now be interested in finding out? Keep in mind that future students are looking for directions for their projects, so what would you suggest they do if they are interested in pursing this topic further?
E. Conclude the paper with a clear and succinct paragraph that summarizes your research study and ends on a catchy note.
9. References: You must provide a full citation using the fourth edition of the Publication Manual of the American Psychological Association (APA) (see the text and go to www.homestead.com/profjims/jimsclasses.html and click on the "Help with APA" link at the bottom of the page] for each source cited in the paper. Do not provide citations for sources that were not mentioned in the paper.
10. Appendix: Provide a clean copy of the instrument(s) that you used in conducting the research study. No other information should be included in the appendix.

Other Suggestions

A. Write these papers in a scholarly, academic manner. Try to write like the studies you reviewed from the academic journals. Do not, however, write in too complex a manner. Make sure that the points you make and the sentences you construct are clear.
B. Everything should be written in text form, except for the research question or hypothesis, which is indented the same as a paragraph. There is no reason, for example, for incomplete sentences, bullet points, and so forth.
C. There are only limited reasons for quoting material. Almost everything can be paraphrased while still giving credit to the author(s). Quotes might be useful for explaining some general points and for providing definitions for the variables studied. Watch out, however, for paraphrasing without giving credit, or paraphrasing when quoting exact material. These are instances of plagiarism and lead to automatic failure on the assignment, as well as the course.
D. Please type your paper on fairly heavyweight paper, as written comments on lightweight paper smudge. No handwritten papers, or parts thereof, will be accepted.
E. Please use double spacing for all text in the body of the paper. Single spacing may be used for the references, if you wish.
F. Please reread your work and make sure there are no spelling errors, no awkward sentence constructions, and that the paper flows in a clear manner. Effective editing undoubtedly is the most important difference between high- and low-quality papers.

G. Do not use the first person pronoun ("I) anywhere in the paper. Please write in the third person.
H. Use six centered subheadings in the paper: Introduction, Review of the Literature, Research Question or Hypothesis, Methods (with subheadings of Research Participants and Procedure), Results, and Discussion.
I. The research prospectus will not be accepted late. Failure to turn the prospectus in on time constitutes failure on both the research prospectus and the final paper for the course.
J. Two copies of the final paper must be submitted on the due date. (Only one copy of the prospectus is turned in.) Failure to turn the final paper in on time constitutes failure for this assignment.

Student Data Preparation and Term Paper Checklist

The first part of this handout identifies data preparation tips. These should be completed prior to our meeting and my analysis [both Dr. Frey and I perform the data analysis for our students].

The second part of the handout addresses key expectations and questions about the final paper.

<u>Data Prep Tips</u>
1. Bring all completed questionnaires/tape recordings to our meeting.
2. Number the questionnaire/tape recordings by participant; that is, participant 1, 2, 3 etc.

Questionnaires Only (some modification is necessary if the data is nominal or ordinal)

3. Calculate and be able to show the sum of each participant's scores, mean, variance, and standard deviation on the respective scales. Ditto for entire sample. Create a table that visually displays the data in sequence from high to low across the items indicated (e.g., means, variances, standard deviations).

4. Calculate and be able to show the kurtosis and skewness of the sample data.

5. If your group is testing for differences, have the questionnaires separated (e.g., high and low intercultural communication competence levels). Create a table that visually displays the data in sequence from high to low across the items indicated (e.g., means, variances, standard deviations) **for the two groups**.

6. If your group is testing for association, have the summed raw scores for the variables listed from high to low in a visual table. This association test can only occur for two variables.

7. I will help you write most of the results section; however, your group will need to report the demographics in terms of raw numbers and percentages. Also, your group will **have to**

make the decisions during hypothesis/RQ testing. I will perform the necessary calculations to aid your analysis.

Interviews Only

8. Be able to describe in the appendix most of the interview responses.

9. Summarize the themes from the recorded interviews (refer to Query & Kreps, 1993). Use verbatim exemplars.

10. I will help you write most of the results section; however, your group will need to report the demographics in terms of percentages only. Also, your group will have to make the decisions during categorization of themes. I will serve as a "sounding board" to aid your analysis.

****

To receive full consideration, the following items must be turned in with the completed research paper. I have also provided some clarifications as necessary.

General Mechanics

- All papers must be double-spaced and typed.

- A title page is presented first. On the following page, the abstract follows. Neither of these pages are paginated.

- The introduction begins the third page and is not paginated.

- The fourth page of the paper is paginated.

- The remaining pages including the bibliography are paginated. Please use the APA Wizard [go to www.homestead.com/profjims/jimsclasses.html] to help you build citations. Appendices, however, are not paginated.

- Refer to the appendices in the paper by stating something like "see Appendix A"...etc. Only the appendix containing the graded prospecti is not referred to in the paper.

- Please do not bind your papers.

- Turn in two copies of the paper.

- Turn in only one complete set of appendices. These should be collated and attached together, but not stapled to the paper.

What is included in the appendices?

— a copy of your graded prospectus

— a clean copy of all data-collection tools

— a clean copy of the consent form

— a copy of every signed consent form

— a copy of each completed questionnaire

— visual data displays and calculations which may be handwritten

— detailed summaries of interviews

Query, J.L., & Kreps, G. L. (1993). Using the critical incident method to evaluate and enhance organizational effectiveness. In S. L. Fish and G. L. Kreps (Eds.), <u>Qualitative research: Applications in organizational communication</u> (pp. 63-77). Creskill, NJ: Hampton Press.

INFORMED CONSENT FORM*
Observing and Measuring Communication Behavior, CMUN 248
Department of Communication
Loyola University Chicago

STUDY TITLE: to be filled in by the research team.

PRINCIPAL INVESTIGATOR: insert student name(s), and professor's office number.

FACULTY SUPERVISOR: to be filled in by course instructor along with his or her business address

This is to certify that I, **[study participant or site coordinator's name]**_____,
hereby agree to participate in a social scientific communication study under the supervision of **[fill in]**...

I understand that the purpose of this research is to investigate and describe **[must focus on message behavior; to be completed by each student or group]**...

I understand that the procedures of the study are not intended to be used to diagnose or treat any medical or psychological disorder. I understand that I should not use the results as substitutes for any consultations with appropriate medical or psychological professionals.

I understand that information obtained from or about me will be kept confidential in the case of interviews or anonymous in the case of observations. The information will be used for scientific purposes and the results will only be reported in general trends. No report, oral or written, will identify me personally. While my group may be identified by name---such as a support group within AA---it will be impossible to make a more precise identification.

I understand that I am free to refuse to participate in any procedure, or to refuse to answer any question, at any time without prejudice to me. I understand that I am free to withdraw my consent and to withdraw from the study at any time without prejudice to me.

I understand that by agreeing to participate in this research and signing this form, I do not waive any of my legal rights.

I understand that the research investigator(s) named above will answer my questions about the research procedures, and my rights as a research participant.

_____   _____
Signature of Participant or   Date
Site Coordinator

*Please consult with your Institutional Review Board to ensure that the form is in compliance with their guidelines.

POTENTIAL NET PAPER SITES FACILITATING PLAGIARISM

SOURCE
www.coastal.edu/library/papermil.html
 Page author: Margaret Fain, Assistant Head of Public Services
Commnts or questions regarding this website?
E-mail the WebDiva, traw@coastal.edu
Page last updated: 22 June 1999

Internet Paper Mills

12,000 Papers.com
 http://www.12000papers.com/literature9.htm

1 Stop Research Paper Shop
http://members.tripod.com/%7ETexasTwister/

A1 Termpapers
www.a1-termpaper.com

Absolutely Free Online Essays: Student Essay Network(free)
www.elee.calpoly.edu/~ercarlso/papers.htm

Academic Research Group
http://www.web-marketing.org/cgi-bin/nph-tame.cgi/termpapers/index.tam

Academic TermPapers
www.academictermpapers.com or www.researchcentral.com/

ACI NetGuide to TermPapers
http://member.aol.com/aciplus/netguide.htm

ACI Writing Assistance Center
http://www.aci-plus.com/

AmericaCorp (submit paper to get free ones)
http://america.simplenet.com/

BigNerds
www.bignerds.com/

Brain Trust
http://www.nh.ultranet.com/~lmccann/the_brain_trust.html

The Cheat Factory
http://cheatfactory.hypermart.net/

Cheater.com
www.cheater.com/

Chris Pap's Essay Database(free)
http://www.chrispaps.freeserve.co.uk/wrk-samples.htm

ChuckIII's College Resources (free)
http://www.chuckiii.com/

Collegiate Care Research Assistance
http://www.papers-online.com/

Coshe's Reports
http://www.coshe.com/

Copiale! (Spanish Language)
http://www.geocities.com/Athens/Acropolis/5757/

CyberEssays
http://www.cyberessays.com

The Doctor
http://www.serve.com/doctor

Dorian's Paper Archive (free)
http://www.fas.harvard.edu/~dberger/papers/

Essay Depot (free)
http://www.essaydepot.com/

Essay Organization (free)
http://www.essay.org/

Essay Powerhouse
http://olympia.fortunecity.com/relay/655/index.html

Essays International
http://www.jerryeden.com/esa/

EssayMan(free)
http://come.to/essayman

Essaybank
www.essaybank.com/

Essayworld (free)
www.essayworld.com/

Evil House of Cheat
www.CheatHouse.com/

Free Reports and Essays(free)

http://stormloader.com/freereports/main.htm

Genius Papers
http://www.geniuspapers.com/

Global Essays
http://www.geocities.com/CollegePark/Square/9223/

Homework Help
http://www.angelfire.com/ca3/homeworkhelp/index.html

Jungle Page
http://www.junglepage.com

Knowledge Reports
http://www.knowledge-reports.com

Lazy Students
http://www.lazystudents.com/

Net Essays
www.netessays.net/

Paper Store Enterprises
www.termpapers-on-file.com/ or www.paperwriters.com/intro.htm

Papers 24-7
http://www.papers24-7.com/

Papers Inn
www.papersinn.com/

Research Papers Online
www.ezwrite.com/

Research Assistance.com
http://www.research-assistance.com/

Saxty's Essayz
http://top30list.hypermart.net/index.html

School Sucks
http://www.schoolsucks.com/

Schoolpapers.com
http://www.schoolpapers.com/

Smart Essays
http://www.FreeEssay.com/smart/

SAXTC.com
http://www.essayxstacy.com/

Studyworld
http://studyworld.com

Superior Term Papers
http://www.superior-termpapers.com/

TermPaper Experts
http://www.termpaper-experts.com/

Terms n Papers
http://www.termsnpapers.com/

Thousands of Papers (T.O.P.)
http://www.termpapers-on-file.com/papers/categories.htm

Totally Free Papers
http://www.totally.net/totallyfreepap/index.htm

Uittreksels.com (Dutch)
http://www.uittreksels.com/

Potential Assignments in a Qualitative Communication Methods Course

1. Exams/Quizzes
2. Participation: Active classroom participation and contribution; completion of any in-class or additional out-of-class assignments.
3. Review of a Study: Students describe and critique an actual qualitative communication research study.
4. Research Proposal: Students propose a research study, which includes the purpose and rationale for the study, review of relevant literature, explanation of the setting, overview of the data collection methods to be employed, and discussion of potential findings and their significance.
5. Research Study: Students conduct (individually or in pairs or groups) a qualitative research study that is reported in written and/or oral form at the end of the semester. (Students can be asked to turn in "Project Updates" throughout the course of the term.)
6. Mapping of a Field Site: Students draw a map, a visual representation of an actual data collection site in some detail and write a brief summary of the effects different areas of this site has on data collection.
7. Field Notes/Data Log: Students keep field notes/data log while conducting research in the field. (Students can also be asked to keep a "personal journal" of their experiences in the field.)
8. Observation Report: Students carry out a brief observational study in a context (typically an unfamiliar one). They identify a researchable problem, describe the methodology used in carrying out research on the problem, generate observational data in the form of field notes, and provide a brief analysis of these field notes.(This can also be a "project update" if students are conducting a research study.)
9. Interview Report: Students conduct and report on an interview. The interview is typically conducted with one individual, but a focus group interview can also be conducted. (This can also be a "project update" if students are conducting a research study.)
10. Transcription: Students transcribe 5-30 minutes of an audiotaped interview (one given by the instructor or one taped by students), and submit a typed transcript. When students conduct the interview, both the tape and the transcripts should be submitted to the instructor so that the tapes may be compared to the transcripts.
11. Analysis of Transcription: Students develop a transcript based on some transcription system (e.g., Jefferson). Students describe the transcription method used together with the resulting transcript and preliminary analysis.

12. Textual Analysis: Students collect a document from a research site and analyze it (e.g., semiotic analysis).
13. Coding Data: Students are given data (e.g., interview transcripts) and a general purpose, and then develop and apply a coding scheme.

Student Information About Writing A Qualitative Communication Research Paper

A. General Comments

1. Write the paper in a scholarly, academic manner, keeping in mind that the primary audience for the paper is communication scholars, and, in particular, communication scholars who do naturalistic research. As such, you should write the paper in a similar manner to the academic journal article(s) you read for this class.
2. Try to weave together thick description of behavior with theoretical/conceptual points, and be sure to embed those explanatory/interpretive points within the available literature(s) on the points being discussed. The paper should, thus, be a seamless integration of description, explanation, and reference to other scholars' work. You should, of course, also feel free to engage in criticism and action advocacy, if they are appropriate.
3. It is very important to keep in mind that this paper is being written for a communication class, and hence, communicative behavior should be privileged in the paper. Make sure that you focus your thick description, interpretation/explanation, and so forth, on communicative behavior.
4. Try to produce a compelling narrative to the paper; that is, a story that needs to be told. That narrative should also be coherent and well-developed in the sense of being organized effectively, such that sections flow smoothly from one to the other.
5. Think carefully about how to embed yourself into the narrative. In some cases, this may demand a lot of your first-person perspectives, but in other cases, this may be minimal.

B. More Specific Comments

1. Try to construct a title for the paper that provides a context for the rest of the paper. The title should hook people in and should represent a dominant theme that is then played out in the work.
2. Use subheadings throughout the paper to walk the reader through in a coherent and conscientious manner. Those subheadings can be traditional ones (e.g., Introduction, Review of the Literature, Methods, etc.), or

they can be nontraditional headings, such as those used by Adelman and Frey (1997).
3. Some people use epigraphs--a quote from another scholar or from a member of the population you studied--to start subsections. You certainly are free to do this, but don't feel compelled to do so.
4. Use the 4th edition of the American Psychological Association Publication Manual to cite reference sources, both in the text and in the reference section (see handout).
5. Use justify left margin (as is done here) rather than justified right margin when writing the text.
6. All text should be double spaced. This includes the distance between (sub)headings and text, as well as indented quotes. Indent quotes (from the reference material or from participant interviews) if they are 40 words or more. If they are less, place them in the body of the paragraph.
7. The paper should be anywhere from 15-30 pages, not counting references and any footnotes. If you use footnotes selectively, do so selectively. This is not a place to dump a lot of extra material. (For example, notice that the Adelman & Frey text does not use footnotes.)
8. Type your paper on fairly heavy-weight paper, as written comments on light-weight paper smudge. No handwritten papers, or parts thereof, will be accepted.
9. Please reread your work and make sure there are no spelling errors, no awkward sentence constructions, and that the paper flows in a clear manner. Effective editing undoubtedly is the most important difference between high- and low-quality papers.
10. Two copies of the paper are due; I will keep one to show future students and return the other one to you.
11. No late papers are accepted.
12. A 5-7 minute oral presentation is due on the day the paper is submitted. Those presentations will be given in alphabetical order starting with last name. The purpose of this oral presentation is to provide an overview of what you were interested in, what you did, what you found, and what you now think.

Adelman, M. B., & Frey, L. R. (1997). <u>The fragile community: Living together with AIDS.</u> Mahwah, NJ: Lawrence Erlbaum Associates.

PROFESSOR EXERCISE

A. Purpose: To illustrate some of the basic elements of the research methods process. To provide students with a chance to learn something about the professor.

B. When to Use: The first or second day of class.

C. Time Required: 45min.-1 hour

D. Steps

1. Have students write 3 anonymous questions about the professor. Tell them that they can ask anything they want; there are no limits.
2. Examining the Questions
   A) Content Analysis of Questions: One question that concerns communication scholars might be, "What types of questions do people ask when they want to get to know another person?" Content analysis is a method that can be answer this question.
      1) Rubin (1979), for example, categorized questions into 5 categories: knowledge (questions dealing with requests for information known to most people and unrelated to the individual); experience; demographic; values & opinions; and personality.
   B) The Effects of Input Variables on Question Asking: There are a variety of input variables (variables that precede communication) that influence the nature of how we ask questions (or any communicative behavior), including the context (see Rubin study), characteristics of the people (e.g., demographic, personality) asking the questions, and relationship between interactants.
   C) Discussion of Relationship Between Variables and What Makes a Project a Communication Study: Communication projects typically either describe communication behavior, relate input variables to communication behavior, or relate communication to outcome variables.
3. Methods for Obtaining Answers: Have students suppose that 10 questions are picked out and given as an assignment to be answered for the next class session. The grade will be based on the number of correct answers. What are the ways (methods) by which students could obtain the answers?:
   A) Interview Professor
   B) Interview Students and Other Professors (Talk about sampling)
   C) Administrative Records (i.e., course catalogue might contain some demographic information) (Relate to historical and archival research methods)
   D) Textual Analysis of Written Work
   E) Follow and Observe Professor (Naturalistic Inquiry; could mention the study of garbology)
   F) Implicit Personal Theory Mini-Experiments: Find out answers by relating other information to the questions. For example, a student could go to the professor's office and make judgments based on the pictures, furniture, etc., or the student could ask another question in which the answer is thought to be "related" to an answer for a question posed on the assignment.

4. Students Answer Questions: Researchers aren't naive; they often expect certain answers based on information they know (i.e., they develop hypotheses or predictions). Pick out 10 questions from the set (vary the types of questions, by including, for example, both open-ended and closed-ended questions) and ask students to answer them in writing. Even though students have not had much experience with the professor, they should be able to make some educated guesses at some of the questions.
    1) This is also a good time to point out that the form of the question is related to the correctness of the answer. Some questions are easier to answer correctly (and to judge as correct answers) (such as yes/no questions) than are others (i.e., open-ended questions).
5. Professor Answers Questions: The professor should go through each of the questions, have students offer answers (tell them answers won't be held against them), and then answer them. If the professor does not wish to answer one of the questions, then this can lead to a valuable discussion about the types of questions people won't answer. (Bogus question added by professor can be used to discuss research ethics, such as manipulation of data.)
6. Effects of Answers: Communicative behavior has many effects. What are the types of effects that might occur based on the answers to the questions given:
    A) Additional Perceptions of Professor
    B) Increased Liking or Disliking of Professor
    C) Motivation to Perform in the Class
    D) Future Behavior Toward Professor

Rubin, R. B. (1979). The effect of context on information seeking across the span of initial interactions. *Communication Quarterly, 27*, 13-20.

Possible Class Interview Exercise

A. Purposes

1. To illustrate the use of in-depth interviewing to elicit information from another person.
2. To illustrate the process of representing another person through narrative/portrait.
3. To provide a way of getting to know the people in this class.

B. Procedures

1. Match people up with a partner (dyadic interactions).
2. Provide time for people to write down some initial questions they would like to ask the other person.
3. Provide time (approximately 20 minutes per interview) for the partners to interview one another, asking the questions and probing for more information. (Might ask them to move out of

the classroom and take a walk or remove themselves from the immediate classroom context).

4. Provide time (5-10 minutes) for each partner to construct a coherent narrative/portrait of the other person.

5. Have those narratives/portraits presented to the rest of the class. After each one, ask the person being "narrated" how that narrative does or does not represent him/her, and whether there is any additional information he or she would like to provide about him/herself to the class members.

C. Discussion Points

1. Process the interviews, such as how people felt asking questions, their ability to probe deeper, what problems were encountered, and so forth.
2. Process the narratives/portraits created and presented, such as the degree of depth, the ability to represent the other, and so forth.

Hollywood Squares Simulation: A Template
Possible Responses for Celebrities

A. Purpose: To help students grasp and better appreciate material that they otherwise might find as mundane or daunting. Hence, the questions below incorporate material from several chapters.

B. When to use: The second week of class or thereafter.

C. Time required: The time needed can vary from 15-30 minutes based in part on the number of questions and the length of the bluffs.

D. Steps

- One person serves as the game show host reading the questions to the "celebrities" as they are selected by the two contestants.
- One male and one female student serve as the contestants and the simulation can end after a certain number of questions. In this manner, the remainder of the class can serve as "celebrities" since the goal is to achieve the most "Xs" or "Os".
- Contestants earn the "square" by ascertaining if the celebrity is giving the correct answer or a bluff. Contestants typically reply with, "I agree or I disagree." Celebrities may only give the correct answer or one bluff.
- Celebrities can use notebook paper to place an "O" on one side and "X" on the opposite side.

- Some of the questions and bluffs can be modified to appear on exams and quizzes further reinforcing the saliency of the material
- Many of my students make their own game up while studying for quizzes and exams.

E. Sample Questions

Q1---Standard scores aid investigators by indicating the:
Correct Answer---distance between scores and the mean/std. deviation

Bluffs
relationship between skewness and kurtosis
relationship between scores and variances
relationships between scores and medians

Q2---Z-scores are a type of standard score with a mean of:
Correct Answer---0 and standard deviation of 1

Bluffs
1 and standard deviation of 2
2 and standard deviation of 4
-1 and standard deviation of -4

Q3---A z-score of 2.6 reveals that a score is:
Correct Answer---2.6 standard deviations away from the mean.

Bluffs
to the left of the mean
+3 standard deviations away from the mean
-3 standard deviations away from the

Q4---Why are z-scores not always practical when reporting results?
Correct Answer---the perception that the average (0) means lack of a given trait

Bluffs
the popular perception that ratio data is inferior
the calculations are tedious and highly complex
the variances are more important than z-scores

Q5---When reporting the results to lay individuals, which standard score should be used?
Correct Answer---T-scores

Bluffs
Y-scores
X-scores
W-scores

Q6--- T-scores are a type of standard score with a mean of:
Correct Answer---50 and standard deviation of 10

Bluffs
10 and standard deviation of 40
20 and standard deviation of 60
-20 and standard deviation of -40

Q7---To calculate T-scores, one must have the appropriate:
Correct Answer----z-scores

Bluffs
Y-scores
X-scores
W-scores

Q8---According to the Central Limit Theroem, the mean of the sampling distribution of means is equal to the mean of the:
Correct Answer---population from which the samples were drawn

Bluffs
population with negatively skewed scores
population with positively skewed scores
sum of squares

Q9---The standard error of the mean allows investigators to determine:
Correct Answer---the location of a sample means

Bluffs
how incorrect the mean is
how incorrect the median is
how incorrect the mode is

Q10---What percentage of scores reside within +/- 1 z-scores under the normal curve?
Correct Answer---68.26%

Bluffs
58.26%
78.26%
95.44%

Q11---Confidence intervals are useful primarily because investigators often:
Correct Answer---test hypotheses at 95% levels

Bluffs
test hypotheses at 85% levels
test hypotheses at 90% levels
test hypotheses at 100% levels

Q12---Content validity aids investigators by providing a/an:
Correct Answer---index of effectiveness for assessing conceptualizations

Bluffs
bridge between internal validity and reliability
bridge between external validity and reliability
bridge between concurrent validity and Cronbach's alpha

Q13---Criterion validity is very persuasive since it demonstrates the _____ between a new measurement technique and an already established and valid technique
Correct Answer---positive relationship

Bluffs
negative relationship
ambiguous relationship
inverse relationship

Q14---Concurrent validity is a key component of:
Correct Answer---criterion validity

Bluffs
content validity
construct validity
interrater reliability

Q15---The Educational Testing Service primarily attempts to create tests that have high:
Correct Answer---predictive validity

Bluffs
alternative procedure reliability
content validity
ecological validity

Q16---Which type of validity is most closely linked to theorizing?
Correct Answer---construct validity

Bluffs
ecological validity
content validity
concurrent validity

Q17---Quantitative measures can be used to provide numerical indexes of:
Correct Answer---reliability

Bluffs
internal validity
predictive validity
content validity

Q18---Which of the following types of research is unlikely to involve the researcher personal attribute effect (RPAE)?
Correct Answer----unobtrusive measures

Bluffs
survey research
ethnographic research
experimental research

Q19---A key strategy to reduce the likelihood of RPAE is to use:
Correct Answer---several research associates

Bluffs
female research associates
male research associates
well-educated research associates

Q20---The case of Hans the Wonder Horse primarily demonstrated that:
Correct Answer---the researcher unintentional expectancy effect (RUEE)

Bluffs
some animals can communicate
some animals are intelligent
humans are generally superior to animals

Q21---When is sensitization most likely to occur?
Correct Answer---during research designs having pretests and posttests

Bluffs
during research designs having independent and moderating variables
during research designs having control groups
during research designs having the Hawthorne effect

Q22---When is history most likely to occur?
Correct Answer---during longitudinal research designs

Bluffs
during cross-sectional research designs
during random research designs
during experimental research designs

Q23---When is a data analytic threat most likely to occur?
Correct Answer---when variable data type is erroneous

Bluffs
when variable type is independent
when variable type is dependent
when variable type is nominal

Q24---All of the possible cases in a study is defined as the:
Correct Answer---universe

Bluffs
sample
population
parameter

Q25---The primary advantage of random sampling is its:
Correct Answer---bias reduction
Bluffs
convenience
clustering
practicality

Research Process Exercise: Using the Scientific Method

A. Purpose: To illustrate how difficult it is to understand and explain a real-life event focusing on the message behavior of the participants. To provide students with the opportunity to apply the scientific method.

B. When to use: The third or fourth week of class.

C. Time required: 30-40 minutes in-class time and students can also work on the exercise outside of class.

D. Steps

1. Distribute the case below and have students form small groups to process the assignment completing the remaining steps.
2. Identify the target behavior and its communicative manifestations/links.
3. Devise at least three communication-based RQs about the target behavior.
4. Advance three communication-based hypotheses about the target including a directional hypothesis, nondirectional hypothesis, and a null hypothesis.
5. Specify how to conceptualize and operationalize the variables of interest within the hypotheses.
6. Suggest at least two ways to test the hypotheses. These should be consistent with your conceptualizations and operationalizations.
7. Identify at least two biases which influenced your analysis of this situation. Hint---in what ways do your hypotheses reflect personal biases?

Situation

Angela Kay and Heather Lee are best friends and 22 years of age. They regularly "hang" and cruise together. Many outsiders often comment about how similar Angela Kay and Heather Lee are in terms of their tastes in clothes, cars, movies, and music. Additionally, the two are usually characterized as outgoing and personable.

During the past week, however, their friends have noticed some atypical behaviors. For example, Angela Kay has "blown up" several times without any apparent justification. These outbursts have also occurred when Chase comes around and makes "small talk" with Heather Lee. Although Heather Lee and Chase are not the targets of these scathing polemics, Heather Lee has become withdrawn. Indeed, she seems off in the "twilight zone."

Puzzled by this behavior, you search for clues. Subsequently, your investigation uncovers the following information:
(A) Angela Kay and Heather Lee have been listening to Judas Priest practically 8 hours a day;
(B) Angela Kay and Heather Lee have been toking and drinking steadily for the past five days;
(C) Angela Kay and Heather Lee have forged a suicide pact.

Current Event Article Analysis: Possible Homework Assignment

General Overview (see syllabus)
Working individually or in groups, you will draw from furnished editions of the *Chicago Sun-Times* and *Chicago Tribune*, identify and cut out relevant current event articles that help better illustrate some aspect of naturalistic research. Provide a brief glimpse into the articles (4-5 total) using "bullets" to help us hone in on the key features of the article. Be sure to explain how the article is helpful and briefly identify any key ramifications.

Some Thoughts From a Student, Nikki
Nikki: "Current event article work, huh?...Now Jim, come on dude, get a life. After all, this seems like busy work or tasks better suited for journalists and grad school aspirants. You Communica tion profs....sheesh"

Jim: I understand your skepticism and welcome it. *Smile*

Nikki: "Jim, are you feeling okay??"

Jim: Yes I am and thank you. Anyway, after working with your group, you should have developed a much better appreciation for how "reported research" helps shape public opinion and often in negative and misleading ways.

Nikki: Ok, I'll give a try. *Smile*

Assignment Explication (completed over the semester)
1. Using 4-5 sentences, explain the thesis or main idea of the article.
2. On a scale of 1-7, with 1 being Strongly Agree, 4 Undecided, and 7 Strongly Disagree, indicate the extent to which your group (or self) believes this article to be appropriate and illustrative for future research classes. Try and develop a range of articles to include the poor, mediocre, and the best write-ups.

3. Identify and define any "special" or research jargon terms. These may be implicit [such as when an article indicates the independent and dependent variables, but does not use the preceding terminology.
4. Based on the article's thesis (see 1 above), which content that we have covered does this write-up best exemplify? Identify the page numbers and provide a brief justification for your reasoning.
5. Create 4-5 "Bullets" using "sound bytes" to garner the attention of future readers.

Films For Understanding Research Methods

A. General Research Methods

1. "Scientific Methods and Values" (1990): Introduces the fundamentals of scientific methods and values from ancient history to the present, and emphasizes to secondary and college level science students the uniqueness and relevance of science to life on earth today. Madison, WI: Hawkhill Associates.

B. Research Ethics

1. "Do Scientists Cheat?": NOVA Program

2. "Evolving Concern: Protection for Human Subjects"
   "Balancing Society's Mandates: IRB Review Criteria"
   "The Belmont Report: Basic Ethical Principles and Their Application"
   To obtain copies of the three videotapes and User Guide, contact:
   Office for Protection from Research Risks
   National Institutes of Health
   Building 31, Room 4B09
   9000 Rockville Pike
   Bethesda, MD 20892
   Attention: Videotapes

C. Experimental Research

1. "The Psychologist and the Experiment"" (1975): Introductory Psychology Series, CRM Films Collection, McGraw Hill. To obtain copies, contact CRM Films, 1-800-421-0833.

D. Statistics

1. Against All Odds Videorecording: Inside Statistics (1989): 26 programs (30 min. each) on 13 videocassettes. Presents the why as well as the how of statistics using computer animation, colorful on-screen computations, and documentary segments. Santa Barbara, CA: Intellimation.

   A) "What is Statistics?"
   B) "Picturing Distributions"

C) "Describing Distributions"
D) "Normal Distributions"
E) "Normal Calculations"
F) "Time Series"
G) "Models for Growth"
H) "Describing Relationships"
I) "Correlation"
J) Multidimensional Data Analysis
K) "The Question of Causation"
L) "Experimental Design"
M) "Blocking and Sampling"
N) "Samples and Surveys"
O) "What is probability?"
P) "Random Variables"
Q) "Binomial Distributions"
R) "The Sample Mean and Control Charts"
S) "Confidence Intervals"
T) "Significance Tests"
U) "Inference for One Mean"
V) "Comparing Two Means"
W) "Inference for Proportions"
X) "Inference for Two-Way Tables"
Y) "Inference for Relationships"
Z) "Case Study"

To obtain copies of the "Against All Odds Series," contact:
COMAP and Chedd/Angier; Santa Barbara, CA: Intellimation [distributor] 1989. Annenberg/CPB Collection.

Films For Understanding Qualitative Methods

"The Pilgrim Must Embark: Living in Community" (1991) (Mara Adelman & Peter Shultz, Producers): A 25-minute ethnographic video documenting life in a residential facility for people living with AIDS (Bonaventure House, Chicago, IL). The video focuses on the inherent tensions of community living that permeate the practical, personal, and communal lives of residents. Issues of membership, diversity, everyday living, house maintenance, group governance, social attachment, death and dying, and rituals for grieving are addressed. Interviews with residents and staff, woven together with extensive footage of the home environment, social activities, and various community rituals, present a sensitive detailed look at community life for people living with AIDS. Available for $75.00 (with a portion of the proceeds going to residents) from

Lawrence R. Frey, Ph.D., Department of Communication, Loyola U Chicago, Chicago, IL 60626 (773-508-3730).

"The Heart Broken in Half" (1990) (Taggart Siegel & Dwight Conquergood, Producer): A 60-minute video of Conquergood's longitudinal ethnographic research on gang communication in Chicago. The film reveals the symolic practices of gang members and deepens and complicates our understanding of gang culture. Available from Siegel Productions, 5345 N. Winthrop, Chicago, IL 60640 (312) 271-9335.

"Between Two Worlds: The Hmong Shaman in America" (1985) (Taggart Siefel & Dwight Conquergood, Producers): Captures rare and dramatic footage of the Hmong shaman in the United States from Conquergood's ethnographic fieldwork. The film shows that the traditions of this displaced people are in danger of being lost, and shows a people caught between two worlds. Available from Siegel Productions, 5345 N. Winthrop, Chicago, IL 60640 (312) 271-9335.

"Voices From Inside" (1996) (Karina Epperlein, Producer/ Director): A 60-minute video that follows German-born theatre artist Karina Epperlein into a federal women's porison where she teaches weekly classes as a volunteer. Her racially mixed group of women prisoners becomes a circle of trust and healing. Four women prisoners write their own poety and songs for a theatre piece performed inside the prison, and can be used to illustrate performance studies. Available from Transitt 2000, 641 Euclid Avenue, Berkeley, CA 94708 (510-588-8892).

"Nobody's Business" (1996) (Alan Berliner, Producer/ Director): A 60-minute video where Berliner taks on his reclusive father as a relunctant subject of this poingant and graceful study of family history and member. Illustrates hostile interviewing situations and autobiographical/ autoethnographic work, including the use of many types of historical texts. Available from Mileston Film & Video, 275 West 96th Street, Suite 28C, New York, NY 10025 (800-603-1104)

Methods Reference Sources

A. Readings on Communication Research Methods and Reading Research

Anderson, J. A. (1987). <u>Communication research: Issues and methods.</u> New York: McGraw Hill.

Babbie, E. (1989). <u>The practice of social research (5th ed.).</u> Belmont, CA: Wadsworth.

Emmert, P., & Barker, L. L. (1989). <u>Measurement of communication behavior.</u> New York: Longman.

Frey, L. R., Botan, C. H., Friedman, P. G., & Kreps, G. L. (1991). <u>Investigating communication: An introduction to research methods.</u> Englewood Cliffs, NJ: Prentice Hall.

Frey, L. R., Botan, C. H., Friedman, P. G., & Kreps, G. L. (1992). <u>Interpreting communication research: A case study approach.</u> Englewood Cliffs, NJ: Prentice Hall.

Hayes, J. R., Young, R. E., Matchett, M. L., McCaffrey, M., Cochran, C., & Hajduk, T. (Eds.) (1992). <u>Reading empirical research studies: The rhetoric of research.</u> Hillsdale, NJ: Lawrence Erlbaum.

Hsia, H. J. (1988). <u>Mass communications research methods: A step-by-step approach.</u> Hillsdale, NJ: Lawrence Erlbaum.

Katzer, J., Cook, K. H., & Crouch, W. W. (1982). <u>Evaluating information: A guide for users of social science research (2nd ed.).</u> Reading, MA: Addison-Wesley.

Leedy, P. D. (1981). <u>How to read research and understand it.</u> New York: Macmillan.

Rubin, R. B., Rubin, A. M., & Piele, L. J. (1990). <u>Communication research: Strategies and sources (2nd ed.).</u> Belmont, CA: Wadsworth.

Smith, M. J. (1988). <u>Contemporary communication research methods.</u> Belmont, CA: Wadsworth.

Tucker, R. K., Weaver, II, R. L., & Berryman-Fink, C. (1981). <u>Research in speech communication.</u> Englewood Cliffs, NJ: Prentice Hall.

Wimmer, R. D., & Dominick, J. R. (1991). <u>Mass media research: An introduction (3rd ed.).</u> Belmont, CA: Wadsworth.

B. Readings on Full Experimental Research

Aronson, E., & Carlsmith, J. M. (1968). Experimentation in social psychology. In G. Lindzey & E. Aronson (Eds.), <u>Handbook of social psychology: Vol. II. Research methods</u> (2nd ed., pp. 1-79). Reading, MA: Addison-Wesley.

Campbell, D. T., & Stanley, J. C. (1963). <u>Experimental and quasi-experimental designs for research.</u> Chicago: Rand McNally.

Hsia, H. J. (1988). <u>Mass communications research methods: A step-by-step approach.</u> Hillsdale, NJ: Lawrence Erlbaum.

Kirk, R. E. (1968). <u>Experimental design: Procedures for the behavioral sciences.</u> Belmont, CA: Brooks/Cole.

Myers, J. L. (1972). <u>Fundamentals of experimental design.</u> Boston: Allyn & Bacon.

Poole, M. S., & McPhee, R. D. (1985). Methodology in interpersonal communication research. In M. L. Knapp & G. R. Miller (Eds.), <u>Handbook of interpersonal communication</u> (pp. 100-170). Beverly Hills, CA: Sage.

C. Readings on Field Experimental Research

Bickman, L., & Henchy, T. (1972). <u>Beyond the laboratory: Field research in social psychology.</u> New York: McGraw Hill.

Campbell, D. T. (1957). <u>Factors relevant to the validity of experiments in social settings.</u> Psychological Bulletin, 54, 297-312.

Campbell, D. T., & Stanley, J. C. (1966). <u>Experimental and quasi-experimental designs for research.</u> Chicago: Rand McNally.

Cook, T. D., & Campbell, D. T. (1976). The design and conduct of quasi-experiments and true experiments in field settings. In M. Dunnette (Ed.), <u>Handbook of industrial and organizational psychology</u> (pp. 228-293). Skokie, IL: Rand McNally.

Cook, T. D., & Campbell, D. T. (1979). <u>Quasi-experimentation: Design & analysis issues for field settings.</u> Boston: Houghton Mifflin.

Frey, L., O'Hair, D., & Kreps, G. L. (1990). Applied communication methodology. In D. O'Hair & G. L. Kreps (Eds.), <u>Applied communication theory and research</u> (pp. 23-56). Hillsdale, NJ: Lawrence Erlbaum.

D. Readings on Survey Questionnaire Research

Babbie, E. R. (1973). <u>Survey research methods.</u> Belmont, CA: Wadsworth.

Belson, W. R. (1981). <u>The design and understanding of survey questions.</u> Aldershot, England: Gower.

Berdi, D. R., & Anderson, J. F. (1974). <u>Questionnaire design and use.</u> Metuchen, NJ: Scarecrow.

Converse, J. M., & Presser, S. (1986). <u>Survey questions: Handcrafting the standard questionnaire.</u> Beverly Hills, CA: Sage.

Fink, A., & Kosecoff, J. (1985). <u>How to conduct surveys: A step-by-step guide.</u> Beverly Hills, CA: Sage.

Labrow, P. (1980). <u>Advanced questionnaire design.</u> Cambridge, MA: Abt Associates.

Sudman, S., & Bradburn, N. (1982). <u>Asking questions: A practical guide to questionnaire design.</u> San Francisco: Jossey-Bass.

E. Readings on Survey Interview Research

Beed, T. W., & Stimson, R. J. (Eds.). (1985). <u>Survey interviewing: Theory and techniques.</u> Boston: George Allen & Unwin.

Fowler, F. J., Jr., & Mangione, T. W. (1990). <u>Standardized survey interviewing: Minimizing interviewer-related error.</u> Newbury Park, CA: Sage.

Frey, J. H. (1989). <u>Survey research by telephone (2nd ed.).</u> Newbury Park, CA: Sage.

Guenzeel, P. J., Berkmans, T. R., & Cannell, C. F. (1983). General interviewing techniques. Ann Arbor, MI: Institute for Social Research

Steward, D. W., & Shamdasani, P. N. (1990). Focus groups: Theory and practice. Newbury Park, CA: Sage.

F. Readings on Rhetorical Criticism

Andrews, J. R. (1990). The practice of rhetorical criticism (2nd ed.). New York: Macmillan.

Black, E. (1978). Rhetorical criticism: A study in method. Madison, WI: University of Wisconsin Press.

Brock, B. L., Scott, R. L., & Chesebro, J. W. (Eds.). (1989). Methods of rhetorical criticism: A twentieth-century perspective (3rd ed.). Detroit: Wayne State University Press.

Campbell, K. K., & Jamison, K. H. (Eds.). (1978) Form and genre. Falls Church, VA: Speech Communication Association.

Foss, S. K. (1989). Rhetorical criticism: Exploration & practice. Prospect Heights, IL: Waveland.

G. Readings on Content Analysis

Berelson, B. (1952). Content analysis in communication research. New York: The Free Press.

Budd, R. W., Thorp, R. K., & Donohew, L. (1967). Content analysis of communication. New York: Macmillan.

Holsti, O. (1969). Content analysis for the social sciences and humanities. Reading, MA: Addison-Wesley.

Kaid, L. L., & Wadsworth, A. J. (1989). Content analysis. In P. Emmert & L. L. Barker (Eds.), Measurement of communication behavior (pp. 197-217). White Plains, NY: Longman.

Krippendorf, K. (1980). Content analysis: An introduction to its methodology. Newbury Park, CA: Sage.

Stempel, G. H., III (1989). Content analysis. In G. H. Stempel III and B. H. Westly (Eds.), Research methods in mass communication (2nd ed., pp. 124-129). Englewood Cliffs, NJ: Prentice Hall.

Weber, R. P. (1990). Basic content analysis (2nd ed.). Newbury Park, CA: Sage.

H. Readings on the Study of Conversation

Heritage, J. (1989). Current developments in conversation analysis. In D. Roger & P. Bull (Eds.), Conversation: An interdisciplinary perspective (pp. 21-47). Clevedon, England: Multilingual Matters Ltd.

McLaughlin, M. L. (1984). Conversation: How talk is organized. Beverly Hills, CA: Sage.

Nofsinger, R. E. (1991). Everyday conversation. Newbury Park: CA: Sage.

Poole, M. S., Folger, J. P., & Hewes, D. E. (1987). Analyzing interpersonal interaction. In M. E. Roloff & G. R. Miller (Eds.), Interpersonal processes: New directions in communication research (pp. 220-256). Beverly Hills, CA: Sage.

Rogers, L. E., & Farace, R. V. (1975). Relational communication analysis: New measurement techniques. Human Communication Research, 1, 222-239.

Tracy, K. (1991). Discourse. In B. M. Montgomery & S. Duck (Eds.), Studying interpersonal interaction (pp. 179-196). New York: Guilford.

I. Readings on Ethnographic Observational Research

Bakeman, R., & Goteman, J. M. (1986). Observing interaction: An introduction to sequential analysis. Cambridge, England: Cambridge University Press.

Donaghy, W. (1989). Nonverbal communication measurement. In P. Emmert & L. L. Barker (Eds.), Measurement of communication behavior (pp. 296-332). New York: Longman.

Fetterman, D. (1989). Ethnography: Step by step. Newbury Park, CA: Sage.

Jorgensen, D. L. (1989). Participant observation: A methodology for human studies. Newbury Park, CA: Sage.

Sillars, A. (1991). Behavioral observation. In B. Montgomery & S. Duck (Eds.), Studying interpersonal interaction (pp. 197-218). New York: Guilford.

J. Readings on Ethnographic Interview Research

Brenner, M. (Ed.) (1985). The research interview. London: Academic Press.

Douglas, J. (1985). Creative interviewing. Newbury Park, CA: Sage.

McCracken, G. (1988). The long interview. Newbury Park, CA: Sage.

Mishler, E. G. (1986). Research interviewing: Context and narrative. Cambridge, MA: Harvard University Press.

Morgan, D. L. (1988). Focus groups as qualitative research. Newbury Park, CA: Sage.

INVESTIGATING COMMUNICATION 2nd edition: CHAPTER OUTLINES

PART I CONCEPTUALIZING COMMUNICATION RESEARCH

CHAPTER 1: INTRODUCTION TO THE RESEARCH CULTURE

I. Introduction
A. We live in an "information society" with a wealth of information at our fingertips.
B. Information is no longer a luxury; it is a necessity on which we depend for survival.
   1. The economy of the United States, once driven by agriculture and later by service, is now based on information.
C. Not all information is created equally; some information is better than other information because it has been tested and shown to be valid; the key word here is "tested," which means that some *research* has been conducted about it.
D. If we are to distinguish good from bad information, we need to become competent consumers of how information is produced.
   1. Chapter goals
      a. Explore the importance of knowing research methods.
      b. Examine some common, everyday ways of knowing to distinguish these from the research process.
      c. Explore some characteristics of the research culture.
      d. Distinguish good research from pseudo research and bad research.
II. The Importance of Knowing Research Methods
 A. We have become a "research-based" culture.
   1. Research has become perhaps *the* most important stamp of approval in our society.
   2. Research has become part of the ongoing business of doing business.
   3. A United States Department of Labor report identifies "ability in information-acquiring and evaluating data" as one of the five competencies necessary for performing most jobs.
   4. Statements from people working in the real world (see Figure 1.1) show that the communication research methods course they took in college was one of the most important-- if not *the* most important--course they took in terms of being successful in their profession.
   5. Policy decisions made by community organizations, educational institutions, and federal, state, and local governments, to name but a few, are now made, in part, on the basis of original research conducted and/or extensive reviews of what the available research shows.
   6. Understanding research methods might help one's personal life; for example, being able to read and understand research reports that compare products, such as those published in the magazine, Consumer Reports, can help people make better choices about the products they buy.
III. Making Claims and Offering Evidence
 A. If there is one thing that researchers, common folk, politicians, educators, top-level corporate executives, snakeoil salespeople have in common, it is that all make

claims, that is, assertions or conclusions.
1. Most claims are supported with some form of **evidence**, or reason.
2. The validity of a claim obviously is related, to a large degree, to the validity of the evidence in its favor.
   a. The validity of the evidence offered depends to some extent on the situation.
   b. The validity of a claim and the evidence offered for it also depends on the validity of the often-unarticulated **warrant**, a statement (another claim) that logically connects the claim and the evidence.
      i. Some evidence or backing must be given for the warrant as well.
      ii. The warrant is particularly important, for if it is not valid, the argument advanced by the claim and evidence usually falls apart.
3. This text is primarily concerned with understanding and evaluating the claims, evidence, and warrants that are made by researchers about what people do, why they do it, what influences them to do it, and what effect it has on them and others.
   a. Critical thinking skills are taught for evaluating research-based arguments; the specific focus is on research about people's communication.

IV. Everyday Ways of Knowing
A. The acceptance of information at face value is called **everyday ways of knowing**; when we rely on knowledge that we have not questioned or tested, we are using everyday ways of knowing.
B. Five common everyday ways of knowing are: (a) personal experience; (b) intuition; (c) authority; (d) appeals to tradition, custom, and faith; and (e) magic, superstition, and mysticism.
   1. **Personal experience**: Experiencing something firsthand.
      a. Personal experience can be an excellent starting point for the testing of knowledge, but it does not always serve us well.
         i. We often believe that what's in our minds and social encounters is generally true.
         ii. Some research indicates that we form inaccurate opinions about everyday events because we are limited in our ability to think about the information available to us; we jump to conclusions on the basis of limited knowledge and although information derived from the study of many people's lives in more trustworthy, it is also remote and pallid, and, therefore, easily ignored.
   2. **Intuition**: Believing something is true or false simply because it "makes sense."
      a. Intuitive hunches sometimes pay off in useful ideas, but it is often just plain wrong.
         i. One area where intuition leads people astray is with regard to calculating statistics, especially the probability of the occurrence of events; people typically underestimate the probability of what appears to be highly unlikely circumstances.
         ii. Common everyday intuitive thinking often results in mistaken perceptions and judgments.
            (a) *Cognitive conservatism* is a proclivity whereby we hold onto conclusions we reach even when presented with contradictory information.
            (b) *Pareidolia* is perceiving meaning in the face of meaningless objects or stimuli,

such as discernible images in clouds.
- (c) The *tunnel effect* describes perceptual tricks of the mind that accompany intuitive reasoning through which against our will, our mind enters a tunnel in its reasoning.
3. **Authority:** Believing something because of our trust in the person who said it.
   a. Numerous studies of the persuasive effects of source credibility, the characteristics that make a person believable, show that who says something may be even more important that what is said.
   b. There are certainly many cases in which we must rely on authorities, but respected authorities, make mistakes.
   c. Some people also claim and/or are assumed to be experts simply because they hold positions of power, like the boss of a company, although we all probably know instances in which the boss simply is wrong.
   d. In other cases, determining who is and who isn't an authority can be quite problematic.
4. *Appeals to tradition, custom,* and *faith*:
   a. **Tradition** and **custom** involve believing something simply because most people in a society assume it is true or because it has always been done that way.
      i. Some customary beliefs we now know from research make very good sense, such as cuddling babies and playing word games with them.
      ii. But custom can also lead to cognitive conservatism that ultimately cuts off the inquiry process and subsequent growth of knowledge, and leads us to cling tenaciously to the beliefs we hold.
      iii. Custom may also lead people to cling to racist or sexual stereotypes, such as "Women are less capable than men of being top managers"; when pressed about why they hold this belief, prejudiced people might respond, "Because it's always been that way."
   b. **Appeals to faith** involve a belief that does not rest on logical proof or material evidence.
      i. Asking someone to accept something because of the person whom says it or because it has always been done that way in the past are two types of appeal to faith.
5. **Magic, superstition, and mysticism:** As when we use the word *mystery* to explain an otherwise unexplainable event.
   a. Many of these so-called mysteries are actually easily explained.
   b. The mystical/superstitious belief that appears to have caught hold the most in the general public is *astrology*, the "study" (and we use that term loosely) of the positions and aspects of heavenly bodies in the belief that they have an influence on the course of human affairs; there is absolutely no scientific basis or evidence for astrology.

V. The Research Process
A. **Research** is what we call the form of disciplined inquiry that involves studying something in a planned manner and reporting it so that other inquirers can potentially replicate the process if they choose.
   1. Two types of research:

a. **Proprietary research** is conducted for a specific audience and is not necessarily shared beyond that audience.
   b. **Scholarly research** is conducted to promote public access to knowledge, as when researchers conduct and publish studies about the effectiveness of various means of persuasion or new vaccines for treating diseases.
B. Characteristics of (scholarly) research
   1. Research is based on curiosity and asking questions.
      a. Research starts with a person's sense of curiosity, a desire to find an answer to a puzzling question posed.
      b. **Research methods** may be viewed as the strategies researchers use to solve puzzling mysteries about the world; they are the means used to collect evidence necessary for building or testing explanations about that which is being studied.
   2. Research is a systematic process.
      a. Research proceeds in a careful step-by-step manner, employing an ordered system of inquiry.
      b. The communication research process can be viewed as an ongoing cycle of five interrelated phases of research activities:
         i. **Conceptualization:** Involves forming an idea about what needs to be studied, which includes identifying a topic worth studying, reviewing the relevant literature to learn what is already known about the topic, and phrasing the topic as a formal research question or hypothesis (prediction).
         ii. Planning and designing research: Researchers need a systematic plan for conducting their research.
            (a) Moving from the conceptualization phrase to planning and designing research demands that researchers transform abstract concepts into operational, or measurement, terms; **operationalization** is the process of determining the observable characteristics associated with a concept or variable.
         iii. Methodologies for conducting research: Conducting careful research demands understanding and adhering to the specific assumptions and requirements of the methodology chosen: experiments, surveys, textual analysis (rhetorical criticism, content analysis, interaction analysis, and performance studies), and naturalistic research.
         iv. Analyzing and interpreting data
         v. **Reconceptualization:** The part of the research process in which researchers formally connect their studies with previous studies on a specific topic and set the stage for future research.
   3. Research is potentially replicable.
      a. Because research follows a systematic plan, other scholars can potentially replicate, or reproduce, the entire inquiry process.
      b. The words "potentially replicable" are used because scholars who wish to replicate another's research study need to have the appropriate resources to do so.
   4. Research is reflexive and self-critical.
      a. Research is reflexive in that researchers explicitly examine their methods to discover

and report flaws or threats to the validity of any findings from a study.
5. Research is cumulative and self-correcting.
   a. The accumulation of information from research allows for knowledge to evolve and grow.
   b. Research, thus, leads to more research.
6. Research is cyclical.
   a. Research proceeds in stages and ends up back where it started; new questions emerge from answers to previous questions.

VI. Research as Culture

A. Like any culture, research has its own language, rules, and social customs.
B. Research Cultures: Researchers do not necessarily share the same worldview or the same assumptions about how people and communication should be studied.
   1. At the most general level, there are three such cultures: The physical sciences, humanities, and the social (human) sciences.
      a. **Physical sciences:** Scholars study the physical and natural world.
      b. **Humanities:** Scholars produce creative products and study the achievements of creative people.
      c. **Social sciences:** Scholars apply scientific methods to the study of human behavior.
   2. Communication overlaps, in part, each of these three research cultures.
   3. Positivist versus Naturalistic research: Two major **paradigms**, or worldviews, characterize social-scientific research.
      a. The **positivist paradigm** is essentially concerned with how to apply some of the methods used in the physical sciences to the study of human behavior.
      b. The **naturalistic paradigm** is essentially concerned with the development of methods that capture the socially constructed and situated nature of human behavior.
   4. Key differences between the positivist and naturalistic paradigms in terms of five basic assumptions that have important implications for the research process (see Figure 1.4).
      a. *Ontological assumption*: Proponents of the positivist paradigm see reality as *singular* and *objective*; proponents of the naturalistic paradigm contend that there are *multiple realities* that are constructed between and among people (intersubjective).
      b. *Epistemological assumption*: Proponents of the positivist paradigm see this relationship as *independent*, in the sense that what is to be known is independent of any researcher per se; proponents of the naturalistic paradigm believe that the researcher is *interdependent* with that which is being studied in that what can be known depends on who's doing the knowing.
      c. *Axiological assumption*: Proponents of the positivist paradigm believe that research can be *value-free* and *unbiased*; proponents of the naturalistic paradigm argue that research is inherently *value-laden* and *biased*.
      d. Methodological Assumption
         1. Research conducted from the positivist paradigm generally tends to use *deduction*, moving from the general to the specific; searches for *cause*

and effect relationships between variables; typically uses a *static design* in which the specific research procedures are all worked out ahead of time and the researcher sticks to that plan carefully and conscientiously; most often conducted within a *researcher-controlled setting*, a setting created and controlled by a researcher; typically uses *quantitative methods*, research methods that focus on the collection of data in the form of meaningful numbers; yields *context-free generalizations*, conclusions that can be generalized to people, situations, and time periods other than the ones studied; and allow researchers to *explain*, *predict*, and *control* phenomena.
    2. Research conducted from the naturalistic paradigm tends to use *induction*, moving from the specific (the evidence) to the general (tentative explanations); goal is to gain a *wholistic understanding* of the patterns and behaviors that characterize human beings; uses an *emergent design*, planning out the research, but then taking advantage of opportunities that present themselves during the research process; conduct research in the natural setting, rely primarily on *qualitative methods*, research methods that focus on the acquisition of data that take the form of symbols other than meaningful numbers; yield *context-bound findings*, findings that apply to the particular people, situation or time period studied; and provide a rich *understanding* of that social context and, in some cases, serve the purpose of promoting social change.
  e. *Rhetorical assumption*: Positivist research reports tend to have a *formal structure* and are written in an *impersonal* (*third-person*) voice in line with the view of research as an *objective* endeavor; naturalistic research reports tend have an *informal structure* and include the *personal* (*first-person*) voice of the researcher.

VII. Research as Conversation
A. Research can be thought of as a form of conversation.
  1. There are conversations that take place between researchers and the people (or texts) they study; the nature of that conversation is shaped, in part, by the paradigm that researchers adopt and the specific methods they employ.
  2. There are conversations that take place between researchers and a variety of other audiences: colleagues in the field, grant application, gatekeepers of publication outlets, general public, research participants, conversations among research participants, and conversations at the public level.

VIII. The Importance of Distinguishing Research from Pseudo-research
A. If we are to become competent consumers of research, we must be able to distinguish research from pseudoresearch and just plain bad research because we are being exposed every day to more and more research findings, and it is getting hard to separate the valid information from that which is not.
  1. To the extent that we are ignorant of the way research is produced, and the many potential problems that can jeopardize the validity of research findings, we have no basis for accepting or rejecting research-based claims and evidence.
B. The inability to differentiate valid from invalid research-based information is having

some terrible effects at the societal level.
  1. **Pseudo-research** or **junk science** looks, smells, and tastes like real science, but it isn't.
     a. Federal rules of evidence essentially opened the door for anyone with some minimum qualifications, such as a college degree, to be an expert.
     b. So-called junk scientists, whose theories, methods, and procedures sound valid to the naive listener but are not considered so by scientists in the field can now be hired to testify (some of even said "hired to lie") as expert witnesses.
     c. Stopping the spread of false information is not just the responsibility of individual scientists, the media, the government, and the courts--it is everybody's business.

IX. Conclusion
 A. If we are to be knowledgeable and critical consumers of research, we must understand the processes used to conduct it.
 B. To do that, we have to learn about the research culture—its assumptions about how the world words, the various methods employed, and the rules of conduct to be followed.
 C. Once we know the code of research conversations, we have a better chance of distinguishing valid from invalid information.

TEST ITEMS

CH1

1. It has been suggested that we live in the "information age." Which of the following **best** supports this conclusion?
   - (A) new communication mediums are replacing less reliable channels
   - (B) it is impossible to exist in an information vacuum
   - (C) more than 55% of the GNP for the U.S. flows from information-based products and services
   - (D) the quality of disseminated information is easily ascertained
   * (E) none of the above

2. The primary justification for holding *research screenings* is that the movie industry:
   - (A) sees the process as good PR
   * (B) desires to pre-test potential plots with a representative sample
   - (C) perceives the process as a way to placate movie critics and potential adversaries
   - (D) desires to pre-test potential plots with the viewing population
   - (E) views the process as a preemptive strategy against future lawsuits

3. According to the U.S. Labor Department (1991), all of the following are competencies crucial to performing most jobs EXCEPT:
   * (A) earning an advanced degree
   - (B) understanding key technology
   - (C) demonstrating good interpersonal skills
   - (D) understanding relevant systems
   - (E) acquiring and evaluating data

4. The authors of the text contend that one should most likely take a research methods courses if he or she:
   - (A) plans to work for a marketing firm
   - (B) will be attending graduate school
   - (C) seeks to make informed choices across the life span
   - (D) plans to work for a Research and Development firm
   * (E) all of the above

For items 5-6, consider the following.
i. Safe sex, using a condom for example, reduces one's chances of contracting HIV.
ii. HIV, the AIDS virus, is transmitted through the exchange of body fluids.
iii. Condoms, while not foolproof, are an effective strategy against becoming infected with HIV.

5. Statement ii **best** exemplifies which of the following?
* (A) evidence
   (B) claim
   (C) warrant
   (D) backing
   (E) assertion

6. Statement iii **best** exemplifies which of the following?
   (A) evidence
   (B) claim
* (C) warrant
   (D) backing
   (E) assertion

7. One of the primary purposes of research is to:
* (A) verify and/or debunk popular beliefs
   (B) exclude the less fortunate in society
   (C) promote the use of certain products
   (D) prove theories
   (E) none of the above

For item 8, consider the following.
Blue: "You know Rosie, you're just like Sarah, Missy, Erica, and Leslie. Sheesh....women!!"
Rosie: "Get a life...I don't even know them. And just because they lied to you doesn't mean I will!!"

8. Blue is most likely relying on _____ to reach his conclusion.
   (A) authority
   (B) intuition
* (C) personal experience
   (D) appeals to faith
   (E) cannot answer as more information is needed

9. According to the authors of the text, a primary reason many individuals underestimate some event's probability of occurrence is that:
   (A) math phobia is more prevalent than public speaking phobia
   * (B) intuitive reasoning in such situations is generally wrong
   (C) most folks do not carry pocket calculators
   (D) the experiment conducted by Paulos (1988) supports this claim
   (E) cognitive conservatism is widespread among younger individuals

10. According to the authors of the text, all of the following characterize scholarly research EXCEPT:
    (A) systematic
    (B) reflexive
    (C) cynical
    (D) question-driven
    * (E) all of the above are characteristics of scholarly research

For item 11, consider the following.
Laura Jeanne: What a compelling lecture, huh? It was great to hear Sandra Day O'Connor--the first female Supreme Court judge--talk about the importance of perseverance; even in the face of all that sexism she encountered.
Jim: Yes, I too enjoyed her talk very much. She convinced me that things were a lot worse back than now. Sheesh....

11. Laura Jeanne is most likely relying on _____ to reach her conclusion.
    * (A) authority
    (B) intuition
    (C) personal experience
    (D) appeals to faith
    (E) cannot answer as more information is needed

12. Conceptual and operational definitions may be best viewed as:
    * (A) assessing connotative and denotative variable dimensions
    (B) assessing the impact of independent variables
    (C) examples of naturalistic research
    (D) assessing the impact of dependent variables
    (E) examples of positivistic research

For item 13, consider the following.
Assume you are about to conduct an investigation concerning how it feels to be communicatively apprehensive (CA) among 300 college freshmen.

13. Which of the following statements will best describe your view of CA?
    (A) communication apprehension is grounded in theory
* (B) communication apprehension is a fluctuating range of interview scores
    (C) communication apprehension is inductively derived
    (D) communication apprehension is similar to shyness and avoidance
    (E) communication apprehension is a fixed range of interview scores

For items 14-15, consider the following.
At a shopping mall, several individuals are randomly asked to evaluate the meaning of the Vietnam War. Their **distinct** responses follow.

Nikki: "Wow, it was a great waste of life and resources!"
Colleen: "We sure taught those commies a lesson and I am proud to be an American!"
Pat: "The 'smart' ones really turned out to be the draft dodgers..."
Lyle: "I am still not sure what the purpose was..."

14. Since the target of description--Vietnam War--is the same, and the responses are distinct, which theoretical assumption is at work here?
    (A) axiological assumption
    (B) epistemological assumption
* (C) ontological assumption
    (D) social scientific assumption
    (E) cause and effect assumption

15. Which research paradigm would be best suited to uncover the diverse meanings and the role of the context on the messages above?
* (A) naturalistic paradigm
    (B) positivist paradigm
    (C) wholistic paradigm
    (D) researcher-controlled paradigm
    (E) axiological paradigm

True/False
F   16. Information is a luxury and not essential for survival.
F   17. Policy decisions at local, state, and federal levels are rarely informed or shaped by existing research.
F   18. The validity of a claim is related only a small degree to the validity of the evidence in its favor.

T	19.	Everyday ways of knowing are based on acceptance of information at face value.
T	20.	Cognitive conservatism is a tendency whereby individuals hold onto conclusions even in the face of contradictory information.
T	21.	To be considered "research," the knowledge claims advanced must have been tested.
F	22.	Proprietary research is conducted for a specific audience and is usually shared with the general public.
F	23.	Proponents of the positivist paradigm see reality as multidimensional and objective, whereas proponents of the naturalistic paradigm see reality as singular and intersubjective.
T	24.	Research conducted by organizations trying to promote their products would typically exemplify psuedoresearch.
F	25.	When evaluating the strength of a knowledge claim, researchers look to the judicial system to render a decision by issuing a warrant.

Short-Answer/Essay Questions
1. Identify the five everyday ways of knowing discussed in the textbook. For each way of knowing, discuss one strength and one weakness.
2. Explain the fundamental difference between everyday ways of knowing and research using the following sentence form: Everyday ways of knowing are based on _____, whereas research is based on _____.
3. Explain the difference between proprietary research and scholarship.
4. Match the following characteristics of scholarship with their appropriate definition: (A) Question-oriented; (B) Systematic; (C) Potentially replicable; (D) Reflexive and self-critical; (E) Cumulative and self-correcting; (F) Cyclical.
   1) Scholarship proceeds in stages and ends up back where it started
   2) Scholarship follows a plan that should be able to be duplicated by other scholars
   3) Scholarship leads to more scholarship
   4) Scholarship follows a planned process of investigation
   5) Scholarship explicitly examines itself to discover and report flaws or threats to its accuracy and it is open to examination, questioning, and criticism by everyone
   6) Scholarship begins by asking something important
   ANSWERS: 1 = E; 2 = C; 3= F; 4 = B; 5 = D; 6 = A
5. Explain how research may be viewed as a "culture."
6. Identify and explain two differences between the positivist and naturalistic paradigms with regard to methodological practices. Write each of your 2 different answers like this: The positivist paradigm uses _____, which means _____, whereas the naturalistic paradigm uses _____, which means _____. (Note: The difference between the

positivistic and naturalistic paradigm within each sentence must be with respect to the same type of concern; you also must explain what the term means and not treat it as self-evident.)

7. Discuss how positivist and naturalistic approaches to research represent different ways of studying communicative behavior by addressing the main thrust of each paradigm and explicating its key assumptions and tenets.

8. Explain how research may be viewed as a "conversation" and at least two types of research conversations that take place.

9. Define/explain the term pseudoresearch, discuss some of the problems with relying on pseudoresearch, and some of the solutions for overcoming it.

CHAPTER 2: ASKING QUESTIONS ABOUT COMMUNICATION

I. Introduction
 A. Research begins with curiosity.
  1. Researchers notice something about communication and wish to learn more about it.
 B. Researchers move from that sense of curiosity to formulating a question that can be answered by engaging in a research project. .
  1. The questions we ask suggest what information we will gather ("in"-put), and the conclusions we will draw ("out"-put) are based on that information.
II. Defining Communication
 A. Defining the term **communication** is like trying to describe a three-ring circus to a child-- how can we put into a sentence or two everything that goes on when so *much* goes on?
  1. A variety of images come to mind when you tell people you are studying communication.
   a. They react so variably because communication is an umbrella term that covers numerous, apparently disparate, activities.
  2. The term communication, historically, is derived from the Latin word, *communis*, which means "to make common."
  3. Today, most definitions of communication emphasize one of two different views about making things common.
 B. Those who focus on the process of *making* things common adopt what can be called an **information exchange** perspective.
  1. They are primarily concerned with how communication can be used as a tool to transfer information from one person or place (a source) to another (a receiver).
 C. Those who emphasize that which is made *common* adopt what can be called a **meaning-based** or **constitutive perspective**.
  1. They are concerned with how perceptions of reality are shaped by communication processes.
 D. We acknowledge these two views on "making things common" with our definition.
  1. Communication refers to the processes by which verbal and nonverbal messages are used to create and share meaning.
III. What Constitutes Communication Research?
 A. A traditional model of communication--*people exchanging messages through channels within a context*--provides a useful way to focus on the types of research done by communication scholars.
  1. The *model* contains four important components: *people, messages, channels*, and *contexts*.
  2. The pivotal element of the four is messages.
   a. **Messages** are the usual target of communication researchers--messages we send to ourselves, to others, within small groups or organizations, via the media, or within and between cultures.
  3. The other three components of the model--people, channels, and contexts--are usually studied only as they influence messages.

      a. We depend on scholars in other disciplines to study the psychological, biological, and many other dimensions of human life.
         i. Studying how people's self-esteem changes as they grow older is more appropriate for psychology researchers than for communication researchers because the focus isn't on message behavior.
         ii. Studying how self-esteem affects communication apprehension (fear of communicating, such as fear of public speaking) is appropriate for communication research because the focus is on message behavior and not just on psychological variables.
         iii. To make the other elements of people, channels, and/or contexts relevant to communication interests, researchers must relate them to message behavior.

IV. Areas of Communication Research
  A. Message behavior covers a large array of processes and little can be said about "communication in general."
    1. Researchers' first step involves carving out and defining the precise slice of the big communication pie they will investigate.
      i. They identify the **research topic**, the novel idea they consider worth studying and hope to understand better.
  B. The communication realm can be divided in many ways.
    1. Scholars affiliate with colleagues studying similar topics within the **professional associations** in the communication discipline.
      i. The National Communication Association (NCA), the International Communication Association (ICA), and the Association for Educational Journalism and Mass Communication (AEJMC) are major associations.
      ii. There are four regional associations--the Central States, Eastern, Southern States, and Western States Communication Associations.
      iii. There are many state associations.
  C. Professional associations are organized into different interest areas, each of which addresses the common concern(s) of a group of scholars (see Figure 2.1).
    1. Professional associations often publish academic journals (see Chapter 3).
    2. The interest areas of the communication discipline are reflected in the courses taught at universities and colleges, and, in some cases, in the concentrations offered for communication majors.
      i. Within each interest area, several general topics attract scholars' attention (see Figure 2.2).
      ii. Existing interest areas within the communication discipline suggest fruitful directions for research.
         (a) Officially designated interest areas are not mutually exclusive compartments within which all communication research can be neatly classified.

V. Basic Versus Applied Communication Research Topics
  A. One distinction communication scholars make is between **basic** and **applied research**.
    1. *Basic research*: research designed to test and refine theory.

2. *Applied research*: research designed to solve a practical problem.
B. People often misinterpret the word theory, sometimes contrasting it negatively with practical knowledge.
   1. A *theory* is simply a generalization about a phenomenon, an explanation of how or why something occurs.
   2. There is an important difference between "commonsense" theories and "scientifically tested" theories.
      i. Scholars are more systematic in the way they develop and test theories.
      ii. The purpose of **basic communication research** is to increase our knowledge about communication phenomena by testing, refining, and elaborating theory.
C. Numerous theories have been developed to explain a wide array of communication events and processes, far too many to catalogue in this chapter.
   1. Not all theories proposed by scholars are equally worthwhile.
      i. The value of a given theory is judged by the extent to which it explains an important phenomenon satisfactorily, organizes knowledge, predicts certain outcomes, focuses research efforts, and excites inquiry (see Figure 2.3).
      ii. The process of testing a theory is relatively straightforward (see Figure 2.4).
         (a) The first step involves the selection of a research topic.
         (b) The next step is the choice of an appropriate theory to help explain important aspects of the research topic.
         (c) A hypothesis (or hypotheses) is then derived from the theory, and the accuracy of that prediction is tested in a study.
         (d) Data are collected an analyzed, and they are used to gauge the merits of the prediction.
         (e) If the findings confirm the or support the hypothesis, the theory has one more piece of support. If the findings do not support the hypothesis, more research may need to be conducted, the hypothesis may need to be revised, and/or the theory may need to be revised or rejected.
   2. One example is that many researchers who study interpersonal communication (an area) are interested in communication behavior during initial interactions (a topic).
      i. One theory that is especially useful for explaining communication during initial interactions is Berger and Calabrese's (1975) Uncertainty Reduction Theory (URT), a theory that describes the relationship between uncertainty and communication.
      ii. The theory starts with the premise that people experience a lot of uncertainty during initial interactions (e.g., about the other person, how to behave etc.) and that they engage in communication to reduce their uncertainty.
      iii. Berger and Calabrese derived a number of hypotheses from this theory.
         (a) The research study conducted by Douglas (1994) shows that a theory is really never complete.
         (b) Theories, like communication, are on-going and ever-changing, and can always benefit from further refinement and elaboration.

D. **Applied communication research** is conducted for the purpose of solving a "real- world", socially relevant communication problem.
   1. Applied communication research seeks to demonstrate the relevance of communication knowledge to a particular event or challenge of everyday life.
      i. Applied researchers start with a communication problem in a specific context and conduct a study to lessen its intensity and/or prevalence.
   2. Many important problems experiences by individuals, couples, groups, organizations, and societies have attracted the attention of communication scholars (see Figure 2.5).
   3. One type of applied research that has important consequences for the study of communication is **action research**, "a collaborative approach to inquiry or investigation that provides people with the means to take systematic action to resolve specific problems" (Stringer, 1996, p. 5).
      i. Action research stresses *participative inquiry*, that is, communication and collaboration with community group members throughout the course of a research study.
      ii. Working with a researcher, stakeholders define a problem in their community, determine the methods to be used to collect, analyze, and reflect on the data, and use their new understandings to design action steps to resolve and manage the problem.
   4. One important type of applied communication research that lends itself well to action research methods is **social justice communication research**.
      i. This research deals with and contributes to the well-being of people who are economically, socially, politically, and/or culturally under-resourced and disenfranchised.
      ii. One way researchers do this is by identifying and critiquing dominant structures that underwrite equality.
      iii. Sometimes social justice communication researchers go beyond identification and critique to actively change an oppressive situation.
VI. An Integrated Model of Basic and Applied Communication Research
A. Although there are some important differences between basic and applied communication research (see Figure 2.6), these should not be treated as unrelated endeavors.
   1. *Theory* and *practice* are inherently intertwined.
   2. The interrelationship of theory and application is especially important in a "practical discipline" such as Communication that has enormous potential to make a difference in people's lives.
B. Kreps, Frey, and O'Hair (1991) advanced a conceptual model that integrates concerns for theory with concerns for practice (see Figure 2.7).
   1. This model employs two axes.
      i. One axis describes the relative emphasis of a particular study on theory.
      ii. The other axis references the relative emphasis on application/practice.
   2. This model is useful for assessing the potential benefits of research studies.
      i. A study low on both theory and application (1/1) is rarely worth doing.
      ii. A study may have relatively high theoretical interest but little practical application (1/9), at least in the short run..

iii. A study rated high on applied value but low on theory (9/1), is one which the research solves an important problem in a particular context, but the findings cannot be generalized to other contexts (see Chapter 5).

iv. Many studies fall between the extremes, of course (5/5 studies for example), but communication scholars should aim to do research that has high concern/potential for both theory and practice (9/9).

VII. Justifying Communication Research Topics

A. R. K. Tucker, Weaver, and Berryman-Fink (1981) argue that all researchers should be prepared to answer the questions: "So what?" and "Who cares?"

1. Researchers, therefore, must develop a clear rationale for why their research topic is worth studying.
2. Research should contribute to the "conversation" between those who conduct research and those who might use their research findings. . .
    i. In that light, research can be addressed to three primary audiences, each of which has slightly different needs: scholars, practitioners, and the general public.
    (a) A research project is important to communication scholars when it investigates an important communication phenomenon/problem, extends previous research by providing a more complete understanding of that phenomenon/problem, tests and refines theory, and suggests directions for future research.
    (b) A second audience is practitioners who apply the knowledge that scholars produce, and they value communication research projects that help them do their job better.
    (c) A third audience is the general public, non-professionals who want to know what messages will help them handle their everyday communication challenges better; therefore, a communication project is important to the extent that it helps them live a more fulfilling life.
    (d) Some communication research has utility for all three audiences.

VIII. Research Questions and Hypotheses

A. In research articles, researchers first explain why they chose their topic, review the relevant literature (see Chapter 3), and then they articulate the research question or statement that guided their investigation.

1. These questions and/or statements usually are designed to accomplish one of two goals.
    i. To describe communication behavior.
    ii. To relate communication behavior to other variables.

IX. Describing Communication Behavior

A. One important purpose of communication research is to describe the nature and characteristics of a particular communication behavior or sequence of communication behaviors.

1. A **research question**, a formal question posed to guide research, of this type essentially asks, "What is the nature of communication behavior 'X'?"
    i. An example is, What receiver behaviors trigger perceived suspicion? (J. K. Burgoon, Buller, Dillman, & Walther, 1995).
    ii. Another example is, What topics do recipients report being teased about? (Alberts, Kellar-Guenther, & Corman, 1997).

iii. A third example is, What are the types of interpersonal rituals reported in friendships and marital relationships? (Bruess & Pearson, 1997).
  2. These questions attempt to categorize a concept, and, thereby, measure it and turn it into a variable (see Chapter 4).
    i. A **variable** is any concept that can have two or more values.
    ii. A single object, therefore is not a variable.
      (a) It becomes a variable only when it exists in different types or in different amounts and we understand those different states.
X. Relating Communication Behavior to Other Variables
  A. Turning a communication concept into a variable makes it possible to examine the relationship between that communication behavior/variable and other important variables.
    1. Researchers can answer specific instances of the general research question, "How is communication variable 'X' related to other variables.
      i. One example: Is affective orientation related to the reported use of specific types of nonverbal comforting behaviors? (Bullis & Horn, 1995).
      ii. Another example: Is the sex of the siblings related to the amount of verbally aggressive messages? (Teven, Martin, & Newpauer, 1998).
      iii. A third example: Are there associations between a woman's surname and men's and women's perceptions of a woman's commitment to the relationship or love for her partner? (Stafford & Kline, 1996).
  B. Independent versus Dependent Variables
    1. When researchers study how two variables are related, they often assume that one of them influences the other.
      i. The variable that is thought to influence the changes in another variable is called an **independent variable (IV)** (sometimes called an **explanatory variable**; in nonexperimental research a **predictor variable**).
      ii. They call the variable thought to be changed by another variable a **dependent variable (DV)** (in nonexperimental research, sometimes called the **criterion variable** or **outcome variable**).
    2. Sometimes researchers suspect a **causal relationship** between variables, believing that changes in the independent variable cause observed changes in the dependent variable.
      i. Researchers sometimes study independent variables that are not about messages, but are thought to influence people's communication behavior.
        (a) Example: The attractiveness of people's appearance may influence how others talk to them.
      ii. Communication behavior, of course, can also be studied as an independent variable that causes changes in the dependent variable.
        (a) Example: Researchers may suspect that certain messages designed to get other people to comply with a request may actually cause people to *resist* doing what was asked rather than agreeing to it.
      iii. It should be pointed out that causality is very difficult to establish.
        (a) We would not want to conclude that a drug cured a disease on the basis of

a single study, or two or three, and the same is true when attempting to establish causal principles for communication behavior (see Chapter 5).
   iv. There are also various models of causal relationships between variables.
      (a) Example: In **recursive causal models**, the causal relationship is one way in that the one variable influences another but not the other way around, that is one is the cause and the other is effect.
      (b) Example: In **nonrecursive causal models**, the causal relationship is reciprocal or two way, in that a variable can be both a cause and effect.
   v. At other times, researchers assume a **non-causal relationship** between variables, meaning that the variables are associated, or occur together, without one necessarily causing changes in the other.
      (a) When posing formal research questions for a study that assesses noncausal relationships, researchers typically designate one variable as the independent variable and the other as the dependent variable, depending on their primary interest.

C. Ordered versus Nominal Variables
  1. Variables can also be differentiated with regard to the values researchers assign to them or the kind of "scale" used to measure them (see Chapter 4).
    i. **Ordered variables** can be assigned numerical values that indicate how much of the concept is present.
      (a) Variables such as age, weight, temperature, and income are ordered variables.
    ii. **Nominal variables** (also called categorical, classificatory, or discrete variables), by contrast, can be differentiated only on the basis of type (nominal means "in name only").
      (a) Variables such as gender (male and female), race (e.g., Caucasian, African American, Hispanic, and Native American), and political affiliation (e.g., Democrat, Republican, and Independent) are nominal variables.
      (b) A nominal variable that can be divided into two categories such as gender is called a **dichotomous** or **binomial** variable.
      (c) A nominal variable that can be divided into more than two categories such as ethnicity is called a **polytomous variable**.
    iii. In some cases, a potentially ordered variable is treated as a nominal variable; however, due to a loss of important information, researchers do not typically turn ordered variables into nominal variables.

D. Research Questions versus Hypotheses
  1. Research studies usually are designed to answer research questions or test hypotheses about relationships between variables..
    i. Questions are typically posed when researchers do not have enough evidence, on the basis of the literature reviewed (see Chapter 3), to predict the nature of that relationship.
    ii. At other times, researchers have a hunch or tentative answer about the nature of the relationship between an independent and dependent variable.
      (a) When researchers feel confident enough to make a prediction, they advance a

hypothesis (Ha is the general symbol for a research hypothesis; H1 is used to refer to a specific research hypothesis), a tentative statement about the relationship between the independent and dependent variables.
- (b) If the hypothesis predicts a relationship between variables without specifying a relationship, it is called a **two-tailed hypothesis** or, less accurately, a **non-directional hypothesis.**
- (c) If the hypothesis predicts a specific relationship between variables, it is called a **one-tailed hypothesis** (sometimes called a **directional hypothesis**) (see Chapter 12).

XI. Posing Research Questions and Hypotheses about Relationships between Variables
 A. How the research question or hypothesis for a communication study is phrased usually depends on two things.
  1. Whether the independent variable is nominal or ordered.
  2. Whether a researcher wishes to pose a research question or a hypothesis about the relationship between the independent and dependent variables.
  3. We use two hypothetical examples to demonstrate: The effects of gender on self-disclosure and the effects of age on self-disclosure.
   i. When the independent variable is nominal, divided into categories, the research questions asks whether there is a difference between *a* (the first category of the nominal independent variable) and *b* (the second category of the nominal independent variable) with respect to *c* (the dependent variable).
   ii. In studying the effects of gender (the independent variable) on self-disclosure (the dependent variable), the research question asks whether there is a difference between males (*a*, the first category of the nominal variable) and females (*b*, the second category of the nominal variable) with regard to the self-disclosure (*c*, the dependent variable).
   iii. Some actual examples: Will females provide more sensitive comforting messages than males? (Hoffner & Haefner, 1997); How do doctors and patients differ in their covert responses during the medical interview? (Cegala, McNeilis, McGee, & Jonas, 1995); and Do program enrollees and nonenrollees [in a Breast and Cervical Cancer Control Program] differ in their preference for persuasive messages delivered through mass media, one-to-several interpersonal channels, or one-to-one interpersonal channels? (A.A. Marshall, Smith, & McKeon, 1995).
 B. A hypothesis for a nominal independent variable predicts the nature of the difference between the two (or more) categories of the independent variable.
  1. It takes the form: *a* (the first category of the nominal independent variable) will be greater (or less) on *c* (the dependent variable) than will *b* (the second category of the nominal independent variable).
   i. Regarding the effects of gender on self-disclosure, the hypothesis might state that "men self-disclose more than women" (or "men self-disclose less than women").
    (a) Note: Like most research hypotheses, this statement is one-tailed.
    (b) A two-tailed hypothesis would state: "Men and women self-disclose differently."
   ii. Some actual examples: Women report more than men that verbal interactions

contribute to their relational closeness (Floyd & Parks, 1995); employees provided with justifications will perceive the manager's actions as fairer than employees provided with excuses or no social accounts (Tata, 1996); older people will evaluate their communication with young family adults more positively than young people in general (Cai, Giles, & Noels, 1998).

C. When the independent variable is *ordered*, measured in sequenced numbers, the research questions asks whether there is a relationship between x (the independent variable) and y (the dependent variable).
 1. To ascertain how age (x, the independent variable) affects self-disclosure (y, the dependent variable)--with age being an ordered variable--the research question asks whether there is a relationship between the variables of age and self-disclosure.
   i. Actual example: How are proportions of argument complexity associated with perceptions of communication satisfaction? (Canary, Brossman, Brossman, & Wegner, 1995)
   ii. Actual example: What is the association between leadership evaluations and specific types of leadership-relevant talk? (Pavitt, Whitchurch, McClurg, & Petersen, 1995)
   iii. Actual example: What is the relationship between perpetrator message affect and negotiator affect behavior? (Rogan & Hammer, 1995)

D. A hypothesis for an ordered independent variable specifies the nature of the relationship between the independent and dependent variable.
 1. Independent and dependent variables may be related in quite a few ways; however, we focus on two types of relationships.
   i. A **positive relationship** (also called a **direct relationship**) in which increases in an independent variable are associated with increases in a dependent variable (e.g., the more hours one spends studying before an exam, the higher one's scores will be).
   ii. A **negative relationship** (also called an **inverse relationship**) in which increases in an independent variable are associated with decreases in a dependent variable (e.g., the more hours one spends "partying" the night before an exam, the lower one's exam scores will be).
   iii. A hypothesis, thus, takes the form: x (the independent variable) is positively (or negatively) related to y (the dependent variable).
     (a) For the effects of age on self-disclosure, the hypothesis might be either "Age is positively related to self-disclosure" or "Age is negatively related to self-disclosure".
     (b) A two-tailed hypothesis would state: "Age and self-disclosure are related."
   iv. Actual example: Cognitive efficiency will be positively related to interaction involvement (Jordan, 1998).
   v. Actual example: Increases in the amount of gaze, smiles, head nods, and forward lean will be positively correlated with increases in amount of liking toward the actor (Palmer & Simmons, 1995).
   vi. Frequent viewing of nonviolent children's programs leads over time to an

increase in children's positive-intense daydreaming (Valkenburg & van der Voort, 1995).
- E. Some independent variables are obviously nominal or ordered, such as the variables of gender and age above, but others can be treated as ether nominal or ordered.
  1. As a general rule, if a variable can be measured either way, it should be treated as ordered and a scale should be used to measure it.
- F. Researchers are often interested in the effects of *multiple* independent variables on a dependent variable (an even multiple dependent variables).
  1. In such situations, researchers are especially interested in **interaction effects** (also called **conditioning**, **contingency**, **joint**, and **moderating effects**; sometimes known as **multiplicative reactions** in nonexperimental research---effects due to the unique combination of the independent variables that make a difference to on the dependent variable(s).
     - i. Interaction effects are due to the effects of multiple independent variables working together, in contrast to the effects of each independent variable working alone (called **main effects**).
     - ii. Actual RQ: Do argumentativeness and verbal aggression interact to predict an individual's reported use of evidentiary appeals to respond to refusal of a request? (Ifert & Bearden, 1998)
     - iii. Actual H: The combination of interpersonal communication apprehension and receiver apprehension is more strongly associated with sexual communication satisfaction for women than men in sexually intimate, heterosexual relationships. (Wheeless & Parsons, 1995)

XII. Conclusion
- A. Research does not occur in a vacuum. Communication researchers must examine what is already known.
- B. Determining the "lay of the land" will require finding and evaluating a wide variety of information sources.
- C. The research process does not stop at the "end" of a study as the process is cyclical beginning anew.

TEST ITEMS

CH2

For item 1, consider the following.
(I) What personality attributes shape one's resistance to using crack cocaine?
(II) Is there a relationship between poor communication skills and being adopted?

1. In sequence, statements I and II should primarily be characterized as:
   (A) psychological and biological research questions
   (B) historical and sociological research questions
 * (C) psychological and communication research questions
   (D) historical and biological research questions
   (E) biological and historical research questions

2. Which of the following best describes the role of questions in research in general, and communication, in particular?
   (A) questions have little effect on the outcome of a study
   (B) questions are very similar to one-tailed hypotheses
 * (C) questions shape all aspects of a research endeavor
   (D) questions have little effect on a study's operationalizations
   (E) questions are primarily geared toward providing answers

3. Which approach to communication inquiry supports the "communication as tool" analogy?
 * (A) the information-exchange perspective
   (B) the systems perspective
   (C) the constitutive perspective
   (D) the naturalistic paradigm
   (E) more information is needed

4. According to the authors of the text, the usual target of communication researchers is:
   (A) contexts
   (B) people
 * (C) messages
   (D) channels
   (E) more information is needed

For item 5, consider the following.
Heather has learned that Eugene's friend, Sarah, is about to be laid off from her job. Acting quickly, she faxes the information to Eugene. Upon its arrival, all Eugene focuses on is whether it got through "loud and clear," and in its entirety.

5. Similar to Fisher's (1978) view of communication, Eugene is operating from the _____.

*   (A)   the information-exchange perspective
      (B)   the systems perspective
      (C)   the constitutive perspective
      (D)   the naturalistic paradigm
      (E)   the three-dimensional communication model advanced by the text's authors

For item 6, consider the following.
While perusing a study, you notice that the researcher is examining how people's self-esteem changes as they grow older.

6. According to the authors of the text, this study <u>excludes</u> a key component of behavior crucial to communication investigations and that component is:
      (A)   contexts
      (B)   people
*   (C)   messages
      (D)   channels
      (E)   more information is needed

7. Generally speaking, a sound theory enables investigators employing the positivist paradigm to:
      (A)   predict outcomes
      (B)   test cause-effect relationships among variables
      (C)   control the conditions undergirding a study
      (D)   advance deductive statements
*   (E)   all of the above

For item 8, please consider the following.
A research team to which you belong expects its investigation to reveal that people with high communication apprehension (CA) will report a lower amount of social support than individuals with low levels of CA.

8. This statement primarily reflects a/an:
   (A) nondirectional hypothesis with CA as the dependent variable
   (B) directional hypothesis with CA as a continuous variable
   (C) non-directional hypothesis and inductive statement
   (D) research question awaiting data collection and testing
 * (E) directional hypothesis with CA as the independent variable

For item 9, consider the following.
To have the greatest impact on understanding and knowledge, research conducted within the positivist paradigm builds on prior studies. Yet, within any one study, the testing of hypotheses are *limited to that point in time and particular sample*.

9. In light of these snap-shot features, the logic of hypothesis disconfirmation best supports which of the following positions?
 * (A) knowledge and reality should be viewed as having a fixed nature
   (B) knowledge and reality should be viewed as consensually constructed
   (C) knowledge and reality should be viewed as inductively derived
   (D) knowledge and reality should be viewed as contextually-bound
   (E) knowledge and reality should be viewed as channel and people dependent

10. Assuming a line of research progresses through initial, middle, and late stages, ID the order of Research Questions (RQs), non-directional hypotheses (hys), and directional hys:
   (A) non-directional hys, RQs, directional hys
   (B) directional hys, RQs, non-directional hys
   (C) RQs, directional hys, non-directional hys
   (D) non-directional hys, RQs, non-directional hys
 * (E) RQs, non-directional hys, directional hys

For items 11-12, consider the following.
An investigator decides to represent a variable, "illness," as follows: 650= chronic; 651= temporary; 900= adult; 901= childhood.

11. This variable is best characterized as:
    (A) ordered
　* (B) nominal
    (C) ordinal
    (D) ratio
    (E) interval

12. If this variable is represented by the length of time a person has had the illness, it should be classified as:
    (A) ordered
    (B) independent
    (C) nominal
    (D) ratio
　* (E) interval

For items 13-14, consider the following.
A research team is attempting to ascertain what influence, if any, listening to Mozart has on intelligence in young children.

13. "Intelligence" is best defined here as a/an:
    (A) ordered variable
    (B) independent variable
    (C) nominal variable
　* (D) dependent variable
    (E) interval variable

14. "Listening to Mozart" is best defined here as a/an:
    (A) ordered variable
　* (B) independent variable
    (C) nominal variable
    (D) dependent variable
    (E) interval variable

15. In a typical, social scientific investigation, the <u>most powerful test</u> of the underlying theory is provided by:
    (A) justifying and using a two-tailed hypothesis
    (B) proving a one-tailed hypothesis
    (C) justifying and using a RQ
    (D) proving a two-tailed hypothesis
  * (C) justifying and using a one-tailed hypothesis

True/False

F 16. The term communication is derived from the Latin word, *communis*, which means "to make visible."

T 17. According to the definition given in the text, "communication" refers to the processes by which verbal and nonverbal messages are used to create and share meaning.

T 18. A theory is simply a generalization about a phenomenon, an explanation of how or why something occurs.

F 19. When the findings from a study confirm or support a hypothesis, derived from a theory, the underlying theory has been proven.

T 20. Social justice communication research is conducted for the purpose of contributing to the well-being of people who are underresourced and disenfranchised.

T 21. Basic and applied communication research should not be treated as unrelated endeavors, for theory and practice are inherently intertwined.

F 22. A research question makes a prediction about the nature of the relationship between two variables.

F 23. A variable can be a single object.

F 24. The variable that is thought to influence the changes in another variable is called a dependent variable.

T 25. When the independent variable is nominal, the research question or hypothesis asks about the differences between the categories of the nominal variable.

Short-Answer/Essay Questions

1. Explain the two different views regarding the term "communication."
2. Identify the textbook authors' definition of communication.
3. Match the following types of studies with the titles below: (A) Person ? Message; (B) Context ? Message; (C) Message ? Person; (D) Channel ? Message
    1) The Effects of Compliance-Gaining Strategies on Buying Behavior
    2) The Effects of Age on the Management of Conflicting Communication
    3) Informational Differences Between Face-to-Face and Computer-Mediated Communication

        4)   Television Coverage of President Clinton's Address to the Nation in the United States and Iraq
             ANSWERS: 1 = C; 2 = A; 3 = D; 4 = B

4. Support or reject the argument that basic and applied research are distinct, yet also interdependent.
5. Explain what is meant by "social justice communication research."
6. Identify the two goals of research questions and or statements.
7. Define the terms "nominal variable" and "ordered variable" and provide a common, everyday example of each.
8. Using the nominal independent variable of couple satisfaction (divided into "satisfied couples" and "dissatisfied couples" for the purposes of this question) and the dependent variable of the number of arguments they have, construct a relevant research question and a one-tailed hypothesis.
9. Using the ordered independent variable of number of television soap operas watched and the dependent variable of loneliness, construct a relevant research question and a one-tailed hypothesis.

CHAPTER 3: FINDING, READING, AND USING RESEARCH

I. Introduction
 A. Doing good research requires being able tog et the information we need, when we need it, and being able to understand and use it.
  1. Most readers of this textbook are probably already comfortable working on a computer, getting information off CD-ROMS or though the Internet.
  2. In fact, it's not uncommon for readers like you to be much more at home in the age of electronic information than many of your teachers or textbook authors.
  3. Your comparatively greater skill in handling information is a result of being the first true generation of the Information Age.
 B. We assume a certain familiarity with various popular sources of information, and focus attention on how the information needed for good research differs from other kinds of information with which you are already familiar, as well as how to find, understand, and use this research-relevant information.
II. Reasons for Reviewing Previous Research
 A. Researchers don't work in a vacuum.
  1. Their research is a result of previous work on a topic.
  2. Knowing what others have done and found helps to avoid "reinventing the wheel."
  (a) This is true whether one is conducting scholarly research (public knowledge) or proprietary research (research for a private company or organization; see Chapter 1).
 B. Even those who don't conduct research per se often need to know what the findings from relevant research show.
  1. Before implementing a total quality management (TQM) program decision makers would want to see what the research shows about the effects of TQM, or other programs like it, on such outcomes as worker satisfaction and productivity.
  2. Competent consumers also find that reviewing relevant research proves quite helpful.
 C. Regardless of the communication topic of interest, it's likely that there is some relevant research that has been conducted in the past.
  1. Even for brand new topics that have not been studied before, researchers still consult the literature, searching for sources that can help them to understand the new topic.
 D. Reviewing previous research is bound to shape a new study in a number of ways.
  1. The purpose of one's study may be affected.
  2. Previous research invariably is used to provide support for, or shape, the formal research question or hypothesis posed.
  3. As researchers review relevant literature, they also look at how those studies were conducted, gathering ideas for the design of their own study.
  4. Prior work, thus, provides the foundation on which researchers build.
  5. Anyone interested in studying communication phenomena, whether as a producer or a consumer, should find out what has already been done and learned about the topic(s) of interest.
III. The Search for Research
 A. The search for previous research (see Figure 3.1) begins by understanding the types of

research available and where they can be found.
   1. Once they have been found, the information contained within them needs to be understood and evaluated.
   B. Finding, reading, and evaluating research usually leads researchers to rethink and revise the original topic they considered worth studying, and this often makes it necessary to find additional, more focused research.
      1. This cyclical process of finding, reading, and evaluating research enables researchers to select and review the most appropriate research until they are ready to pose a formal research question or hypothesis.
      2. At that point, researchers are ready to write a review of the literature.
IV. Types of Research Reports
 A. There are two general types of reports.
    1. A **primary research report** is the first reporting of a research study by the person(s) who actually conducted the study.
    2. A **secondary research report** is a report of a research study by someone other than the person who conducted the study or a later report by the person who conducted the study that cites or uses the primary report that has already appeared elsewhere.
 B. We're starting with secondary reports because what you know about most topics comes from them, and these appear in a variety of forms.
    1. Textbooks, like this one, are the main way college students learn about course-relevant research findings.
       (a) The studies you read about in textbooks and any other books that review previously published research are secondary research reports.
    2. Most people's exposure to secondary research reports comes from the mass media--the newspapers and magazines they read, the radio programs they listen to on the way to school or work, the television news programs they watch during the dinner, and/or the Internet they surf at night.
    3. Secondary research reports are quite adequate most of the time.
    4. Scholars, too, frequently find secondary research reports helpful.
       (a) Well-written reviews, such as those in *Communication Yearbooks* 19 and 20, help researchers understand the work done in an area and formulate ideas about what needs to be done and provide them with valuable reference sources to find and read.
 C. Scholars and conscientious individuals, however, aren't content to rely on secondary research reports.
    1. They know that such reports, and we're talking especially about those presented by the media, too often give only a brief overview of the research study, simplify complex findings into a "sound bite," or worse, report inaccurate findings.
    2. Therefore, they read primary research reports--actual studies as reported for the first time by the person(s) who conducted the research.
    3. There are three general sources that provide primary research reports: scholarly journals, scholarly texts, and conference papers.
 D. The most important source for locating primary research report is **a scholarly journal**, a

periodical publication (often called *periodicals* and/or kept in that section of libraries) that prints scholarly essays and research studies.
1. Scholarly journals date back to the creation of the *Journal des scavans* in January 1665, in France, and shortly thereafter, in March 166, the *Philosophical Transactions* in England, both regular publications that contained descriptions of research.
2. There are well over 100,000 scholarly journals around the world, publishing more than six million articles each year (Shermer, 1997).
3. Each academic discipline has many journals devoted to topics that interest these scholars.
  (a) The field of Communication is no exception; there are a great many journals that report original communication research studies (see Figure 3.2).
4. Communication researchers also frequently find relevant articles in journals from related fields, such as advertising, anthropology, business and management, etc.
5. The main advantage of scholarly journals is that, unlike some other sources, the importance and accuracy of the reported results have been reviewed by experts in the field before being published.
E. A second source of primary research reports is a **scholarly text**, a text authored or edited by a scholar that is intended primarily for other scholars to read.
  1. Some authored scholarly texts report original research.
  (a) A common type of scholarly text that features primary research reports is edited texts.
  (b) Many edited texts contain both primary and secondary research reports.
F. The final source of primary research reports is a **conference paper**, a manuscript presented at a scholarly conference/convention.
  (a) Conference papers do not have the same prestige, or "stamp of approval" as scholarly journal articles, but they can still be a valuable source of primary research reports.
  (b) Obtaining copies of conference papers cited in research reports, however, can be difficult.
V. Finding Research Reports
A. Primary and secondary research reports may be found in many places; however, we focus on *two* locations.
  1. Libraries, as we all know, are locations set aside specifically to store knowledge in an organized fashion.
  (a) The knowledge stored in libraries can take traditional and electronic forms.
  (b) Libraries have a long and rich tradition.
  2. There are many types of libraries that differ in terms of purpose, content, and access.
  (a) **Public libraries** are municipal libraries operated by a city, town, or local government that are accessible to members of the general public.
    i. Seldom do public libraries stick scholarly journals and texts that report original research studies.
  (b) **Academic libraries** are attached to universities/colleges and support their research and teaching needs.
    i. These libraries stock both primary and secondary research reports, in addition to some nonfiction texts, popular periodicals, newspapers, and recorded materials.
  (c) **Special-use libraries** contain materials that meet specific needs.

  i. Many of these special-use libraries are operated by private organizations, such as historical societies, religious societies, and even business corporations.
  ii. Some special-use libraries are or contain **archives**, where **primary source materials**, original records and documents, housed.
  iii. *Primary source materials* should not be confused with *primary research reports*; the first term means any original records and documents, whereas the latter term references reports of original research studies.
B. Finding research reports in academic libraries.
 1. Academic libraries are the primary place where researchers spend their time.
 2. To enjoy the resources of such a library---rather than wandering around in confusion or searching futilely down blind alleys---you need to know where to find what you're there to obtain.
 3. Libraries organize their holdings using some type of **cataloguing system**.
  (a) Most academic libraries use the *Library of Congress System* (see Figure 3.3).
  (b) Public libraries use the *Dewey Decimal System* which employs 10 numbered categories as general headings, subdivided as many times as necessary to assign a unique call number to each book (see Figure 3.3).
   i. A card catalogue contained cards for each book in the holdings that were cross-referenced in three ways: by author, title of work, and subject area.
   ii. Most libraries today have this information filed electronically in a database, information stored in machine-readable form that can be retrieved by a computer located in the library or elsewhere.
 4. Electronic library searches as illustrated by Loyola's library information service (LUIS).
  (a) Users are presented with a screen that allows them to search for a book or journal by title, simply by typing the letter "t" followed immediately by an equals sign "=" and the followed immediately by the title of the book.
  (b) One can also search by author (a= name of author), and/or call number (c=call number).
  (c) If more general searches are desired, users can enter a keyword (k=keyword) or a subject (s=subject).
  (d) Locating articles in scholarly journals demands a little more effort.
   i. At Loyola University Chicago, the best way to access a social science article is through the PsycInfo database, copyrighted by the APA and it can be entered into through the InfoTrac database, an **on-line database**, copyrighted by Information Access Company.
   ii. Many databases are available on **CD-ROMs**, which stands for "compact disk-read only memory."
   iii. The best CD-ROM for locating articles in communication journals is CommSearch (2nd ed.), a database copyrighted by the National Communication Association (NCA; previously Speech Communication Association or SCA).
   iv. The most important printed source for finding communication journal articles is Matlon and Ortiz's (1997) text, *Index to Journals in Communication Through 1995* (published by NCA).

v. One final print resource, possibly available electronically through the First Search database at one's academic library, is *Communication Abstracts*; a quarterly publication that prints abstracts (one paragraph summaries) of communication-related articles in various journals and books over the previous 90 days.
vi. One of the main advantages, in comparison to print searches, is the ability to engage in free-text searching (or keyword searching), searching for key words regardless of where they appear in a record; the downside though is that such searches often result in numerous *false hits* or *false drops*.
vii. One useful set of commands are **Boolean operators**, words that allow one to narrow or broaden a search or to link to related terms; and there are also **positional operators** that can be used to make sure that records are searched with regard to particular word orders.
ix. In addition to learning the set of commands for conducting such searches, there is a lack of standardization of commands across databases.
5. Internet Resources, such as the **Internet**, consists of interconnected networks of computers such as BITNET (for universities) and MILNET (for the military).
(a) The **World Wide Web (WWW or the Web)** is a portion of the Internet that uses hypertext language to combine text, graphics, audio, and video.
 i. The growth of the Web was nothing short of astounding.
 ii. From a scholar's perspective, the main advantage of the Internet and Web is the ability to locate primary and secondary research reports quickly and efficiently.
 iii. Although the Internet and Web offer vast resources relevant to research, they also create new challenges for finding reliable, accurate, and specific information; therefore it's important to check the veracity of resources acquired through the Internet and Web whenever possible.
(b) These resources fall into three general categories:
 i. electronic journals (and other such sources);
 ii. academic and professional associations and public and private organizations whose web pages provide information about accessing their archives, publications, conventions, and other research-related resources;
 iii. Listserv discussion groups, which promote the exchange of dialogue and information about research by delivering messages to all subscribers, and newsgroups, "bulletin boards" where users go to read messages placed by other users.

VI. Using the Internet and World Wide Web Resources for Research
 Diane F. Witmer, California State University, Fullerton
A. Most Web resources have clear instructions and simple menus for online help.
 1. To access a Web page, simply type the URL (Uniform Resource Locator or Web address) into your web browser, taking care to type it exactly as shown, including capitalization and punctuation marks.
 2. Once you enter the correct URL, your browser will link you directly to the resource (usually one depresses the enter key to activate the link).
B. One way to begin your online research is with a Web-based search engine.

1. If one knows how to conduct a simple search, these engines can point you to both primary and secondary resources that may not be available in traditional libraries.
2. Each search engine has its own cataloguing system and search strategies, so it's best to use a combination of several.
    (a) Four of the best known search engines are: **Alta Vista, Infoseek, Lycos, and Yahoo.**

C. A variety of online journals (e-journals), magazines, "e-zines," newspapers, and news media appear on the web.
  1. Of particular importance to communication researchers are the following e-journals: **The American Communication Journal; EJC/REC: Electronic Journal of Communication/La Revue Electronique do Communication; Journal of Computer-Mediated Communication**; and **M/C.**
  2. A variety of services exist for finding the many other e-journals now published in virtually every discipline; some are free and some require paid membership: **Committee of Institutional Cooperation (CIC) Electronic Journals Collection; Blackwell's Electronic Journal Navigator; Ingenta;** and **University of Houston Libraries.**

D. Many academic and professional organizations and public and private organizations provide help in locating research studies, have their own archives of specialized research information, or offer other resources useful when conducting research (as well as many other services and products).
  1. Several organizations are particularly helpful for the study of communication (see text).

E. Free Internet-based discussion lists offer opportunities to exchange information, debate topical issues, and find other research resources.
  1. Both good "netiquette" and the expectations of other members dictate that questions and comments reflect basic background research and an understanding of list norms.
  2. The following are of particular interest for conducting communication research: **CRTNET News (Communication and Theory NETwork); Comserve Hotlines; and METHODS.**
  3. There are literally thousands of newsgroups and Internet discussion lists; three sites in particular are useful for finding and accessing online discussions that focus on specific topics: **Deja News; Onelist; and Tile.Net.**
  4. The Communication Ring---http://www.nonce.com/commring/---is a ring that organizes a group of Web sites, and this ring is dedicated to the study and teaching of communication.

VII. How Research Is Presented: Reading Scholarly Journal Articles

A. Scholarly journals present the most current research in the field, research that has passed the test of review.
  1. Scholarly journal articles report the results obtained from the methodology employed in a particular study.
  2. There are articles about experiments performed, surveys taken, texts analyzed, and research conducted in naturals settings.
    (a) Experimenters, surveyors, and sometimes textual analysts collect **quantitative data**, numerical data.

(b) Other textual analysts and naturalistic researchers collect **qualitative data**, data using symbols other than numbers.
3. Journal articles that analyze qualitative data are so varied that it is difficult to discuss a single model for how these results are written (see Chapter 10).
4. One particular format is well established for presenting the results obtained from analyzing quantitative data.

B. A typical quantitative scholarly journal article contains a number of important subheadings (see Figure 3.4).
1. Understanding the accepted format will help you to know where to look in an article for the information you need to avoid wasting valuable time (see Frey, Botan, Friedman, & Kreps, 1992).
   (a) The preceding text examines actual scholarly journal articles that employ various methodologies.
2. The eight subheadings contained in a typical quantitative scholarly article follow.
   (a) **Title**: The most straightforward title presents the topic, and specifically, the variables studied by the researcher.
      i. The title has two parts with the first part specifying the general topic and the second part the specific variables studied.
   (b) **Abstract**: Most journal articles start (either in the article itself or in the table of contents for that issue of a journal) with a summary of the important points in that article; usually one-paragraph long.
      i. An abstract can be a researcher's best friend because it encapsulates the most important information contained in an article, such as the purpose of the study, methods used, key findings from the study, and/or contribution the study makes (see Figure 3.5).
   (c) **Introduction**: The introduction begins the actual body of a journal article.
      i. This section, frequently no longer than a page or two, orients the reader to the topic and why it is important that it be studied.
   (d) **Review of the Relevant Literature**: The literature review is one of the most crucial sections of a journal article.
      i. A researcher identifies the previous work done by scholars that is relevant to the topic.
      ii. Each literature review reflects many factors, including the author's personal style.
      iii. If the research blazes a new path in the discipline, probably little research will be cited.
      iv. If the research builds on topics that have received considerable attention, the literature review is targeted specifically to the research that addresses that topic directly.
      v. At the end of the literature review, either as part of that section or in a separately titled section, the author poses a formal research question or hypothesis (see Chapter 2), with the author explaining how the literature review informed the hypothesis or research question.
   (e) **Methodology**: The methodology section is where the author explains exactly how

the research was conducted and this section usually contains three formal subheadings.
- i. The *methodology section* typically starts by describing the **research participants** (or **subjects,** designated Ss), the people who participated in the study, and/or **texts**, the recorded or visual messages studied.
- ii. The *procedures section* explains the specific procedures used to conduct the research by providing a straightforward account of what was done with the research participants/texts.
    - (a) The author explains exactly how the independent and dependent variables were operationalized (put into observable terms) and measured (see Chapter 4), and if relevant, manipulated (see Chapter 7).
- iii. The data treatment section is sometimes included, as a final part, to the methodology section and it explains the ways in which quantitative data were analyzed.

(f) **Results**: The results section of a journal article explains what was found.
- i. This section is typically a short, straightforward account of the findings without attempting to interpret or discuss them.

(g) **Discussion**: In this section, the author interprets the results reported in the preceding section.
- i. This is where the author explains the significance of the results and what they mean addressing three items.
    - (a) The meaning and importance of the findings are examined;
    - (b) The problems and limitations of the study are identified on the basis of hindsight;
    - (c) The findings are used to suggest new topics worth studying, new questions worth asking, and new procedures worth trying.

(h) **References:** Because scholarly research is cumulative (see Chapter 1), readers have a right to know two things: who should get credit for each idea presented and what is the track record of each idea.
- i. This disclosure of indebtedness takes the form of *references,* a complete and accurate list of all sources cited in the text.

VIII. Writing A Literature Review

A. Once researchers have located and synthesized relevant research, they use that information to revise the topic they are studying.
1. This process of finding, reading, evaluating, and revising may be necessary several times until researchers are ready to pose a formal research question or hypothesis.
2. There are five things involved in preparing a research prospectus.
    - i. **Title**: Construct a clear title for the paper that captures the essence of your intended research study.
        - (a) Most projects examine *differences between groups* or the *relationship between variables.*
    - ii. **Introduction**: This is a relatively short part of the paper that establishes the purpose and significance of the study.
        - (a) Start with an introduction to the general area of research under which the

specific topic you are examining falls, followed by a paragraph that explains the specific purpose of your research.
- (b) This section concludes by pointing out the potential significance/importance of your research study for communication scholars, practitioners, and/or the general public.

iii. **Literature Review**: This literature review section varies a great deal depending on how much specific information there is on the topic you are studying.
- (a) To write a good review of the literature, you must first understand the two purposes this section should serve with one purpose being to summarize what is known about your topic, and the other being to use previous evidence for the argument you are going to make by posing a research question or hypothesis.
- (b) Establish the organizational scheme for this section, so the reader knows how the review is being organized.
- (c) Not everything written on the topic can be covered so your job is to pick out the research that is most relevant to the topic (variables) you are studying and the research question/hypothesis you will pose, and then to pull out of each piece the ideas that are most useful.
- (e) You must cover research relevant to all the variables being studied, with the best possible research to review being the studies that link the specific variables that interest you.
- (f) Keep your eyes open for any *meta-analytic studies* about the topic being investigated noting that **meta-analysis** is a procedure used to identify patterns in findings across multiple studies that examine the same research topic or question.
- (g) Meta-analyses can be affected by the **file drawer problem**, a potential problem affecting meta-analyses and literature reviews that occurs because studies that yield non-significant results are often not published, so the significant effects found may seem to happen more often than they actually do (see Figure 3.6).
- (h) If you review a specific study in detail, make sure to explain the purpose of the study, the methods, findings, and the significance/implication of those findings, in that order.
- (i) When reviewing studies, write in the past tense, except when discussing their significance/implications, which should be written in the present tense.
- (j) Use some organizational scheme to review the selected research studies and this order could take one of several forms: topical; chronological; problem-cause-solution; general-to-specific; known-to-unknown; comparison-and-contrast; and/or specific-to-general.

iv. **Research Question/Hypothesis**: Five suggestions follow.
- (a) Start by summarizing what the reviewed literature showed in terms of what has been done, what has not been done, and what needs to be done.
- (b) It is preferable to advance a hypothesis as opposed to a research question,

    because statistical procedures, in a sense, make it easier to find support for a hypothesis (see Chapter 12).
   (c) Phrase research questions or hypotheses with regard to *description, significant differences between groups, and/or relationships between variables.*
   (d) If there is more than one independent variable being studied, one option is to put them together in one research question or hypothesis.
   (e) Indent a formal research question of hypothesis to the start of a new paragraph (six spaces from the left margin).
  v. **References**: On a separate page, with a centered-upper-and lowercase heading (i.e., References), list all sources cited in the literature review in alphabetical order by the first author's last name only including those sources actually cited in the text itself.
   (a) Quantitative research reports typically use the style sheet recommended by the American Psychological Association (APA) (see Figure 3.7).
   (b) You can also purchase and download the APA-Style Helper at http://www.apa.org/apa-style/
   (c) You may also use an interactive web site, developed by Lyle J. Flint, that builds your citations at http://www.stylewizard.com/apa/apawiz/html

IX. Conclusion
 A. The research process may seem daunting as it involves what may be new steps to you and a myriad of potential sources.
 B. Good researchers and consumers, however, work diligently to cull the best information possible from extant literature and then advance research questions and/or hypotheses. Only in this manner can informed decisions be made about the merits of particular explanations and theories.

TEST ITEMS

CH3

1. All of the following are ways in which a review of previous research shapes a new study except:
   - (A) the direction of the hypothesis may be affected
   - (B) the decision to use a research question instead of a directional hypothesis may be affected
   - (C) the new study's foundation may be influenced
   - (D) the choice to employ particular data-collection strategies may be affected
   - *(E) all of the above are ways in which a review of previous research shapes new studies

For item 2, consider the following.
While conducting some background research online, you find and read a scholarly journal article in its entirety. The authors of the article share their findings and, in the discussion section, seek to explain their ramifications.

2. According to the authors of the text, the preceding source is best classified as a:
   - (A) secondary research report
   - (B) preliminary research report
   - (C) computer-mediated research report
   - *(D) primary research report
   - (E) archival research report

3. Which one of the following is or can be an example of a secondary research report?
   - (A) college textbooks
   - (B) local newspapers
   - (C) state-of-the-art literature reviews
   - (D) magazines
   - *(E) all of the above can be secondary research reports

4. Reports of cutting-edge scholarly research are most likely to be found in:
   - (A) public libraries
   - *(B) academic libraries
   - (C) special-use libraries
   - (D) archives
   - (E) cannot answer as more information is needed

85

5. The Internet and World Wide Web (WWW) are comparable to a double-edged sword primarily because:
   (A) while difficult to use, a wealth of information can be obtained
   * (B) while fast and efficient, the veracity of the information must be corroborated
   (C) they often disenfranchise those who do not have computer resources
   (D) while intimidating to laypersons, researchers have little difficulty culling sound information
   (E) cannot answer as more information is needed

6. According to the authors of the text, which of the following are well-known search engines?
   (A) Alta Vista
   (B) Infoseek
   (C) Lycos
   (D) Yahoo
   * (E) all of the above

7. In a quantitative research article, we should expect the theoretical and pragmatic justification for the study to be explained in the:
   (A) results section
   (B) abstract section
   * (C) introduction section
   (D) discussion section
   (E) methods section

8. In a quantitative research article, we should expect the sample's characteristics, such as average age and biological sex, to be reported in the:
   (A) results section
   (B) abstract section
   (C) introduction section
   (D) discussion section
   * (E) methods section

For item 9, consider the following.
The authors of a study report that absenteeism is high, with meaningful interaction between managers and employees being rare. The authors then <u>suggest</u> that managers and employees participate in communication skill workshops, and that <u>interviews should be conducted</u> to ascertain whether employee communication skills have improved.

9. In scholarly journals, we should expect the authors' <u>recommendation for additional evaluation</u> to be explained in the:
   (A) introduction section
   (B) results section
   (C) abstract section
   * (D) discussion section
   (E) methods section

10. In a quantitative research article, we should expect the reporting of the findings to appear in the:
   * (A) results section
   (B) abstract section
   (C) introduction section
   (D) discussion section
   (E) methods section

11. In a quantitative research article, we should expect the operationalizations of the variables studied to appear in the:
   (A) results section
   (B) abstract section
   (C) introduction section
   (D) discussion section
   * (E) methods section

12. *All things being equal*, a meta-analysis will be perceived as more powerful than a particular study because it:
   (A) typically is conducted by a research team
   * (B) evaluates a series of studies and identifies consistent findings
   (C) typically is done on super computers
   (D) typically employs complex statistical procedures
   (E) cannot answer as more information is needed

For item 13, consider the following.
After perusing several scholarly journals, Shoshanna noted how the meta-analyses she found showed statistically significant results for the variables being studied. She is impressed that so many researchers knew they would confirm their hypotheses.

13. Although all the research studies found statistically significant results, the meta-analysis could still be problematic because of the:
    (A) faulty description syndrome
    (B) null hypothesis nullification syndrome
    * (C) file drawer problem
    (D) meta-analytic crisis
    (E) cannot answer as more information is needed

For items 14-15, consider the following
Drawing from the 4th edition of the American Psychological Association Publication Manual, identify the correct sequence for the following information.

(i) 329-347
(ii) Western Journal of Communication
(iii) Croft, S. E.
(iv) [Special issue]
(v) 63
(vi) Croft, Sharon E.
(vii) (1999)
(viii) Creating locales through storytelling: An ethnography of a group home for men with mental retardation

14. The correct sequence is:
    (A) vi, vii, viii, ii, v, i
    (B) iii, vii, viii, ii, v, i
    (C) vii, vi, viii, iv, ii, v, i
    (D) iii, vii, iv, viii, ii, v, i
    * (E) iii, vii, viii, ii, v, i

15. The volume number for this citation is:
    (A) 1999
    * (B) 63
    (C) 329
    (D) 347
    (E) none of the above

88

True/False

T 16. Information needed for conducting good research differs from other kinds of information with which you are already familiar.

F 17. The findings of previous research rarely shape the nature of the research questions and/or hypotheses in a new study.

F 18. Locating, reading, and evaluating published research is a linear process in that once one activity (such as finding research reports) is completed, the researcher moves to the next step.

T 19. When someone describes in writing what other investigators have found, they are providing a secondary research report.

F 20. A textbook most often serves as a primary research report.

F 21. Primary source reports and primary research reports are very similar.

F 22. It is quite likely that a researcher will find the scholarly journals he or she needs in a public library.

T 23. The Internet and World Wide Web offer vast resources relevant to research, but they also create new challenges for finding reliable and accurate information.

T 24. There is a particular format that is well established for presenting the results obtained from analyzing quantitative data.

F 25. The results section of a scholarly journal article interprets the findings of a study.

Short-Answer/Essay Questions

1. Explain two ways in which a review of previous research might shape a new research study.

2. Explain some differences between primary research reports and secondary research reports with regard to information recency, authorship, credibility, and retrieval location.

3. Discuss why scholarly journals are considered the most important source of primary research reports.

4. Identify the three main types of libraries and explain their relevance, or lack thereof, for scholars conducting a review of research.

5. Discuss some of the challenges for finding reliable, accurate, and specific information over the Internet and World Wide Web.

6. To help a friend about to enroll in a communication research methods course, explain to him or her the typical structure (that is, the appropriate headings and subheadings) of a quantitative scholarly journal article.

7. Define the term "meta-analysis" and identify one potential advantage and one potential disadvantage to using such a study in a review of literature.

8. Identify one type of organization scheme for reviewing selected research studies in a literature review and show how that organization

would look if one were studying the topic of "the effects of violent television on children's aggression."

9. Put the letters for the following citation in the correct order according to the 4th edition of the American Psychological Association Publication Manual: (A) 569-588; (B) Human Communication Research; (C) 25; (D) O'Sullivan, P; (E) Bridging the mass-interpersonal divide: Synthesis scholarship in HCR; (F) 1999.
ANSWERS: D; F; E; B; C; A

CHAPTER 4: OBSERVING AND MEASURING COMMUNICATION VARIABLES

I. Introduction
  A. If you meet an old friend after a long separation and ask, "how ya' doing?" you're likely to get the bland and disappointing answer, "Fine."
    1. Vague questions most often yield uninformative responses.
    2. So how might you learn more about your friend's life?
      (a) You would ask pointed questions about specific issues.
      (b) In so doing, you're taking the overall goal, "learning about your friend's life," and dividing it into some of its main components.
  B. The process of variable identification and measurement in the work of communication researchers has a similar goal---learning about particular elements of communication in people's lives.
II. Conceptual Versus Operational Definitions
  A. When researchers start to operationalize an abstract term, they take word definition a step beyond our commonsense view of it.
    1. A **conceptual definition** describes what a concept means by relating it to other abstract concepts.
    2. An **operational definition** describes a concept in terms of its observable and measurable characteristics or behaviors, by specifying how the concept can be observed in actual practice. wheel."
      (a) As an example, notice that we've focused on communication-related indicators of love such as saying "I love you" and "staring into another's eyes."
      (b) Had we been psychologists, we might have operationalized love in terms of cognitive or emotional states, such as how much a person reports feeling close, physically attracted, and committed to another person.
      (c) It is theoretically possible to operationalize any abstract concept.
      (d) While simple concepts, like the volume or pitch of a voice, may be operationally defined by a single observable characteristic, no single characteristic stands very well for complex concepts.
      (e) An operational definition represents the most readily available way of specifying the observable characteristics of an abstract concept that we currently know, but operational definitions rarely capture completely all the dimensions of sophisticated concepts.
      (f) When many observable characteristics are included in an operational definition, researchers must decide which ones are more essential than the others for defining the abstract concept.
    3. The first step in research, then, is moving from the abstract, conceptual level to the concrete, operational level; and only after defining a concept operationally can researchers examine it.
  B. Evaluating Operational Definitions: Researchers use a conceptual definition as the basis for devising a good operational definition.
    1. Good conceptual definitions describe the primary elements of the research topic being

investigated and researchers often refer back to them to assure that the behaviors they observe and measure in their studies actually reflect the conceptual components of their research topic.
   2. Researchers try to retain in the operational definition the essential meaning of a conceptual definition.
      (a) This strong linkage between a conceptual and an operational definition is referred to as **conceptual fit**.
      (b) The closer the conceptual fit, the more likely it is that researchers are observing the phenomenon they intend to study.
      (c) The looser the conceptual fit, the greater the danger that researchers are observing a phenomenon different from the one they intended to study.
      (d) Researchers may differ about how a concept should be operationally defined and measured.
   3. Barker (1989) suggests keeping the following questions in mind when evaluating researchers' operational definitions:
      i. Is the definition or operationalization *adequate*?
      ii. Is the definition or operationalization *accurate*?
      iii. Is the definition or operationalization *clear*?

III. Measurement Theory
 A. After researchers specify the observable characteristics of the concepts being investigated, they must determine the ways to record and order in a systematic way observations of those behavioral characteristics.
   1. **Measurement** is the process of determining the existence, characteristics, size, and/or quantity of changes in a variable through systematic recording and organization of the researcher's observations.
      (a) Increasingly precise measurement and statistical analysis of behavior are relatively recent developments, pioneered in the nineteenth century and refined in the twentieth century.
 B. Quantitative and Qualitative Measurements: One way measurements are distinguished is with respect to whether they employ meaningful numerical symbols.
   1. **Quantitative measurements** employ meaningful numerical indicators to ascertain the relative amount of something.
   2. **Qualitative measurements** employ symbols (words, diagrams, and nonmeaningful numbers to indicate the meanings (other than relative amounts) people have of something.
   3. Quantitative and qualitative measurements provide researchers with different but potentially complementary ways of measuring operationally defined concepts.
      (a) *Quantitative measurements* provide numerical precision about such properties as amount and size.
      (b) Qualitative measurements provide useful information about people's perceptions.
 C. There has been much debate in communication research about whether quantitative or qualitative measurement is more persuasive.
      (a) Baeslar and Burgoon (1994) found that all forms of evidence were initially persuasive

when compared to no evidence.
- i. Statistical evidence was more persuasive than story evidence, and this held constant at 48 hours and even 1 week for the vivid statistical evidence.
- ii. The persuasiveness of statistical evidence is also supported by M. Allen and Priess' (1997) meta-analysis, which shows that across 15 investigation, statistical evidence was more persuasive than narrative evidence.
- iii. There are some studies that support the persuasiveness of other forms of qualitative evidence besides narratives.
- iv. One example is reported by Kazoleas (1993) who found that while both types of evidence were equally effective in changing attitudes, the qualitative evidence was significantly more persuasive over time, with people also recalling the qualitative evidence better than the quantitative evidence.
- v. It could be that quantitative and qualitative measurements affect people in different ways.

D. The debate between quantitative and qualitative measurements is by no means settled.
1. Many researchers and practitioners actually use both types of measurements to enhance both the precision of the data gathered and an understanding of contextual influences on those data.
2. Studying something in multiple ways within a single study is called **triangulation,** which means calculating the distance to a point by looking at it from two other points.
3. There are four types of triangulation.
    (a) *Methodological triangulation* involves the use of and comparisons made among multiple methods to study the same phenomenon.
    (b) *Data triangulation* is where a number of data sources are used.
    (c) *Research triangulation* is when multiple researchers are used to collect and analyze data.
    (d) *Theoretical triangulation* involves using multiple theories and/or perspectives to interpret the same data.
    (e) Communication researchers often use triangulation to increase their understanding of the phenomenon of interest, and one way to methodologically triangulate research findings is to combine quantitative and qualitative measurements.

E. Levels of Measurement
1. In Chapter 2, we described a variable as an observable concept that can take on different values.
2. These different values are measured by using a **measurement scale**, "a specific scheme for assigning numbers or symbols to designate characteristics of a variable" (F. Williams, 1986, p. 14).
3. Stevens (1958) identified four levels of measurement scales used to describe the type, range, and relationships among the values a variable can take: nominal, ordinal, interval, and ratio.
    (a) These levels of measurement are arranged hierarchically---each level has all the characteristics of the preceding level, and each provides increasing measurement precision and information about a variable.

(b) **Nominal** variables are differentiated on the basis of type or category: hence, **nominal measurement** scales classify a variable into different categories.
   i. The term "nominal" is derived from the Latin nomen, meaning "name", and the categories of a nominal scale may be named by words or by numbers.
(c) A variable measured at the nominal level must br classifiable into at least two different categories.
   i. The categories must be mutually exclusive; otherwise, comparisons between them are misleading.
   ii. With regard to communication research, the problem of constructing mutually exclusive categories is illustrated in Christenson and Peterson's (1988) study of college students' perceptions of "mapping" music genres (see Figure 4.1).
   iii. The categories must be equivalent; otherwise, we will be comparing apples and oranges.
   iv. The categories must be exhaustive; otherwise, they will not represent the variable fully.
(d) Many communication researchers measure variables, especially independent variables using nominal measurements (see Chapter 7).
   i. Many **background variables** (also called **classification, individual-difference, organismic,** or **subject variables**), "aspects of subjects' [research participants] 'backgrounds' that may influence other variables but will not influenced by them" (Vogt, 1993, p. 16), such as one's nationality and ethnicity are measured using nominal scales.
(e) Researchers also sometimes measure dependent variables nominally.
   i. The most basic way is asking people to answer "yes" or "no" to questions.
   ii. Another nominal form of measurement is asking people to choose between two or more responses from a checklist.
   iii. Many communication researchers measure variables, especially independent variables using nominal measurements.
   iv. Researchers also sometimes measure a dependent variable nominally by first asking people to respond to open-ended questions and then classifying their responses into categories.
   v. Counting the frequency of use of nominal categories may reveal important findings, but it also limits the quantitative data analyses that can be performed and the conclusions that can be drawn.
(f) **Ordinal measurement scales** not only classify a variable into nominal categories but also rank order those categories along some dimension.
   i. The categories can then be compared because they are measured along some "greater than" and "less than" scale.
   ii. An ordinal scale in which a particular rank can only be used once is referred to as an **ipsative scale**; a scale that allows ranked ties is called a **normative scale**.
   iii. Ordinal measurements provide more information about a variable than nominal measurements because they transform discrete classifications into *ordered* classifications.

iv. Ordinal measurements are still quite limited, for they only rank order a variable along a dimension without telling researchers *how much* more or less of the variable has been measured.
v. The points on an ordinal scale are, thus, arranged in a meaningful numerical order, but there is no assumption that the distances between the adjacent points on that scale are equivalent; a variable measured by an interval or ratio scale is sometimes called a *continuous, metric, or numerical variable*.

(g) **Interval measurement scales** not only categorize a variable and rank order it along some dimension but also establish *equal distances* between each of the adjacent points along the measurement scale.
   i. Interval measurements also include and arbitrary zero point on the scale; however, a zero rating does not mean the variable doesn't exist.
   ii. Interval measurements provide more information than nominal or ordinal measurements.
   iii. There are a number of scales used in the social sciences for measuring variables at the interval level.
   iv. **Likert scales** identify the extent of a person's beliefs, attitudes, or feelings toward some object.
      (a) The traditional Likert scale asks people the the extent to which they agree or disagree with a statement by choosing one category on a 5-point scale that ranges from "strongly agree" to "strongly disagree" (See Figure 4.2).
      (b) Any adaptations that resemble, even superficially, the Likert scale are loosely referred to as **Likert-type** (or **Likert-like**) scales (See Figure 4.3).
      (c) Most Likert and Likert-like scales include a middle neutral point because sometimes people legitimately neither agree nor disagree or don't know how they feel.
      (d) Some researchers use visual Likert-type scales to measure people's attitudes or feelings (See Figure 4.4).
      (e) Researchers also use Likert and Likert-type scales to rate/evaluate people's behavior.
      (f) Likert and Likert-type scales typically are scored by assigning the number 1 to the category at one end of the scale and consecutively higher numbers to the next categories, up to the number 5 (or 7, etc.) at the other end of the scale, and these numbers can be sometimes summed.
   v. **Semantic differential** scales were developed to measure the *meanings* people ascribe to a specific stimulus.
      (a) Semantic differential scales present a stimulus item at the top of a list of (usually) 7-point scales representing polar opposites.
      (b) Respondents choose a single point on each scale that expresses their perception of the stimulus object (See Figure 4.5).
      (c) Semantic differential scales are used frequently in communication research.
      (d) The selection of the bipolar adjectives for semantic differential scales is not arbitrary or random.

(e) Most measure three dimensions: evaluation, potency, and activity.
(f) The research population must also see the paired adjectives as opposites, which may be problematic.
(g) The construction of effective semantic differential scales, therefore, requires careful pre-testing.
(h) Like Likert and Likert-type scales, semantic differential scales are scored with numbers 1 through 7 assigned to the points on a scale.
(i) Many scholars question, however, whether the distance between the points on these scales actually are equivalent (e.g., whether the distance between "strongly agree" and "agree" is actually equal to the distance between "agree" is actually equal to the distance between "agree" and "neither agree or disagree").

vi. One type of scale that attempts to ensure that the distances are equal is the **Thurstone scale.**
  (a) To construct a Thurstone scale, a researcher first generates many statements, usually several hundred, related to the referent being investigated.
  (b) A large number of judges, usually 50 to 300, then independently categorize the statements into 11 categories, ranging from "extremely favorable" to "extremely unfavorable".
  (c) The researcher selects those statements, usually about 20, that all judges code consistently into a particular category.
  (d) While the Thurstone scale is superior to Likert and Likert-type, and semantic differential scales, it takes a lot of time and energy to construct; and this is probably why it is seldom used in social-scientific research.
  (e) In actual practice, researchers use Likert, Likert-type, and semantic differential scales, and assume that the distance between adjacent points on these scales is equivalent.
  (f) This assumption allows them to use advanced statistical procedures that require interval-level data (See Chapters 13 and 14).

vii. **Ratio measurement scales** not only categorize and rank order a variable along a scale with equal intervals between adjacent pints but also establish an *absolute*, or *true, zero point* where the variable being measured ceases to exist.
  (a) Because of the absolute zero point, ratio measurements cannot have negative values, since the smallest value on ratio scale is zero.
  (b) Ratio measurements are common in the physical sciences, but rare in the social sciences.

F. Measuring Unidimensional and Multidimensional Concepts
  1. Many concepts/variables can be measured by asking only one question on a single-item scale.
  2. Measuring complex concepts requires multiple items.
    (a) These several indicators are then combined in some manner to yield the desired measurement.
    (b) When all those indicators relate to one concept, that concept is called

Unidimensional.
- (c) When indicators relate to several subconcepts, the concept that unites them is called *Multidimensional.*
- (d) The statistical procedure that reveals whether a concept is unidimensional or multidimensional is called **factor analysis** (See Chapter 14).
3. **Unidimensional concepts** are measured by a set of indicators that can be added together equally to derive a single, overall score.
    - (a) A scale comprised of such items is called a **summated scale**.
    - (b) S. Booth-Butterfield and Booth-Butterfield (1991) took 17 observable characteristics associated with the variable of humor orientation (HO), and asked 275 people to indicate on a Likert scale the extent to which each one applied to themselves.
    - (c) A factor analysis revealed that responses to these 17 items were related to each other and, therefore, they were measuring a unidimensional concept (see Figure 4.6)..
4. Many communication concepts are composed of a number of different subconcepts, called **factors**.
5. Concepts that incorporate more than one factor and, therefore, must be measured by more than one set of scale items are called **multidimensional concepts.**

IV. Measurement Methods
  A. Researchers use three general measurement methods: self-reports, others' reports, and observing behavioral acts.
    1. Most researchers use **self-reports** to measure their target characteristics/behaviors.
      (a) They ask people to comment on themselves.
    2. There are both advantages and disadvantages to using self-reports.
      (a) Self-reports are an efficient way to ascertain respondents' beliefs, attitudes, and values.
        i. These are psychological characteristics that exist inside of people's heads, which makes them impossible to observe directly, so asking people what they think, like, or value makes sense.
      (b) Self-reports can also sometimes be a good measure of how people behave.
        i. The researcher asks them how often they do something.
        ii. Some social scientists distrust self-reports of behavior and believe that observations of behavior are more accurate.
        iii. It is not the measurement method per se that is better, it is a matter of which method yields the most valid information about people's behavior (see Chapter 5).
        iv. People also may provide inaccurate information when asked to step outside themselves and comment on behaviors they not normally think about or remember.
          (a) You've probably met people who don't remember what they sais two minutes before, let alone what they said last week, last month, or last year.
          (b) Those people who pay more attention to their verbal and nonverbal behaviors, a practice called *self-monitoring.*
          (c) Sometimes people don't report the truth.
          (d) Self-reports about controversial issues or deviant behavior are questionable, due in part, to a **social desirability bias,** the tendency for people to answer

in socially desirable ways.
- (e) A social desirability bias potentially compromises the validity of many self-reports).

B. Others' Reports
1. A second general method for measuring how much people demonstrate particular characteristics/behaviors is through **others' reports**, that is, asking people to describe other people.
   - (a) In some cases, others' reports may be more accurate than self-reports.
   - (b) But others' reports can be as susceptible to inaccuracy as self-reports.
   - (c) To compensate for the strengths and weaknesses of self-reports and others' reports, researchers sometimes use triangulated measurement. Thus, when respondents and others agree that they behave in particular ways, researchers have more confidence in the accuracy of their measurements.

C. Behavioral Acts
1. Researchers can sometimes observe a person's *behavior* to assess an operationally defined concept.
   - (a) Most researchers believe that direct measures of a person's behavior are more accurate than self-report or others' reports.
   - (b) In two instances, however, behavioral acts aren't as useful to researchers as self-reports or others' reports: first behaviors show what people do, not what they feel or believe, and secondly, researchers must be sure that the behaviors observed accurately represent the concept of interest.

V. Measurement Techniques
A. Three specific measurement techniques are used in conjunction with self-reports, others' reports, and behavioral acts.
   1. *Questionnaires*: The presentation of written questions to evoke written responses from people;
   2. *Interviews*: The presentation of spoken questions to evoke spoken responses from people;
   3. *Observations*: The systematic inspection and interpretation of behavioral phenomena.
      - (a) Researchers have developed many **instruments** for using these measurement techniques; that is specific, formal measurement tools together data about research variables.

B. Questionnaires and Interviews
   1. **Questionnaires** are probably the measurement technique used most frequently in communication research.
   2. **Interviews** are employed in many of the same situations as questionnaires.
   3. The use of questionnaires and interviews presents three important issues: closed versus open-ended questions; question strategies and formats; and the relative advantages and disadvantages of both measurement techniques.

C. Closed versus Open Questions
   1. **Closed questions** (also called **closed-ended questions**) provide respondents with preselected answers from which they choose or call for a precise bit of information.

2. **Open questions** (also called **open-ended questions** and **unstructured items**) ask respondents to use their own words in answering questions.
3. Because closed questions provide limited options or seek quantitative responses, respondents answer using terms *researchers* consider important, and, thereby, give direct information about researchers' concerns.
4. Open questions are more time consuming for researchers to administer and for respondents to answer.
5. Researchers sometimes use both open and closed questions in the same study.

D. Question Strategies and Formats
1. Questionnaires and interviews are structured in a variety of ways, depending on the type and arrangement of questions.
2. **Directive questionnaires and interviews** present respondents with a predetermined sequence of questions.
3. In **nondirective questionnaires and interviews**, respondents' initial responses determine what they will be asked next.
4. The list of questions that guide an interview is referred to as the **interview schedule**, or **protocol.**
   (a) **Structured interviews** list all questions an interviewer is supposed to ask, and interviewers are expected to follow that schedule consistently so that interviews conducted by different interviewers and with different respondents will be the same.
   (b) **Semi-structured interviews** allow interviewers to ask a set of basic questions on the interview schedule, but they are free to ask probing follow-up questions, as well, usually to gather specific details or more complete answers.
   (c) **Unstructured interviews** provide a list of topics for interviewers, but they have maximum freedom to decide the focus, phrasing, and order of questions.
5. The strategic *sequence* of queries on questionnaires and interviews is referred to as the **question format** and there are three common types.
   (a) **Tunnel format:** Provides respondents with a similar set of questions to answer and researchers with a consistent set of responses to code.
   (b) **Funnel format:** Broad, open-ended questions are used to introduce the questionnaires or interview followed by narrower, closed questions that seek more specific information.
   (c) **Inverted funnel format:** Begins with narrow, closed questions and builds to broader, open questions.
6. Researchers try to structure their question format to avoid **question order effects.**
   (a) These can occur when responses to earlier questions influence how people respond to later questions.
   (b) Researchers also try to avoid, **response set (style)**, that is, the tendency for respondents to answer the questions the same way automatically rather than thinking about each individual question.
7. There are relative advantages and disadvantages to questionnaires and interviews.
   (a) For questionnaires, they usually are more economical than other methods. and reach a large audience in a short period of time with a short turnaround time (See Figure 4.7).

- (b) For interviews, those done by phone can reach remote respondents quickly, and they provide an opportunity to gather observational data, verbal and nonverbal (See Figure 4.7).
- (c) In the final analysis, choosing between questionnaires and interviews (or using both) depends on three factors: The research population, the research questions, and the available resources.

E. Observations
  1. **Observations**, the systematic inspection and interpretation of behavioral phenomena, are also used to gather data about communication variables
  2. **Direct observation:** Researchers watch people engaging in communication.
     - (a) Sometimes these occur in a *laboratory setting*.
     - (b) Other times, researchers go out into the *field* to observe people as they engage in everyday activities.
     - (c) In some cases the people know they are being observed.
     - (d) In other situations, people know a researcher is present, but not that they are being observed.
     - (e) Finally, people may not know that a researcher is present and that they are being observed.
  3. **Indirect observation:** Researchers examine communication artifacts, texts produced by people, as opposed to live communication events (See Chapter 9).
     - (a) These artifacts can include recordings, conversations, books, magazines, tv programs, Internet messages, etc.
     - (b) **Trace measures:** Physical evidence, such as footprints, hair, ticket stubs, or cigarette butts left behind.
     - (c) **Measures of erosion:** These physical signs show how objects are worn down over time (e.g., the wear and tear of a book's pages or faded nature of a couch's fabric).
     - (d) **Measures of accretion:** These physical signs show how traces build up over time (e.g., the number of different fingerprints appearing on a magazine advertisement).
       - i. These measures can be *natural* or *controlled* based on whether the artifacts build up naturally or are set up by a person.
     - (e) Both measures of erosion and accretion, whether natural or controlled, only provide a measure of a physical trace; researchers must interpret what that physical trace means.
     - (f) **Unobtrusive or nonreactive measures:** Both indirect observations and covert direct observations in which people don't know they are being observed, and the presumption is that their behavior will be natural or unchanged.

F. Methods of Observation
  1. There are many ways observations can be recorded systematically including using electronic devices; taking notes and writing down what occurs as it happens, and using audio or video recorders, as well as observing messages sent online through the Internet.
  2. To categorize these multifaceted observations, researchers use **coding schemes**, classification systems that describe the nature or quantify the frequency of particular communication behaviors.

(a) The process of coding observations, like types of questions on questionnaires and interviews, ranges from closed to open.
(b) Researchers using closed coding procedures can sometimes enter their observations directly into a computer program (See EVENTLOG).
(c) Developing effective closed coding schemes is a complex task.
(d) At the other extreme is open coding or categorization during or after observations have taken place.
   i. Ethnographic researchers typically use this procedure when observing people's behavior (See Chapter 10).

VI. Conclusion
A. Observing and measuring behavior is a central part of many communication research studies.
B. Just as people in everyday life hate to be misunderstood and described inaccurately to someone else, it is equally damaging to good communication research for researchers to judge hastily or imprecisely what the people they study say or do.

TEST ITEMS

1. Conceptual and operational definitions can be viewed as:
   * (A) assessing the abstract qualities and observable features of variables examined in a study
   (B) assessing the impact of independent variables examined in a study
   (C) examples of naturalistic research
   (D) assessing the impact of dependent variables examined in a study
   (E) examples of positivistic research

2. A communication scholar could operationalize "love" by measuring all of the following except the:
   (A) number of times one says "I love you"
   (B) length of time spent looking meaningfully into another's eyes
   (C) duration of holding hands
   (D) amount of time spent smiling at one another
   * (E) all of the above could be incorporated and measured

3. Assume you are about to conduct an investigation concerning communication competence (skilled at communicating). Which of the following statements would best describe your operationalization?
   (A) communication competence is genetically grounded and a DNA profile is necessary
   (B) communication competence is similar to persuasive and nonverbal skills
   * (C) communication competence is a fixed range of questionnaire scores
   (D) communication competence is creatively derived
   (E) communication competence is a fluctuating range of questionnaire scores

4. The litmus test for evaluating the relationship between a conceptual and operational definition is:
   * (A) degree of conceptual fit
   (B) whether the target can be tested by through the use of research questions
   (C) whether the target's key attributes can be proven through the scientific method
   (D) whether the target is unique and, thereby, trigger diverse conceptualizations
   (E) cannot answer as more information is needed

5. Barker (1989) suggests all of the following criteria be used to evaluate the merits of operationalizations except:
   (A) adequacy
   (B) accuracy
   (C) comprehensiveness
   (D) clarity
   * (E) all of the above are criteria

6. A sound definition of measurement involves determining a target's _____.
   - (A) size
   - (B) quantity
   - (C) durability
   - (D) changes over time
   * (E) all of the above

For item 7, consider the following.
Suppose two researchers seek to uncover recurring themes, if any, expressed during support group meetings for caregivers of individuals with Alzheimer's disease. The literature clearly indicates that some of the <u>talk</u> will exemplify <u>intense and powerful emotions</u> ranging from guilt to rage.

7. To enhance the explanatory richness of the data, the researchers should <u>most likely</u> use:
   - (A) support group newsletters
   * (B) qualitative data-collection strategies, such as interviews
   - (C) obtrusive videotape cameras
   - (D) quantitative data-collection strategies, such as questionnaires
   - (E) cannot answer as more information is needed

8. The study conducted by Baeslar and Burgoon (1994) centering on messages about juvenile delinquency is illustrative and compelling in that the findings revealed:
   - (A) across 15 investigations, statistical evidence was more persuasive than narrative evidence
   * (B) statistical evidence was more persuasive than narrative evidence even after 1 week had lapsed
   - (C) narrative evidence was more persuasive than statistical evidence even after 1 week had passed
   - (D) statistical evidence was less persuasive with individuals who experienced math phobia
   - (E) cannot answer as more information is needed

9. In a study to ascertain which type of evidence would persuade people to wear seat belts, if any, Kazeolas (1993) found that:
   - (A) people were significantly more persuaded over time by quantitative evidence
   - (B) as the intensity of the focal event escalated (e.g., discussing train and car accidents), quantitative evidence was significantly more persuasive than qualitative evidence over time
   * (C) people were significantly more persuaded over time by qualitative evidence
   - (D) people who worked in the insurance industry were significantly more likely to be persuaded by quantitative evidence over time
   - (E) as the intensity of the focal event decreased (e.g., accidents involving minor injuries), qualitative evidence was significantly more persuasive than the quantitative evidence over time

For item 10, consider the following.
(i) Three researchers are examining the relationships among political party affiliation, reading frequency levels of newspaper editorial sections, and voting behavior.
(ii) To collect the data, these researchers use in-depth interviews, questionnaires, and observations of group meetings held by the Young Democrats and Young Republicans.
(iii) The sample is comprised of Young Democrats, Young Republicans, and Young Independents.

10. Statement ii <u>best</u> exemplifies:
    (A) theoretical scope
*   (B) methodological triangulation
    (C) theoretical triangulation
    (D) data triangulation
    (E) researcher triangulation

11. If the <u>length of time</u> a person has had an illness (e.g., 650 days) is studied, the measurement scale being used is:
    (A) ordinal
    (B) independent
*   (C) interval
    (D) ratio
    (E) nominal

12. A researcher who seeks to measure if individuals wear Levi, Gitano, Dockers, or Blair apparel most frequently is operationalizing clothing as a/an:
    (A) ordinal variable
*   (B) nominal variable
    (C) interval variable
    (D) ratio variable
    (E) predictor variable

For item 13, consider the following.
Suppose a scale was developed to measure the extent to which people feel former President Reagan was a "great communicator" and decision-maker. Respondents evaluate a series of statements and indicate the degree to which they agree or disagree with a particular statement.

13. This scale would <u>most likely</u> be a:
    (A) nominal scale
    (B) Semantic differential scale
    (C) Thurstone scale
    (D) ratio scale
*   (E) Likert-type scale

14. A scale that presents a referent and then requests participants to indicate their reaction along a continuum anchored by bipolar adjectives (e.g., weak-to-strong) is an example of a:
    (A) nominal scale
* (B) Semantic differential scale
    (C) Thurstone scale
    (D) ratio scale
    (E) Likert-type scale

For item 15, consider the following:
A researcher decides to use interviews to collect data from assembly-line workers during the workers' 30-minute break.

15. Which of the following probably best describes this situation in terms of interview schedule type and its justification in this context?
    (A) unscheduled type; and many open-ended questions will be used
* (B) scheduled type; and many close-ended questions will be used
    (C) unscheduled type; and Likert-scale questions will be used
    (D) scheduled type; and deep probing questions will be used
    (E) unscheduled type; and questions about social desirability will be used

True/False

F 16. Both a conceptual and operational definition describe what a concept means by associating with other concepts; however, a conceptual definition describes a concept in terms of its observable and measurable characteristics or behaviors.
T 17. Studies with a high degree of conceptual fit are most likely observing the phenomenon they intend to study.
F 18. Past research clearly suggests that quantitative evidence is superior in all cases to qualitative evidence.
T 19. A measurement scale specifies a scheme to assign numbers or symbols to denote features of a variable.
F 20. The term "nominal" is derived from the Latin nomen, and means bias-free.
T 21. An ordinal measurement scale in which a particular rank can only be used once provides more information than a nominal measurement scale.
F 22. Likert-type scales ask respondents to indicate the extent to which bipolar adjectives, such as weak to strong, describe the target variable being measured.
T 23. A summated scale measures a unidimensional concept.
F 24. Self-report measures are always more accurate indicators of people's actions than Behavioral measures.
T 25. Questionnaires, interviews, and observations often provide different, but complementary, information from/about research.

Short-Answer/Essay Questions

1. A conceptual definition describes the major components or characteristics of a concept, whereas an operational definition describes its _____ characteristics. (Note: use a single word only).
2. Give an example of a conceptual definition and then an operational definition for the concept "communication apprehension."
3. Distinguish quantitative from qualitative evidence and support or reject the argument that quantitative evidence is superior to qualitative evidence.
4. Identify from lowest to highest, explain the characteristics, and provide a common everyday example of each of the 4 levels of measurement.
5. Describe the four types of triangulation and give an example of how two of them might be used to study some aspect of communicative behavior.
6. Explain Likert scales and Semantic Differential scales and discuss whether these should be perceived as interval or ordinal measurement scales.
7. Explain the difference between a unidimensional concept and a multidimensional concept and give what you think is an example of each and justify those choices.
8. Discuss some relative advantages and disadvantages of relying on (a) self-reports, (b) others' reports, and (c) behavioral acts as methods for measuring the extent to which people demonstrate particular characteristics.
9. Define measures of erosion and measures of accretion.

CHAPTER 5: DESIGNING VALID COMMUNICATION RESEARCH

I. Introduction
A. People frequently refer to the concept of validity in everyday conversation, saying things like, "She has a valid point" or "That's not a valid statement."
   1. They are referring to the accuracy of a statement; therefore, the best synonym for the word **validity** is *accuracy*.
II. Internal and External Validity
A. Two general types of validity are important: internal and external.
   1. **Internal validity** concerns the *accuracy of conclusions* drawn from a particular research study.
   (a) Internal validity asks whether a research study is designed and conducted such that it leads to accurate findings about the phenomena being investigated for the particular group of people or texts being studied.
   2. **External validity** concerns the *generalizability of the findings* from a research study.
   (a) External validity asks whether the conclusions from a particular study can be applied to other people/texts, places, and/or times.
   3. The best studies are high on both internal and external validity.
   (a) There are times when a researcher must sacrifice a little of one type of validity to boost the other.
   (b) Validity ranges on a continuum from studies that have internal and/or external validity to those with less.
B. As Figure 5.1 shows, internal validity is potentially compromised by three general threats, each of which contains several specific threats:
   1. How the *research is conducted, effects due to research participants, and/or effects due to researchers.*
   2. Three factors may influence external validity and include: How the people/texts studied were selected, called *sampling*; whether the procedures used mirror real life, called *ecological validity;* and/or the need to *replicate* the findings.
III. Measurement Validity and Reliability
A. Data collected through questionnaires, interviews, and observations are worthwhile only if they are recorded in accurate ways.
   1. **Measurement validity** refers to how well researchers measure what they intend to measure.
   (a) Measurement validity refers to the ability of a measurement technique to tap the referents of the concepts being investigated.
   (b) For any measurement to be valid, it must first be **reliable**, a term that implies both consistency and stability.
      i. **Measurement reliability** means measuring something in a consistent and stable manner.
      ii. Measurement validity and reliability go hand in hand; neither is meaningful without the other.

    iii. A measurement can be reliable, however, but not necessarily valid.
2. **Measurement reliability** is not an absolute measure as indicated by the "friend who usually arrives on time"; there is some variation.
    (a) Even reliable or general consistent measurements have some deviation, or error.
    (b) Observed Measurement = True Score + Error Score which also shape the amount of random error and measurement error (See the text's formula).
        i. **True score component:** In theory, the true score as measured over the course of time.
        ii. **Error score component:** Is the amount of deviation from the true value.
        iii. **Random error** (also called **accidental or chance error**): This is error that cannot be predicted or controlled.
        iv. **Measurement error:** This is error that occurs due to faulty measurement procedures on the times the behavior is measured and, therefore, is more directly under the researchers' control.
            (a) Measurement error can be reduced in several ways, such as conducting a **pilot study**; that is, a preliminary study that tests the questionnaires, interview protocols, observational techniques, and other methods to make sure they are as effective as possible before the main study starts.
    (c) A perfectly reliable measurement would be 100 percent reliable.
        i. The reliability of most measurements ranges between 0 percent and 100 percent.
        ii. A **reliability coefficient** provides a numerical indicator that tells the percentage of time a measurement is reliable.
        iii. Reliability coefficients range from .00 (no consistency) to 1.00 (perfect consistency; 100 percent).
        iv. Several techniques are used to assess the reliability of measurements including: comparing the results from *multiple administrations* of a measurement procedure; comparing the internal consistency of a measurement procedure administered once, called *single administration techniques*; and/or the amount of *agreement between observers* to assess observational measurement techniques.
3. Multiple administration techniques involve assessing the temporal stability of instruments at two or more points in time.
    (a) **Test-retest method:** Administers the *same* measurement procedure to the same group of people at different times.
    (b) The measurement is considered reliable if the results are consistent (usually .70 or greater; called the *coefficient of stability*) from one time to another.
        i. Just because a measurement varies from one time to another does not necessarily mean it isn't reliable.
        ii. **Alternative procedure method:** Involves having the same people complete another, equivalent instrument at the second administration.
            (a) **Coefficient of equivalence:** Statistically comparing scores on these two instruments is the basis for making claims about the reliability of the first instrument.

4. Most measurements are only taken once and involve single administration techniques to assess reliability.
   (a) In single administrations, reliability is assessed by measuring the **internal consistency** of an instrument.
      i. Because most instruments are composed of items measuring the same general concept, researchers can examine whether there is sufficient consistency between how people answer the related items.
      ii. **Split-half reliability:** Assessed by separating people's answers on an instrument into two parts (half the questions in one part and half in the other) and then comparing the two halves.
         (a) *First-half/last-half split* divides the answers at the midway point of the scale.
         (b) Figure 5.2 demonstrates a better technique by showing how to calculate the *odd-even halves* reliability coefficient.
         (c) Researchers can also create *balanced halves* if they are concerned that an item characteristic might make a difference; or *random halves* such that items have an equal chance of being assigned to either half.
         (d) One of the most popular internal consistency methods is Cronbach's (1951) **alpha coefficient method** which assesses the overall relationship among the answers as the reliability coefficient for an instrument.
5. When a measurement instrument is found to not be reliable enough, researchers can measure the relation of each single item to the rest of the instrument, called the **agreement coefficient**, and try dropping problematic items.
6. In observational research, the most common method for assessing reliability is calculating the percentage of agreement between or among the observations of independent coders, which is called **interobserver, interrater, or intercoder reliability.**
   (a) If the observations recorded by two or more individuals who are not aware of the purposes of the study and each other's codings are highly related (showing 70 percent agreement or more), their ratings are considered reliable.
   (b) If the interobserver reliability score is lower than .70, several options are available ranging from modifying the observational system to increasing the length or number of observations sessions until consistent data are obtained.

B. Measurement Validity
   1. There is an important difference between measurement reliability and measurement validity with the former being assesses numerically and the latter being assessed conceptually.
   2. Content validity: A measurement instrument, such as a questionnaire, possesses **content validity** if it measures the attributes of the content being investigated.
      (a) The identification of these attributes ranges from relative ease to great difficulty.
      (b) One way a researcher can establish content validity is to establish **face validity** by generating items that "on the face of it," seem to be accurately reflect the concept being investigated.
      (c) A stronger approach for establishing content validity is a **panel approach**, where

qualified people are recruited to describe the aspects of that variable or to agree that an instrument taps the concept being measured.
3. **Criterion-related validity:** Established when a measurement technique is shown to relate to another instrument or behavior (called the criterion) already known to be valid.
   (a) The first type of criterion-related validity is called, **concurrent validity (also called convergent validity)** is established when the results from a new instrument agree with those from an existing, known-to-be valid criterion.
      i. Concurrent validity can also be established by seeing how a group of experts (called a *criterion group*) perform with respect to a measurement instrument.
   (b) **Predictive validity:** Refers to how well a measurement instrument forecasts or predicts an outcome.
4. **Construct validity** is the extent to which scores on a measurement instrument are related to in logical ways to other established measures.
5. Triangulating validity: Recognizes that content, criterion-related, and construct validity are not mutually exclusive.
   (a) The best way researchers can argue for the validity of a measurement technique is by trying to establish all three types.
   (b) Designing reliable and valid measurement instruments is a crucial part of research that does not come easy.
      i. Researchers must engage in a systematic process of constructing and testing instruments (See the guidelines reported in Figure 5.3).
IV. Threats to Internal Validity
 A. Besides measurement validity, many other threats to internal validity may affect the accuracy of the results obtained from a research study.
 B. These threats fall into three interrelated categories: threats due to *how research is conducted*, threats due to *research participants*, and threats due to *researchers*.
 C. A number of threats are due to the internal validity of a study are due to how research is conducted.
   1. **Procedure validity and reliability:** Conducting research by administering accurate measurement techniques in a consistent manner.
     (a) **Treatment validity and reliability:** Making sure that any treatment a study is investigating is what it purports to be every time it is administered.
        i. To make sure treatments are valid and reliable, researchers conduct **manipulation checks** in which some of the respondents are exposed to a study's independent variable(s), while others in a control group are not exposed.
     (b) **Controlling for environmental influences:** Keeping the setting in which a study is done as consistent as possible.
   2. **History** refers to changes in the environment external to a study that influence people's behavior within the study.
     (a) The threat os history is particularly important for longitudinal research that follows people over a relatively long period of time.
   3. The **sleeper effect** refers to an effect that is not immediately apparent but becomes

evidenced over the course of time.
   4. **Sensitization** (sometimes called **testing, practice effects, pretest sensitizing**) is the tendency for an initial measurement in a research study to influence a subsequent measurement.
      (a) Sensitization is a particularly significant problem that must be ruled out in studies of instructional behavior.
   5. **Data analysis:** An important threat to the internal validity of research has to do with the way n which data are analyzed.
      (a) Researchers sometimes use improper procedures to analyze data, and this may lead to invalid conclusions.
D. A number of threats are due to the internal validity of a study are due to research participants.
   1. **Hawthorne effect:** Any change in behavior due primarily to the fact that people know they are being observed.
      (a) The Hawthorne effect is derived from a famous study about the effects of the amount of light in a room on worker productivity.
         i. Workers produced more not due to the changes in lighting, but due to knowing that they were being observed.
      (b) To the extent that people engage in atypical behavior because they know they are being observed, conclusions about their behavior may not be valid.
   2. **Selection** of people or texts for a study may influence the validity of the conclusions drawn.
      (a) A particular type of selection problem is **self-selection bias,** which can occur when researchers compare groups of people that have been formed on the basis of self-selection.
         i. One of the more insidious problems with selection is that it interacts with many of the other internal validity threats to produce unique effects.
   3. Another way in which selection can threaten the validity of research findings is **statistical regression** (also called **regression toward the mean**), the tendency for individuals or groups selected on the basis of initial extreme scores on a measurement instrument to behave less atypically the second and subsequent times on that same instrument.
      (a) Such an effect is also called a **regression effect** or **artifact**.
      (b) Choosing people on the basis of extreme scores also potentially leads to ceiling and floor effects.
         i. A **ceiling effect occurs** when people have scores that are at the upper limit of a variable, making it difficult to tell whether a treatment has any effect.
         ii A **floor effect** occurs when people have scores that are at the lower limit of a variable, making it difficult to tell whether any treatment has an effect..
   4. **Mortality** (also called **attrition**) is the loss of research participants from the beginning to the end of a research study.
   5. **Maturation** refers to internal changes that occur *within* people over the course of a study that explains behavior.

(a) These changes can be physical or psychological and can happen over a short or long time period.
6. **Interparticipant bias** or **intersubject bias** results when the people being studied influence one another.
   (a) If the people being studied, converse before or during the study, and the result is that the experimental treatment becomes known, a **diffusion of treatments** or **diffusion effect** will occur.

E. A number of threats are due to the internal validity of a study are due to researchers, or **researcher effects**, which refer to the influence of researchers on the people being studied..
   1. The **researcher personal attribute effect** occurs when particular characteristics of a researcher influence people's behavior.
      (a) This effect is likely to occur when the research task is ambiguous, and participants look to the researcher for clues about how to behave.
      (b) This effect is more likely to occur when the task is related to the personal characteristics of a researcher.
   2. The **researcher unintentional expectancy effect** (also called the **Rosenthal** or **Pygmalion effect**) occurs when researchers influence research participants' by inadvertently letting them know the behavior they desire.
      (a) Researchers may smile unconsciously when participants behave in ways that confirm their hypothesis or frown when they behave in ways that don't support the hypothesis.
      (b) Such behavior is often referred to as *demand characteristics*.
      (c) To control for this potential threat, some researchers go to great lengths to remove themselves from the actual conducting of study.
   3. **Researcher observational biases** occur whenever researchers, their assistants, or the people they employ to observe research participants demonstrate inaccuracies during the observational process.
      (a) **Observational drift** occurs when observers become inconsistent in the criteria used to make and record observations.
      (b) A more insidious bias, **observer bias**, occurs when the observers' knowledge of the research (e.g., its purpose or hypotheses) influences their observations.
      (c) The **halo effect** occurs when observers make multiple judgements over time and typically overrate a research participant's performance because that participant did well (or poorly) in an earlier rating.

V. External Validity
A. In addition to knowing that conclusions drawn are valid for the people/texts studied (internally valid), researchers also want to be able to generalize these conclusions to other people/texts, and times.
B. Judgements of external validity, the ability to generalize findings from a study to others, are made on the basis of three issues: sampling, ecological validity, and replication.
   1. Communication researchers are interested in a **population** (also called a **universe** when applied to texts) of communicators, all the people who a possess a particular

characteristic, or in the case of those who study texts, all the messages that share a characteristic of interest.
(a) The population of interest to researchers is often called the **target group**.
(b) The best way to generalize to a population is to study every member of it, or what is called a **census**.
   i. Communication researchers are often interested in large populations where obtaining a census is practically impossible.
(c) Because measuring every member of a population usually isn't feasible, most researchers employ a **sample**, a subgroup of the population.
   i. The results from a sample are then generalized back to the population.
   ii. For such a generalization of be valid (demonstrate **population validity**), the sample must be *representative* of its population; that is, it must accurately approximate the population.
(d) **Random sampling** (also called **probability sampling**) involves selecting a sample in such a way that each person in the population of interest has an equal chance of being included.
   i. No random sample ever represents perfectly the population from which it is drawn, and **sampling error** is a number that expresses how much the characteristics of a sample differ from the characteristics of a population.
   ii. **Simple random sample:** Each person of the population is assigned a consecutive number and then selected from these numbers in such a way that each number has an equal chance of being chosen.
      (a) To conduct a simple random sample, a researcher must first have a complete list of the population.
      (b) Use a formal procedure that guarantees that each person in the population has an equal chance of being selected.
      (c) One strategy is to use a **random number table** (See Appendix A) that lists numbers generated by a computer in a nonpurposive way, which means there is no predetermined relationship whatsoever among the numbers on the table.
      (d) *Sampling without replacement* means if you come across the same number twice, skip it.
      (e) *Sampling with replacement* means replacing the number each time so that it has another chance of being selected.
      (f) Communication researchers often use a simple random sampling procedure because it is an easy way of drawing a relatively representative sample from a population.
      (g) The biggest difficulty in conducting a simple random sample is obtaining a complete list of a population.
(e) A **systematic sample** (also called **ordinal sampling**) chooses every *n*th person from a complete list of a population *after starting at a random point*.
   i. The interval used to choose every *n*th person is called **sampling rate**.
   ii. Systematic samples are often used with very large populations, perhaps because they are easier to employ than a simple random sample.

iii. Systematic random samples usually produce virtually identical results to those obtained from a simple random sample (See Babbie, 1973).
(f) A **stratified sample** categorizes a population with respect to a characteristic a researcher concludes to be important, called a **stratification variable**, and then samples randomly from each category.
   i. Stratified samples are used frequently in research, especially in political polling, because they ensure that different subgroups of a population (a subgroup of a population is called a **stratum**; the plural is **strata**) are represented in a sample.
   ii. **Proportional stratified random sample:** Respondents from stratified categories can be randomly selected in proportion to their representation in the population.
   iii. The frequency with which respondents can be obtained from stratified populations is called the **incidence**.
(g) Each of the preceding types of samples necessitates obtaining a complete list of the population of interest and then randomly selecting members from it.
   i. As noted previously, this is not always feasible; however, in the case of IBM for example, it would be possible to compile a list of all branch offices and then randomly select the units to be studied; a **cluster sample**.
   ii. Many cluster samples involve **multistage sampling**, a procedure for selecting a sample in two or more stages, in which successively smaller clusters are picked randomly.
   iii. Multistage sampling is particularly appropriate for companies that conduct state, regional, or national surveys, such as the Gallup polls or Nielsen ratings.
(h) It sometimes isn't possible to sample randomly from a population because neither a complete participation list nor a list of clusters is available.
   i. When random samples cannot be obtained, **nonrandom sampling** (also called **nonprobability sampling**) is used and consists of whatever researchers do instead of using procedures that ensure each member of a population has an equal chance of being selected.
(i) In a **convenience sample** (also called an **accidental or haphazard sample**), respondents are selected nonrandomly on the basis of availability.
   i. The most popular type of convenience sample for researchers who teach at universities is one composed of students.
   ii. The problem with convenience samples, as with all nonrandom samples, is that there is no guarantee the respondents chosen are similar to the general population they are supposed to represent.
   iii. Sometimes researchers can increase that confidence be making the convenience sample similar in some ways to the population that respondents are supposed to represent.
(j) In a **volunteer sample**, respondents choose to participate in a study.
   i. To recruit volunteers, researchers frequently offer some reward to those people who sign up for studies, especially to university students.
   ii. Researchers must be very wary about generalizing the results from a volunteer sample to the population of interest.

(k) In a **purposive sample** (also called a **deliberate, purposeful,** or **strategic sample**), respondents are nonrandomly selected on the basis of a particular characteristic.
  i. A pruposive sample is similar to a stratification (random) sample in that the characteristic chosen is a stratification variable; yet, the crucial difference is that there is no random selection in purposive samples.
(l) To gather a **quota sample**, respondents are selected nonrandomly on the basis of their known proportion in a population.
(m) In a **network sample** (also called a **multiplicity sample**), respondents are asked to refer a researcher to other respondents, and these people are contacted, included in the sample, and, in turn, are asked for the names of additional respondents.
  i. This type of technique is sometimes called the **snowball technique**, as a network sample becomes larger as a researcher contacts more people.
  ii. The snowball technique is quite popular wiht naturalistic researchers (See Chapter 10).

VI. Ecological Validity
A. **Ecological validity** refers to research that decribes what actually occurs in real-life circumstances.
B. To the extent that research procedures reflect what people do in the contexts in which their behavior normally occurs, confidence in the generaliziability of the findings to other people and situaitons is icnreased.
  1. One way to increse the ecological validity of communication reserch is to study message behavior as it occurs in natural settings (See Chapter 10).
  2. Studying communication behavior in natural ssettings increases the generalizzbility of research because communication processes may be thought of as streams of behavior.
  3. A critical reader must ask serious questions about the validity of findings from research conducted in controlled settings.
  4. This is not to suggest that all research studies conducted in natural settings are more ecologically valid than research conducted in laboratories.
  5. One good way to enhance the generalizability of laboratory findings is to replicate them in natural settings.
    i. Sometimes, **confederates** (persons who pretend to be research participants to help a researcher) are used in such replication attempts.
C. The third criterion in establishing external validity, **replication**, refers to conducting a study that repeats or duplicates in some systematic manner a previous study.
  1. There is no way to ever replicate someone else's study exactly, and there are three types of replication.
    i. An **exact replication** duplicates a research study as closely as possible, with the exception of studying different research participants.
      (a) Exact replications in the social sciences are rare.
  2. A **partial replication** duplicates a previous research study by changing one procedure while keeping the rest of the procedures the same.

i. Partial replications are the most frequent type employed, for they typically are designed to both retest and extend the findings from a previous study.
   ii. One replication does not prove an alternative model.
3. A **conceptual replication** examines the same issue as a previous study but uses entirely different procedures, measurement instruments, sampling procedures, and/or data analytic techniques.
   i. The goal is to see if the same results can be obtained with very different research procedures.
4. While replication is tremendously important, not all studies are worth replicating and not all replications are equivalent.
   i. Rosenthal proposes three criteria for judging the value of a replication: W*hen*, *how*, and *by whom* the replication is conducted.
      (a) He argues that earlier replications are more valuable than later ones.
      (b) He argues that how similar the methodology of a replication is to the original study and how similar the findings are determines the type if information gained.
      (c) He contends that replications by different researchers are more valuable than replications by the same researcher, and that the more the replication is different from the previous researcher, the better.
   ii. In addition to the preceding criteria, the number of replications is important to consider and in general, the more the better, such as three are better than two; however, there is also point of diminishing returns after many replications have been done.
5. There is healthy regard and respect for replication in the physical sciences, where it is a normal part of the way researchers do business.
   i. In the social sciences, such as Communication, replication is viewed in contradictory ways; with some seeing it as a natural part of "science," while others such as many editorial boards of scholarly journals do not see it as necessary or beneficial.
   ii. The danger in not replicating research is that invalid results from a single study may end up guiding behavior.

VII. Conclusion
A. The importance of validity cannot be overestimated.
B. Researchers and consumers must invest the efforts and diligence described in this chapter to produce and evaluate findings that can be trusted.

TEST ITEMS

For item 1, consider the following.
Geiger counter 1 reports that a sample of Kryptonite rates a 1,000 rod rating over six months time.
Geiger counter 2 reports that this same sample has a 3,000 rating over six months time.

1. Which of the following issues is most likely salient here and would potentially explain the discrepancy between the two measurements?
   - (A) varying conceptual definitions
   - * (B) internal validity
   - (C) varying operational definitions
   - (D) ecological validity
   - (E) reliability

2. If a study finds that communication competence influences social support processes among lay caregivers for individuals with Alzheimer's disease, and is very high in external validity, we should most likely expect that the findings will:
   - (A) apply to many health care providers (formal caregivers)
   - (B) be very complex and replicable
   - * (C) apply to many other lay caregivers helping individuals with Alzheimer's disease
   - (D) be limited in their explanatory power
   - (E) apply to caregivers within a 50-mile radius of where the study was conducted

3. In evaluating the relationship between reliability and validity, once should best conclude that:
   - (A) reliability is optional; validity is mandatory
   - (B) validity is subordinate; reliability is superordinate
   - (C) reliability is tied to qualitative methods, whereas validity is tied to quantitative methods
   - (D) validity and reliability are tridimensional
   - * (E) reliability is a necessary but not sufficient condition of validity

4. According to the authors of the text, if a reliability estimate for a measurement instrument, such as a questionnaire is found to be .45, we should best conclude that level of consistency is:
   - (A) excellent
   - (B) strong
   - (C) satisfactory
   - (D) mediocre
   - * (E) poor

For item 5, consider the following.
Assume that four researchers developed a new questionnaire assessing television viewing, newspaper reading, and Internet use among middle-aged adults. During their literature review, they found that other instruments had been used among college students, but not among this population.

5. If the researchers use both the new instrument and an existing older one in the study they are about to conduct, they could attempt to establish _____ validity.
* (A) concurrent
  (B) face
  (C) ecological
  (D) predictive
  (E) construct

For items 6-8, consider the following.
(i) A principal investigator (PI) examines communication apprehension (CA) using a 36-item Likert scale.
(ii) The administrations occur on the seventh day of July 1993, August 1994, and September 1995.
(iii) Prior to inputting the data into a computer and analyzing it statistically, the PI defines CA as having three levels: high, moderate, or low.

6. Situation iii is unique in that it allows the PI to establish _____ reliability.
  (A) alternative procedure
  (B) intercoder
* (C) multiple administration
  (D) Cronbach's procedure
  (E) split-half

7. Situation iii potentially means that the PI should primarily be on guard against which threat to internal validity?
* (A) maturation
  (B) intrasubject bias
  (C) statistical regression
  (D) data analysis
  (E) sensitization

8. Situation iv potentially means that the PI should primarily be on guard against which threat to internal validity?
  (A) maturation
  (B) intrasubject bias
  (C) statistical regression
* (D) data analysis
  (E) sensitization

For item 9, consider the following.
(i) On March 5, 1994, the members of Group A receive a 45-minute lecture on how to reduce their work stress. They then complete a questionnaire.
(ii) <u>Ten weeks later</u>, the members of Group A again receive a 45-minute lecture on how to reduce work stress. They then complete the same questionnaire initially given 10 weeks earlier.
(iii) <u>During both lectures</u>, Group C members were present and complained about the complexity of the information.

9. Situation iii could potentially produce the internal validity threat of:
    (A) sensitization
    (B) mortality
    (C) selection
*   (D) intersubject bias
    (E) maturation

For item 10, consider the following.
At the close of the twentieth century, the U.S. Supreme Court ruled that statistical sampling techniques could NOT be used to derive the Census for the entire country. Its position was that it was possible to include and/or count all of the residents.

10. On the basis of the information above, the fundamental issue underlying this legal ruling is <u>best</u> described as:
    (A) whether convenience sampling can be employed effectively
    (B) whether population sampling can ease future counts
*   (C) whether the measurement of an entire population is feasible
    (D) whether convenience sampling can ease future counts
    (E) whether network sampling can be employed effectively

11. To reduce cost, increase efficiency, and work relatively quickly to study a large population, a researcher should:
    (A) study and collect data from the population of interest
    (B) strive to become a part of the host culture being studied as soon as possible
    (C) strive for exact replication of a previous study
*   (D) study and collect data from a representative sample
    (E) strive for conceptual replication of a previous study

For item 12, consider the following.
A researcher decides to survey any travelers arriving and leaving Chicago O'Hare to investigate the suspected relationship between advocacy advertising from large corporations and consumer satisfaction with the company's degree of social responsibility.

12. The sample/group studied is a:
* (A) convenience sample
   (B) random sample
   (C) purposive sample
   (D) treatment group
   (E) population

13. The chief difficulty with drawing convenience samples is that:
* (A) they may have little similarity with the larger population they are designed to represent
   (B) the possibility for bias to skew the findings is low since these types of samples are random
   (C) they tend to be long drawn-out affairs and very expensive
   (D) one cannot be assured that the participants are responding truthfully
   (E) cannot answer as more information is needed

14. Which one of the following types of sampling techniques ensures that participants reflect particular demographic characteristics on the basis of known levels of occurrence?
   (A) convenience
   (B) network
* (C) quota
   (D) strategic
   (E) random

For item 15, consider the following.
(i) A group of college students are placed together and are told to assume they are on the Titanic, which is sinking. The last lifeboat will only hold 10 individuals and there are 15 students. The group must decide who goes and who stays (no violence please!!!).
(ii) Another group of college students sits quietly in a different room.

15. It could be argued that the findings from any such research are questionable because of _____ validity.
   (A) concurrent
   (B) face
* (C) ecological
   (D) predictive
   (E) construct

True/False

F	16.	The best synonym for the term "validity" is "truth."
T	17.	External validity refers to the generalizability of the findings from a research study.
F	18.	Something can be valid but not reliable, but if it is reliable, it must be valid.
F	19.	The difference between measurement reliability and measurement validity is that the former is a conceptual argument one makes whereas the latter is a mathematical calculation.
F	20.	The test-retest method of establishing measurement reliability involves splitting a questionnaire into halves and having the research participants complete distinct parts.
T	21.	If the internal consistency of an instrument or the intercoder reliability is reported at 70%, then, the measurement is considered reliable.
F	22.	Threats due to how research is conducted include history, maturation, and sampling.
T	23.	The Hawthorne effect demonstrates that research participants often alter their behavior when they know they are being observed.
F	24.	There is no substantive difference between a random and a nonrandom sample.
T	25.	Ecological validity increases the confidence we can have in the findings from a research study because this means that the research describes what actually occurs in real-life circumstances.

Short-Answer/Essay Questions

1. Provide the best synonym (a word that means the same thing) for the term "validity" and the best synonym for the term "reliability."
2. Explain the difference between internal and external validity.
3. Discuss and in your answer give a concrete example of how a measurement scale can be reliable but not necessarily valid.
4. Explain the how the internal consistency of a measurement instrument administered only once may be assessed.
5. Explain content validity and give an example of, and argue for, an item that might demonstrate content validity for a scale that purported to measure communication flexibility.
6. Match the following internal validity threats with the definition/example below: (A) Hawthorne effect; (B) History; (C) Interparticipant bias; (D) Maturation; (E) Mortality; (F) Procedure Validity and Reliability; (G) Researcher Observational Biases; (H) Researcher Personal Attribute Effect; (I) Researcher Unintentional Expectancy Effect; (J) Selection; (K) Sensitization; (L) Sleeper Effect; (M) Statistical Regression.
   ANSWERS: 1 = B; 2 = M; 3 = H; 4 = E; 5 = I; 6 = J; 7 = F; 8 = C; 9 = D; 10 = K; 11 = A; 12 = G; 13 = L
   1) Events happening in the real world that impinge on the people

being studied and influence their behavior
2) The tendency for people selected on the basis of extreme scores to go back toward the mean on a second measurement
3) People answering differently when asked questions by a male or female interviewer
4) Loss of participants due to death in a longitudinal study
5) People responding in a certain way because they are influenced by an interviewer's smiles or frowns
6) Obtaining a biased poll because only Democrats were asked
7) Keeping the setting for a study as consistent as possible
8) People conforming to the ways others behavior in a small group, even though they know that behavior is not right
9) Internal changes that occur in people studied over the course of time that explain their behavior
10) People becoming "test wise" when a similar or identical measurement technique is used twice.
11) People changing their behavior because they know they are being studied
12) Observers' knowledge of the research (e.g., its purpose) influencing their observations
13) The tendency for an effect to not be immediately apparent but to become evidenced over the course of time

7. The most important characteristic of a sample is not its size, but the extent to which it is _____ of the population. (Note: Use a single word only.)

8. Identify the specific type of random/nonrandom sample for each of the following. (Note: Only use an answer once)
   A) Selecting union and non-union newspaper employees nonrandomly in proportion to their representation in the company
   B) Selecting departments at a newspaper company randomly and then selecting employees randomly within those departments
   C) Selecting union and non-union newspaper employees randomly from a complete list of company employees in proportion to their representation in the company
   D) Study any available newspaper employees
   E) Asking newspaper employees selected nonrandomly to identify additional newspaper employees who could participate
   F) Recruiting newspaper employees by placing a note on a bulletin board at that company
   G) Selection 100 telephone numbers randomly from a complete list of newspaper company employees
   H) Selecting union and non-union newspaper employees nonrandomly
   I) Selecting every 100th newspaper company employee from a complete

list of company employees after starting at a random starting point.
9. Identify the three issues that are of concern when evaluating the external validity of a research study.

CHAPTER 6: RESEARCH ETHICS AND POLITICS

I. Introduction
 A. Research may appear at first to be a straightforward, value-free activity, one in which a rational, correct way to operate always is evident to anyone familiar with its procedures.
 B. The reality is that research is a human activity guided by value judgements that have serious moral implications.
II. Ethical Issues in Communication Research
 A. There is a difference between ethical and legal principles.
  1. Laws are usually not universal principles; they are conventions particular to a given culture.
  2. While some act or event may be legal, it's not necessarily ethical.
 B. The word *ethics* is derived from the Greek word *ethos*, meaning "character."
  1. An ethical person is a "good" person.
  2. An ethical communication researcher is a person whose research activities are guided by larger concerns about fairness, honesty, and public good.
  3. Philosophers generally agree that the closest synonym for the word ethics is *morality*, derived from the Latin word *moralis*, meaning "customs."
  4. **Ethics** can be defined at moral principles and recognized rules of conduct regarding a particular class of human action.
  5. **Research ethics** refer to moral principles and recognized rules of conduct governing the activities of researchers.
   (a) To be ethical, communication research should be consistent with fundamental moral principles that apply to all human conduct.
   (b) Communication researchers generally agree that certain forms of behavior are ethically acceptable and others unacceptable when conducting research.
    i. Ethical decisions about research are ones that conform as well as possible to the values and behaviors considered proper by the larger community of researchers.
    ii. Ethical decisions can rarely be judged as right or wrong; they exist on a continuum ranging from clearly unethical to clearly ethical.
 C. There are politics at work in academic research and in other contexts (e.g., government, think tanks, and businesses), each has unique political features that affect the research enterprise.
  1. Most students probably don't fully understand the university system, often thinking that professors are hired only to teach.
  2. That may be true at some schools, but at most schools, that is not the case.
  3. Professors are hired with the expectation they will engage in teaching, research, and service.
   (a) Some universities are oriented toward research and are called *Research I institutions*; often having doctoral programs, including one in communication.
    i. Professors are judged at these universities with regard to quantity and quality of

the research they publish.
- (b) At the other end of the continuum are universities and colleges, including community and junior colleges, that privilege teaching.
  - i. Teaching loads are usually much greater than at research-oriented institutions and teaching effectiveness is often the primary criterion for promotion and tenure.
- (c) Most universities and colleges are somewhere in the middle of this continuum; they promote a balance between teaching and research, with service also considered to be important (although typically less than teaching and research).
- (d) Research is a vital component of most professors' academic lives, and the importance of research is growing at most universities.
  - i. Universities are evaluated at one level by the impact of their faculty's published research.
  - ii. The job market for Ph.D.'s is quite competitive and many "teaching" institutions have had to change their emphasis to research rather than exclusively on teaching.
  - iii. Excellent teaching and research go hand-in-hand.

D. The Effects of Tenure and Promotion on Research
  1. To understand the effects of university politics on professors' involvement with research, you have to understand the reward structure universities employ.
  2. Most universities have in place a tenure and promotion (T& P) system; with **tenure** meaning that a professor is guaranteed a lifetime faculty appointment at a particular institution, except in the most drastic circumstances.
    - (a) Tenure has come under attack recently; but there are at least two reasons why universities award tenure.
      - i. The first reason is economics.
      - ii. The second and much more important reason is *academic freedom*, the ability to teach and research topics that professors consider to be important supposedly without political pressure.
      - iii. Tenure then guarantees that professors can't be fired from what their university for what they teach and research per se; however, this does not mean that political pressures aren't or can't be brought to bear to affect untenured or tenured professors (See UNC example).
    - (b) Not all people who teach at universities have tenure or are on tenure-track lines; some teach part-time or even full-time as instructors, lecturers, or under some other title.
      - i. For those who are on a tenure-track line or have tenure, there are three levels of rank through which they are promoted beginning with Assistant Professor and culminating with Full Professor; a time period usually spanning 12 years or so.
      - ii. If a university demands substantial research to receive T & P, a person must demonstrate that this has been accomplished and in usually a 5 year time period.
      - iii. The T & P system has a tendency to privilege quantity over quality; thus, until a professor receives tenure, he or she may not be able to engage in certain types of research.
      - iv. Most universities expect that promotion to Full Professor means that the person has obtained a national, as opposed to say a regional, reputation with regard to his or

       her research.
      v. There is much pressure on professors to conduct, complete, and publish research.
E. The importance of grant money: A third political influence on professors is the growing importance of acquiring **grant money**, money awarded by public institutions (e.g., government bodies) or private individuals and organizations for the purpose of promoting research.
  1. These grants are extremely competitive, and to succeed in attracting funding, researchers often have to orient their research in particular ways.
  2. Although professors choose to pursue grants, there is tremendous pressure on research universities to acquire grants.
F. Ethical issues involving research participants: Communication researchers often send messages to individuals and measure how they react or they observe how groups of people ordinarily exchange messages among themselves and then make their findings known to others.
  1. While readers of communication research can gain many benefits, the participants of a research project have an entirely different experience and may even accrue more costs than benefits.
  2. Addressing the question of---are participants being treated right?---helps to refocus attention on the ethics of studying human beings in communication research.
  3. There are legal guidelines and these were established primarily in response to serious breaches of ethics evidences in biomedical research (See the Nazi and Tuskegee examples).
  4. The 1960s also witnessed a number of ethically unjustifiable biomedical experiments.
  5. These and other unethical experiments led the Surgeon General in 1966 to establish a committee to review every proposal that sought PHS funding to make sure that research participants would not be harmed and had been informed of any risks.
  6. Other government agencies soon adopted this rule, and in 1974, Congress passed the National Research Act, which required all institutions to create **institutional review boards (IRBs).**
    i. Today, most universities require that research conducted by faculty and students, whether externally funded or not, be evaluated by their IRBs.
    ii. In evaluating a research proposal for approval, an IRB's greatest concern is to insure that the research study does not cause any harm or hardship to the people participating in the study.
    iii. IRBs essentially judge the ethical merits of a research study on a reward/cost basis.
    iv. To make these judgements, IRBs generally rely on a set of ethical guidelines established by governmental and professional associations (See Figure 6.1).
    v. These ethical guidelines are based on four primary principles or rules of conduct commonly advocated by scholars: Provide the people being studied with free choice; protect their right to privacy; benefit, not harm them; and treat people with respect.
G. Whenever possible, researchers first provide **voluntary informed consent** by having research participants voluntarily agree to participate only after they have been fully informed about the study.

1. If for legal reasons participants cannot grant consent (such as in the case of children or those who are mentally disabled), consent must be obtained from the legal guardian.
2. The principle of voluntary informed consent is very important; indeed, it is one of the fundamental principles that guide IRBs.
   (a) Although research participants typically read and sign a consent form, prior to beginning a study, there are exceptions as in the case of "low-risk" large-scale surveys where completion of a questionnaire is viewed as **implied consent**.
   (b) Voluntary informed consent is especially important within the context of research that is designed to be cooperative or empowering.
   (c) When seeking people's consent, researchers ought to provide them with some important information (See Figure 6.2).
   (d) An example of a voluntary informed consent form used by Adelman and Frey (1997) appears in Figure 6.3 (another exemplar is also included in this manual).
   (e) Informed consent also presents a dilemma to communication researchers as once prospective research participants are warned fully about what is being studied and why, that knowledge may distort the data.
3. There are several strategies to lessen the likelihood of data distortion.
   (a) Researchers often omit information, are vague, or even are deceptive regarding what will occur or be measured (this latter approach can pose some ethical concerns).
   (b) Researchers can furnish a complete description of the study to a sample of the population and conduct focus groups to ascertain whether prospective research participants would participate in a study.
   (c) In *prior general consent plus proxy consent*, a researcher first obtains the general consent of a person to participate in a study that may involve extreme procedures.
      i. A proxy selected by the prospective research participant examines the study's procedures in detail and then issues an affirmative or negative response; and in the case of the former, the researcher may proceed as the proxy is stating that the prospective research participant would have given consent.
   (d) Recalling that deception (See a above) poses some ethical concerns, some researchers advocate the use of role playing so that research participants are encouraged to carry out assigned tasks and not merely the behaviors sought by the researchers.
   (e) The issue regarding student participation in faculty/graduate research is unresolved with some saying it is beneficial and others contending only contaminated data result from such studies (see M. Lewin, 1979 for several guidelines).
   (f) In field research where the researchers do not want to encourage the Hawthorne effect, participants are often involved in studies involuntarily.
      i. There is debate about whether such research procedures are ethical.
      ii. The context, such as "streetstyle ethnography" (Weppner, 1977) may also mandate the foregoing of informed consent.
      iii. There may also exist barriers to obtaining informed consent, even in health care contexts.

(g) Some researchers engage in **debriefing** after a study is completed so that every participant receives an explanation of the full purpose of the study, as well as seeking feedback from participants to learn how they perceived the study.
　　i. Debriefing is particularly important in cases where deception has been used.
　　ii. **Desensitizing** is a type of debriefing and necessary when research participants may have acquired negative information about themselves as a result of the research study.
　　iii. **Dehoaxing** is a type of debriefing and necessary when research participants have been deceived; its purposes are to convince the participants that they were actually deceived and to lessen any adverse effects attributed to the deception.
　　iv. Being completely open when informing participants about the results of their investigation during a debriefing is not always beneficial.
　　v. Obtaining voluntary informed consent is not as simple as it may have first appeared.
(h) Researchers usually protect privacy by assuring their research participants of anonymity or confidentiality.
　　i. **Anonymity** exists when researchers cannot connect responses to the individuals who provided them.
　　ii. **Confidentiality** exists when researchers know ho said what, such as in interview research, but promise not to reveal that information publicly.
　　iii. Whenever possible, anonymity is preferable, since research data can leak out inadvertently.
　　iv. While anonymity is an important consideration in the conduct of research studies, surprising little research has been done on such effects.
　　v. When conducting research via interviews, it is virtually impossible to guarantee anonymity to interviewees.
　　vi. In naturalistic research, researchers may well have the right to videotape or photograph people behaving in public places, but there are still questions about the invasion of people's privacy.
(i) The appropriateness of protecting respondents' privacy is sometimes called into question (See the example detailing possible child abuse).
　　i. Researchers are not entitled to professional privilege regarding the disclosure of research information, including research participants' names and their activities, during criminal proceedings; with failure to disclose exposing the researchers to contempt of court charges.
　　ii. Researchers can apply for a **Federal Certificate of Confidentiality**, affording legal protection when they do not disclose research participant information; however, few of these many thousands of requests are granted.
(j) The protection of research participants' privacy also extends to making sure that the acquire data are secure.
(k) In some cases, anonymity and/or confidentiality are not always desired by research participants.
(l) The people being studied should benefit, not suffer, from participating in a research investigation.

i. By providing information, participants contribute to researchers' efforts, and ethical researchers consider how they might reciprocate.
  ii. Some researchers pay people a small fee for their participation.
  iii. The more uniquely and comprehensively the findings relate to particular research participants, the more attention must be given to benefits.
  iv. Berg (1998) identifies seven ways in which research may potentially benefit any of seven kinds of recipients and uses the example of a community to illustrate: *Valuable relationships; knowledge or education; material resources; training, employment, opportunity for advancement; opportunity to do good and to receive the esteem of others; empowerment; and/or scientific/clinical outcomes.*
(m) The flip side of benefitting participants is not causing them harm.
  i. To avoid this danger, one can study people already in that condition.
  ii. A second approach is studying minimal levels of negative states.
  iii. Researchers must be attentive to causing discomfort to their participants inadvertently.
  iv. When communication researchers study how well particular treatments alleviate problems and use control groups that do not receive the treatment (See Chapter 7), they face the ethical dilemma of not benefitting their participants as well as they might.
  v. When publishing the results of their study, researchers must also consider whether they are benefitting or harming their research participants.
(n) An easy trap for researchers too fall into is forgetting to view and treat research participants as individuals worthy of respect.
  i. Some authorities disapprove of the term *subjects*, an expression commonly used to describe research participants and a carry-over from experiments with animals, due to its perceived dehumanizing nature.
  ii. Sexism in research is another manifestation of a dehumanized view of people and Eichler (1988) identifies four major symptoms including *androcentricity, overgeneralization, gender insensitivity, and double standards*.
  iii. Comparable manifestations of bias, in terms of age or race, violate the principle of respecting people.
  iv. Researchers also express their respect for research participants by demonstrating *efficiency*---doing things right---and *effectiveness*---doing the right things.
  v. Researchers are also accountable and must show respect to colleagues in their profession and members of society at large.
H. Ethical Decisions Involving Research Findings
  1. As discussed in Chapter 1, research is cumulative and self-correcting, building on itself in a step-by-step process.
  2. Scholarly journals in the communication discipline typically use a rigorous process of multiple blind review by experts in the field to determine whether research reports are of high enough quality to merit publication (See Chapter 3).
  (a) Only if a majority of the expert reviewers and the journal editor agree that the study

has scholarly merit is the research report published in the journal, and thereby, disseminated to the discipline.
(b) The American Psychological Association (1994) has also established several ethical standards for the reporting and publishing of research findings (See Figure 6.4).
(c) Consumers rarely see the actual data; instead they take the findings on faith and read about the conclusions drawn from the analysis of the data.
  i. Only the researchers see the actual data they collect; therefore, they have an ethical responsibility to make sure that their data are collected in a reliable and valid manner (See Chapter 5), and in the case of quantitative data, that they are analyzed using appropriate statistical procedures (See Chapters 11-14).
(d) Researchers do make mistakes when collecting and analyzing data; worse though, are instances of outright falsification which occasionally occur.
  i. One of the reasons for having reviewers evaluate research reports submitted for publication in journals is to ensure that proper procedures are used in a study and that the data are analyzed using the most appropriate statistical procedure(s).
  ii. Most of the time, these problems are inadvertent and can easily be corrected.
  iii. Some data-analytic deficiencies may actually be encouraged by the nature of academic publications.
  iv. It is also not uncommon for researchers to practice self-censorship, omitting particular facts and features of their research findings for various reasons.
  v. Because it is difficult to evaluate the actual research data, researchers need to be as clear as possible when reporting what they were looking for, how they got the data they did, and how the data were analyzed.
  vi. Researchers must also be careful when presenting the results from research, especially in a public forum.
3. Since this text's focus is on scholarly research, in the public domain, researchers should not withhold the results of their research unless they honestly believe that releasing the results could be damaging or misleading.
(a) Professional ethics require that scholars be free to examine each other's research; this principle does not always apply to proprietary research.
(b) One way researchers can subject their work to public scrutiny is to save their data and make them available to fellow researchers who have an honest need for them.
  i. Researchers have the right to protect themselves from having the fruits oft her labor stolen under the guise of a request to examine data.
  ii. Data should not be destroyed, as in the case of a collegial challenge to the results, thereby allowing the findings to be substantiated.
  iii. The desire to make research public should not compromise the pledge of privacy that researchers make to research participants.
(c) There are a number of common statistical methods used to limit disclosure of such information: **Statistical disclosure limitation methods** (in the United States; **statistical disclosure control procedures**, in Europe).
  i. *Sensitive* cell information when the sample size is so small (e.g., less than 10) is not published as the identity of the research participants more susceptible to

discovery (also called *cell suppression*).
4. Research findings are often used by people taking actions that affect society as a whole.
   i. Researchers have the potential to affect the lives of many people.
   ii. Researchers need to consider the effects of their research on the people who use them or are affected by them.
   iii. The potential for the use of research findings to affect people adversely is particularly true for medical research, which is why it is so important to stamp out fraud when it occurs.
   iv. Not all use of research findings is cut and dry in terms of being right or wrong.

III. Conclusion
  A. Ethical research involves important and complicated moral decisions about appropriate modes of conduct throughout the entire research process.
  B. Ethical research particularly requires taking into account the perspective of research participants.
  C. Ethical researchers go to great lengths to collect, analyze, and report their findings carefully and to consider the impact of their research on their research participants and colleagues, as well as society at large.

TEST ITEMS

1. Traditionally, it was argued that the best research was objective and, therefore, bias free; in contemporary times, however, many scholars argue that all research involving human participants is:
   - (A) cross-sectional
   - (B) experimental
   - * (C) value-laden
   - (D) longitudinal
   - (E) cannot answer as more information is needed

2. The 1949 Nurenberg Code primarily was designed to ensure that:
   - (A) researchers were protected from political persecution
   - (B) research participants were protected from employment loss while taking part in research studies
   - (C) researchers were protected from religious persecution
   - * (D) research participants were protected from unethical and immoral researchers
   - (E) researchers were protected from employment loss while conducting research studies

For item 3, consider the following.
(i) In August, 1999, the University of Illinois at Chicago (UIC) hospital system had its ongoing biomedical research program suspended by the federal government.
(ii) This action was in concert with existing federal laws.
(iii) Federal research auditors discovered that the hospital and its biomedical researchers were not informing the participants of potential health risks involved in the experimental research projects.

3. The preceding situation, see ii and iii above, vividly reflects:
   - * (A) legal and ethical violations
   - (B) legal violations
   - (C) adherence to National Communication Association (NCA) standards
   - (D) ethical violations
   - (E) adherence to American Psychological Association (APA) standards

4. According to the authors of the text, a good working definition of ethics would include all of the following except:
   - (A) morality
   - (B) character
   - (C) communicator credibility
   - (D) commitment to the public good
   - * (E) all of the above

5. According to the authors of the text, ethical dilemmas often arise when the goal of the research is:
    (A)   impersonal
*   (B)   in conflict with research participants' needs
    (C)   in concert with federal and state laws
    (D)   cutting-edge
    (E)   cannot answer as more information is needed

6. By suggesting that ethical decisions be placed on a continuum, the authors of the text are contending that such decisions present:
*   (A)   a number of dimensions requiring flexible alternatives and styles
    (B)   two dimensions requiring fixed alternatives and styles
    (C)   a number of dimensions requiring fixed alternatives and styles
    (D)   two dimensions requiring varying alternatives and styles
    (E)   a "right" and "wrong" dimension

7. It is helpful to realize when one is enrolled at a Research I Institution since:
    (A)   professors are judged primarily for the quantity and quality of their teaching
    (B)   professors are judged primarily for the quantity and quality of their service
*   (C)   professors are judged primarily for the quantity and quality of their research publications
    (D)   professors are judged primarily for the quantity and quality of state-funded grants
    (E)   leading periodicals, such as the U.S. News and World Report, rank and evaluate such institutions periodically

8. The Tuskegee syphilis study, characterized by treatment denial to Black participants, is noteworthy since it demonstrated that:
    (A)   cultural differences were recognized and respected
*   (B)   the U.S. government could fund and sanction unethical and illegal research practices
    (C)   the disease could be easily controlled through medication
    (D)   the Nazis could fund and sanction unethical and illegal research practices
    (E)   the U.S. government could identify and track large numbers of sexual partners

9. The Milgram (1963) studies, which encouraged role-playing participants to role-play teachers who administered punishment, were illustrative <u>primarily</u> since the researcher was:
    (A) acting in accordance with the APA's ethical code
    (B) very concerned about the well-being of the participants
*   (C) involved in deception and pain administration
    (D) balancing promotion and tenure requirements with research participants' well-being
    (E) acting in accordance with the Nurenberg code

10. In 1974, Congress passed the National Research Act and this law mandated:
    (A) use of standardized forms when applying for national/federal grants
    (B) reviews by the National Institutes of Health (NIH) of all research proposals seeking national/federal grants
    (C) use of federally approved data-collection instruments
*   (D) reviews by Institutional Review Boards (IRBs) of all research proposals by institutions sponsoring research
    (E) none of the above

For item 11, consider the following.
(i) Roberta seeks to ascertain if the stories first-graders tell are related to the amount and types of television they watch.
(ii) She plans to conduct and tape record interviews with children.

11. On the basis of ii and in concert with ethical codes of conduct, which of the following should be true?
    (A) all participants' identities will be anonymous
    (B) most participants' identities will be confidential
    (C) most participants' identities will be anonymous
*   (D) all participants' identities will be confidential
    (E) cannot answer as more information is needed

For item 12, consider the following.
A group of five researchers plans to videotape student dyads as they walk on the intramural field in between classes. Their goal is to capture typical nonverbal behaviors of mixed-sex and same-sex dyads.

12. In line with the APA's ethical code, what should the researchers know concerning their responsibility to obtain informed consent?
    - (A) college students are usually exempt from providing informed consent since the research is being conducted by professors at their school
    * (B) naturalistic studies that reasonably pose little harm are exempt from obtaining participants' informed consent
    - (C) naturalistic studies, like their social science counterparts, require informed consent at all times
    - (D) promotion and tenure requirements at Research I institutions allow for informed consent exemptions
    - (E) cannot answer as more information is needed

13. Dehoaxing is perhaps like a "double-edged" sword because the practice is:
    * (A) ethical, yet many research participants may choose to ignore it
    - (B) experimental, yet many research participants may embrace it
    - (C) theoretically rich, yet many researchers refrain from providing it
    - (D) similar to desensitizing, yet only researchers trained in psychology provide it
    - (E) none of the above

14. According to some authorities, such as Eichler (1988), sexism in conducting and reporting research is characterized by:
    - (A) double standards
    - (B) gender insensitivity
    - (C) overgeneralization
    - (D) androcentricity
    * (E) all of the above

15. The line of research at Bonaventure House conducted by Frey and Adelman and associates exemplifies a/an:
    - (A) social action approach
    - (B) overt commitment to empowering research participants
    - (C) ethnographic as well as quantitative approaches
    - (D) strategy to raise external awareness and funds
    * (E) all of the above

True/False
F   16. The word "ethics," is derived from the Greek word ethos, and means certainty.
T   17. When researchers confront ethical dilemmas, they are attempting to balance

competing values.
F 18. Research I institutions emphasize undergraduate teaching.
F 19. Tenure and academic freedom do little to protect professors from political pressure to conduct non-controversial research.
T 20. It is critical to take into account the research participants' perspective when attempting to conduct ethical research.
T 21. Institutional Review Boards seek to ensure that research participants are not harmed.
T 22. Generally speaking, naturalistic observation of everyday public behavior is exempt from the requirement of obtained informed consent from research participants.
F 23. Desensitizing is needed when research participants are faced with complex experimental procedures during a study.
F 24. Anonymity exists when researchers know who said what but promise not to reveal that information publicly, whereas confidentiality exists when researchers cannot connect responses to the individuals who provided them.
F 25. The ethical use of research findings is always cut-and-dry in terms of being right or wrong.

Short-Answer/Essay Questions
1. Define the terms "ethics" and "research ethics."
2. Explain what is meant by a "research I institution" and how working at such an institution affects expectations for how professors will engage in the three major activities of teaching, research, and service.
3. Provide at least two good reasons relevant to research for granting professors tenure (lifetime employment)
4. Describe what an institutional review board (IRB) is, its primary purposes, and discuss whether they are needed or not.
5. Identify the four general ethical guidelines for the treatment of research participants.
6. Define the term "voluntary informed consent" and explain at least one case in which it might be hard to obtain and at least one alternative procedure that could be used under those conditions.
7. Differentiate anonymity from confidentiality.
8. Suppose you wanted to study something that could potentially harm people, such as study communication apprehensive individuals when placed under communication stressful conditions. Explain how might you be able to study this topic while minimizing the harm done to research participants.
9. During World War II, the Nazis conducted unethical experiments on how people are affected by extremely cold weather by subjecting inmates at the Dachau concentration camp to freezing weather and letting them die. Some doctors and researchers have claimed that they can save lives today

by using the knowledge obtained from these experiments. Support or refute whether the information obtained from these studies should be used in this way.

CHAPTER 7: EXPERIMENTAL RESEARCH

I. Introduction
 A. The attribution of causation pervades everyday, common-sense explanations of behavior.
 B. Many researchers are interested in finding the cause(s) of events and behavior.
  1. Just as criminal detective looks for the culprits who committed a crime, researchers interested in attributing causation look for the variable(s) that is responsible for an outcome.
   (a) Recall that the variable thought to produce the outcome is called the *independent variable*; and the outcome variable is called the *dependent variable*.
  2. By conducting **experiments**, researchers assess causal effects of independent variables on dependent variables.
   (a) These systematic investigations are performed under tightly controlled conditions where people are exposed to only the independent variable and the effects of that exposure on the dependent variable are observed.
II. Establishing Causation
 A. It should be pointed out, right at the beginning, that many scholars question the application of principles of causality to explain human behavior, including communication behavior.
  1. One distinction that is helpful to the preceding debate is between *universal laws* and *statistical laws*.
   (a) **Universal laws:** Advance explanations that some event or outcome is always preceded by a particular event or "trigger."
   (b) **Statistical laws:** Suggest that some event or outcome will be followed a some of the time (along a continuum of high-to-low probability) by a particular event or "trigger."
  2. Based in part on Mill's reasoning, there are at least three requirements necessary for attributing a causal relationship between an independent and a dependent variable.
   (a) The independent variable mut precede the dependent variable.
    i. Mistakenly believing something that is chronologically impossible is called an *anachronism*.
    ii. In experimental research, making sure that the independent variable precedes the dependent variable is accomplished by first exposing research participants to the independent variable and then seeing how that exposure affects the dependent variable.
    iii. A **placebo group** believes they are receiving the independent variable being studied, but they are not; *placebo* means "I shall please" and any change that occurs is then called a *placebo effect*.
   (b) The independent and dependent variables must covary, that is they must go together in a meaningful way.
    i. There are many behaviors and events that go together statistically, but are not related in any meaningful manner. These are called **spurious relationships** or

nonsense correlations.
- (c) The changes observed in the dependent variable must be the result of changes in the independent variable an not some other variable.
    - i. If some other variable causes the observed changes, there is an **alternate causality argument** (sometimes called **alternate hypothesis**).

II. Exercising Control in Experimental Research
 A. To establish a causal relationship between an independent and dependent variable, experimental researchers must exercise a good deal of control.
   1. **Control** means that a researcher attempts to exclude other possible causes of the effects that he or she is studying (Kerlinger, 1973).
      (a) Control exists on a continuum, ranging from loosely controlled experiments to those that are very tightly controlled.
      (b) Three factors shape the amount of control.
 B. Exposing Research Participants to the Independent Variable
   1. The first factor, level of exposure, includes researchers who regulate or *manipulate* how participants are exposed to an independent variable (high control), and researchers who only observe without manipulation (low control).
   2. In highly controlled experiments, when researchers control participants' exposure to a variable that variable is called *a manipulated (active or controlled)* variable (See Figure 7.1).
      (a) The examples in Figure 7.1 help illustrate how experiments typically involve various **conditions** or **groups** that receive differential exposure to the independent variable.
      (b) The most basic procedure is to divide research participants into two conditions, one that receives a manipulation (called a **treatment** or **experimental group**) and one that does not (the *control group*).
      (c) A more common and complex way in which researchers manipulate an independent variable is by exposing research participants to different levels or types.
         i. The term, **level**, is generally used to indicate a condition of an independent variable in an experiment, both for nominal and ordered variables.
         ii. The term, **comparison group**, is used in the broad sense to imply any group against which another is compared, such as two treatment groups.
   3. It is not always possible, or even desirable to manipulate an independent variable; some variables, called **attribute variables**, cannot be manipulated (e.g., people's age or gender).
      (a) Other variables can be theoretically manipulated, but researchers would never do so; as in the case of a person living with AIDS and his or her social support network.
         i. No Institutional Review Board (See Chapter 6) would ever approve the manipulation of the HIV virus or one's social support network when it has already been decimated.
         ii. *Natural experiments* allow investigators to observe the independent variable in a naturally occurring context, such as a group residence for persons living with AIDS (See Adelman & Frey, 1994, 1997).

iii. Whenever exposure to an independent variable is not manipulated by researchers themselves, the variable is called an **observed variable**.
C. To further move towards establishing causation, researchers engage in ruling out initial differences between the conditions.
   1. One of the most important things researchers need to know is that people in the different conditions were equivalent at the start of the experiment.
   2. If equivalence cannot be assured, any changes in the dependent variable might be the result of *selection*, in which an unrepresentative sample is used (one that lacks equivalent participants).
      i. Experiments that rule out initial differences demonstrate high control, whereas those low in control cannot rule these differences out as an explanation for the observed effects.
      ii. *Equivalence* often can be achieved through *random assignment* of individuals to treatment, control, and/or placebo groups.
      iii. In *quasi-equivalent* conditions, researchers use pretests in an attempt to establish a higher degree of equivalence among the research participants.
      iv. In *nonequivalent* conditions, no procedures are used and researchers cannot be sure that an change in the dependent variable is the result of the independent variable manipulation.
   3. In **random assignment**, each research participant has an equal chance of being assigned to any particular condition of an experiment.
      i. This procedure attempts to rule out the effects of any initial differences among the prospective research participants.
      ii. Random assignment gives the best possible assurance that the conditions of an experiment start off equivalent because all the initial differences between people should be distributed evenly across the conditions.
      iii. Random assignment is not always the perfect solution to ruling out a selection bias; especially if *mortality* occurs at high levels among the treatment groups, or if only one point in time is being studied.
      iv. *Random assignments* is not the same as *random sampling*. The former term is concerned with how research participants are placed into the different conditions of an experiment.
      v. Random assignment increases the *internal validity* of a study while random sampling increases the *external validity* of a study.
   4. When researchers cannot use random assignment, pretests are often used.
      i. A **pretest** measures research participants on relevant variables that need to be accounted for *before* exposing the treatment group(s) to the manipulation of the independent variable.
      ii. Pretests are used in two primary ways to rule out initial differences between conditions.
         (a) The first is when researchers suspect that some important variable(s) that is not the focus of the study might potentially influence people; pretests can then be used to exclude those individuals who might jeopardize the findings in that they would possess or demonstrate the undesired variable(s).

(b) The second use of pretests is to measure research participants on the dependent variable before the independent variable manipulation occurs.

(c) To assess the impact of a manipulated independent variable, **difference scores** (also called **gain scores**) are computed by subtracting the pretest from the **posttest.**
   i. A posttest is a measurement of relevant variables that occurs after the manipulation of the independent variable.

(d) Using pretests, see "a" and "b" above, is not as effective as random assignment for creating equivalent groups because there may be important differences between the conditions that can't be accounted for by pretests.
   i. In addition, pretests of a dependent variable may also crate a validity threat due to sensitization (See Chapter 5).

5. Controlling for the effects of extraneous influences: The preceding procedures don't control for all the problems that potentially undermine the findings of an experiment.

   (a) With regard to the way experimental research is conducted, one potential threat is a lack of procedural reliability, which makes it unclear whether any observed difference between conditions is due to the independent variable or the different treatments.

   (b) Researchers must also be wary of **threshold effect**, where changes in a dependent variable may not occur until the independent variable reaches a certain level.

   (c) **Experimenter effects** occur when different experimenters consistently administer particular manipulations of the independent variable.
      i. If one experimenter always administers treatment A and another always administers treatment B, it won't be clear whether participants's responses are due only to the differences between the treatments or perhaps the way the experimenters administered them (researcher personal attribute effect).
      ii. To control for the researcher personal attribute effect, researchers commonly use a variety of assistants and **double-blind procedures** that ensure those who administer the different independent variable manipulations and those who receive it do not know (are "blind" to) which participants are getting what manipulation.
      iii. *Confederates*, can also be used, and these are assistants who pretend to be research participants.

   (d) Researchers also attempt to control for such participant threats as the Hawthorne effect, mortality, and interparticipant bias.
      i. Researchers control for the Hawthorne effect by not letting participants know they are being observed or diverting participants' attention away from the purpose of the experiment.
      ii. **Blank experiments** introduce an irrelevant treatment to keep participants from guessing the true purpose of the experiment or becoming automatic in their responses.
      iii. Researchers also want to control for the **John Henry effect**, a type of Hawthorne effect that occurs when research participants in a control group take the

experiment as a challenge and exert more effort than any otherwise would.
- iv. Researchers also employ many participants to minimize the threat of mortality.
- v. Researchers also stress during debriefings the importance of not discussing an experiment with future research participants.
- vi. The bottom-line is that these and other threats to internal and external validity must be controlled for if researchers are to have confidence in the findings from their experiments.

(e) There are a number of other variables that might potentially influence the dependent variable (besides the independent variable being studied).
- i. An **Intervening, intermediary, or mediating variable,** intervenes between the independent and dependent variable to explain the relation between them or provides the causal link.
  - (a) The effects of an intervening variable can be diagramed as:

    Independent variable--->Intervening variable--->Dependent variable
- ii. **Confounding variables** obscure the effects of another variable and there are two types.
  - (a) A **suppressor variable** conceals or reduces a relationship between an independent and dependent variable (See text diagram).
  - (b) A **reinforcer variable** increases a causal relationship between variables (See text diagram).
  - (c) **Lurking variables** are present, often in subtle ways, and can confound the interpretation of the independent to dependent variable relationship (See text diagram).
  - (d) **Extraneous variables** are an umbrella-like term and could include all of the above variables.
  - (e) **Control or concomitant variables** are variables that researchers try to control in order to protect the validity levels of an experiment.
- iii. One way researchers control for such variables is to make them another independent variable in the experiment.
- iv. Another procedure is to use a **matched-pairs design** (also called **participant or subject matching**) in which participants are mated in pairs on some important characteristic.
- v. There are also statistical procedures that can be employed to parcel out the effects of extraneous variables (See Chapter 14), and a variable controlled for statistically is called **a covariate**.
- vi. Step-by-step procedures used in an experiment are called the **protocol**.

III. Experimental Research Designs
A. Campbell and Stanley (1963) identify three types of designs including full experiments, quasi-experiments, and preexperiments.
  1. These designs differ according to whether an independent variable is manipulated or observed, whether random assignment and/or pretests are used to rule out the validity threat due to selection, and what form of equivalence between conditions is created.

(a) These three types of experiments range from highly controlled (full experiments) to loosely controlled (preexperiments). See Figure 7.2.
2. **Full experiments** demonstrate the highest level of control because the independent variable is manipulated by the researcher and random assignment occurs among two or more equivalent conditions; note that full experiments demand that there be two or more conditions.
3. **Quasi-experiments** either manipulate or observe the independent variable and may have one or more conditions. There is no random assignment and pretests are used to assess whether there are some important initial differences between the conditions.
4. **Preexperiments** demonstrate the least amount of control of the three experiments. preexperiments, like quasi-experiments, manipulate or observe the independent variable and may have one or more conditions. There is also no random assignment; however, unlike quasi-experiments there are also no pretests and equivalence is not assumed.
5. The three general experimental designs are not hard and fast categories as what one authority might call a full experiment, another would might label it as quasi-experimental.

B. Preexperimental Designs
1. The simplest preexperimental design is the **one-group post-test-only design** in which a single treatment group is exposed to the independent variable and then assessed on a post-test (See text diagram).
    (a) This is a very problematical design and isn't really used in experimental research unless under unusual circumstances, such as the Challenger disaster.
2. The **one-group only pretest-posttest design** is similar to the previous design except that it adds a pretest (See text diagram).
    (a) Adding the pretest allows researchers to compute a difference score between the pretest (before) and posttest (after) scores (sometimes called *before-after designs*).
    (b) Problems with this design can include sensitization, history, maturation, and/or statistical regression.
    (c) Many of the problems with this and the one-group posttest-only design stem from there being only one condition in the experiment.
3. The **posttest-only nonequivalent groups design** (sometimes called the **static group comparison design**) nonrandomly assigns research participants to a treatment or a control group and then measures them on a posttest (See text diagram).
    (a) *Static* group comparisons pose problems in that we can't be sure whether the treatment really did or did not have an effect, and even if it did, the extent of that effect.
    (b) Confidence is usually lacking in the validity of the supposed causal findings obtained from this design.

C. Quasi-experimental Deigns
1. Quasi-experiments, like preexperiments, either manipulate or observe an independent variable, and have one or more conditions. However, unlike preexperiments, in

both single-and multiple condition cases, pretests are used in a fundamentally different way.
- (a) Quasi-experiments are most often carried out in the field rather than in the laboratory (See the discussion later in this Chapter).
- (b) Quasi-experiments are often used to try and establish at least partial cause-effect relationships by maximizing the real-world transferability of research findings.

2. The **single-group interrupted time series design** (sometimes called **time series design**) involves giving a series of pretests to a single group prior to an experimental treatment, followed by a series of posttests (See text diagram).
   - (a) The multiple pretests in this design help establish an *intragroup baseline comparison,* a way of comparing the same group over time prior to the experimental manipulation.
   - (b) At least three problems are posed by this design: sensitization, the sleeper effect, and the lack of a comparison group.
3. The **pretest-posttest quasi equivalent groups design** nonrandomly assigns research participants to a treatment to control condition, measures them on a pretest, exposes one group but not the other to the treatment, and then measures both groups again on a posttest (See text diagram).
   - (a) The potential problems with this design include selection, sensitization, history, maturation, and/or the various selection-interaction effects (See Chapter 5).
4. The **interrupted time series quasi-equivalent groups design** (sometimes called the **multiple time series design**) combines the previous two quasi-experimental designs by nonrandomly assigning participants to a treatment of control group and measuring them on a series of pretests and posttests (See text diagram).
   - (a) This design does not solve all the validity threats previously discussed since selection sensitization remain a concern, and random assignment is not used to help promote equivalence.

D. Full Experimental Designs
   1. Full experiments are the highest in terms of control because the independent variable is manipulated by researchers and there are two or more conditions to which research participants are randomly assigned.
   2. A traditional full experiment is the **pretest-posttest equivalent groups design** (sometimes called the **pretest-posttest control group design**) that randomly assigns research participants to a treatment or a control group and administers a pretest and posttest (See text diagram).
      - (a) This design provides a high degree of confidence that the findings are due to the treatment and not to initial differences between the conditions; however, sensitization can still be a threat to validity levels.
   3. The **posttest-only equivalent design** (sometimes called the **post-test only control group design**) is the same as the previous design except, that a pretest is not used; participants are randomly assigned to a treatment or control group and given a posttest (See text diagram).

(a) This is a very powerful design, but it is still possible that important initial differences could be missed if random assignment does not work.
4. The **Solomon four-group design** literally combines the posttest equivalent groups and the posttest-only equivalent designs (See text diagram).
   (a) Three primary benefits include: Showing whether random assignment worked; showing whether the pretest worked; and assuming sensitization did not occur revealing whether the pretest combined with the treatment to produce a unique *interaction effect* that id different form the experimental treatment alone.
   (b) This design also requires twice as many research participants as the others and tends not to be used too frequently in experimental research.
5. A **factorial design** occurs when there is more than one independent variable studied, and the multiple independent variables are called **factors**.
   (a) Depending on how they are conducted, factorial experimental designs can be full experiments, quasi-experiments, or preexperiments.
   (b) As the full experimental posttest-only equivalent groups factorial design example reveals (See text diagram), the effects of each independent variable are assessed and the experimenter can ascertain whether the combination of conditions is more effective than one condition alone.
   (c) In theory, researchers can investigate the main and interaction effects of as many independent variables as they deem important.
   (d) Interaction effects among three or more variables are called **second-order or higher order interaction effects**; an interaction effect between two variables when three or more variables are studied is called a **first-order interaction effect**.
       i. Because of the large number of possible interaction effects involved, researchers typically choose only those independent variables they consider most crucial and can examined reasonably within a single study.
       ii. When an interaction effect is found, it typically is considered to be more important than any main effect.
E. Factorial Design Statements and Diagrams
   1. Studies with more than one independent variable are summarized with a **design statement**: A series of numbers, one number for each independent variable in the study, separated by a multiplication sign (x).
      (a) The simplest factorial design statement has two independent variables and two levels for each variable, so there are two numbers (because there are two variables); in this case, both numbers are 2s: a 2 x 2 design.
      (b) More complex factorial designs have more than two independent variables (sometimes called **N-by-M designs** as opposed to the preceding **two-by-two design**).
   2. Both the designs just discussed are **crossed factor designs**, because they involve having every level of one factor appear with every level of the other factor.
      (a) This is the most common factorial design, but in some experiments, the levels of one factor only appear (are "nested") within a single level of another factor and

this is called a **nested factor design**.
  i. When the number of levels for each factor aren't equal, this is known as a **mixed design**.
3. To understand factorial designs and design statements more fully, it's often helpful to depict them visually inn a **design diagram**.
   (a) In a simple, two-factor design, a design diagram is a box with one independent variable represented on the **abscissa**, and the horizontal (or x) **axis** (a line used to construct the graph), and the other on the **ordinate**, the vertical (or y) axis (See Figure 7.3).
      i. A design diagram shows researchers all the possible combinations of the independent variables; each possible combination is called a **cell**.
      ii. The experiment must include research participants for each cell usually equal numbers (where there are an unequal number, it is called an **unbalanced design**); with a generally accepted rule being that at five participants are needed for each cell in a factorial design (Kidder, 1981).
4. A **between-group design (between-subjects design)** are those in which one group of research participants receive one level of an independent variable (such as a treatment) and are compared to another group that receives another level (such as no treatment).
5. A **within-group design (within-subject design)** is one in which a single group of people is tested two or more times.
6. In a **repeated-measures design**, the same participants are given multiple treatments of the independent variable and measured after each exposure.
   i. This design can pose a problem if a **treatment order effect** occurs in which the order of the treatments presented makes a difference; earlier treatments might sensitize participants to later treatments.
   ii. For this reason, researchers randomize the treatment order or **counterbalance** it by making sure that all possible orders are used (See Figure 7.9).
   iii. Researchers using the repeated-measures design must also be sure that there are no **treatment carryover effects**, that is, the effects of each treatment have passed before exposing participants to subsequent treatments.

F. Laboratory Versus Field Experiments
  1. **Laboratory experiments** take place a setting created by researchers, whereas others are **field experiments** conducted in participants' natural setting.
  2. Full experiments, quasi-experiments, and preexperiments can all be conducted in the laboratory or field.
     i. Experimental research typically is conducted in a laboratory.
     ii. A laboratory is actually any research environment that is set up by researchers, including ones created in participants' natural setting.
     iii. Laboratories allow researchers to exercise high control, but often they can minimize external validity (See Chapter 5).
     iv. Sometimes field researchers can conduct full experiments.
     v. At other times, field researchers cannot randomly assign research participants to

conditions or manipulate the independent variable, so they conduct quasi-experiments.
IV. Conclusion
 A. Designing a high-quality experiment is no easy task.
 B. The beauty of the required choreography pirouettes on researchers exercising a high degree of control so that alternate causality arguments for the changes in the dependent variable are ruled out.
 C. By bringing their passion to bear to discover the details---the causes and effect of communication behavior---to steal a phrase, communication research takes one small step for the research participants studied, one giant step in helping people.

TEST ITEMS

For item 1, consider the following.
A group of six researchers observes a series of support group meetings for persons living with AIDS. At each meeting, the researchers note that when the facilitator makes a reflective statement, various members tend to then share personal experiences. Sometimes, however, there is only silence.

1. Which of the following best explains the relationship between the facilitator's reflective statement and subsequent responses?:
   (A) universal laws
   (B) cause-and-effect research approaches
 * (C) statistical laws
   (D) alternate causality arguments
   (E) spurious associations between a dependent and independent variable, respectively

For items 2-3, consider the following.
During a study, you observe the following.
(i) Sixty students first complete a questionnaire about smoking attitudes, smoking ads, and cessation.
(ii) Twenty then watch a videotape that is part of a national smoking cessation campaign.
(iii) Twenty others sit in an adjacent room watching a videotape about how to construct public health campaigns.
(iv) The remaining twenty participants sit in a third room quietly.
(v) Upon completion of the videotapes, all 60 students complete the initial questionnaire again.

2. Which of the following best describes the control group?
   (A) i
   (B) ii
   (C) iii
 * (D) iv
   (E) v

3. Which of the following best describes the placebo group?
   (A) i
   (B) ii
 * (C) iii
   (D) iv
   (E) v

4. Given that "control" is conceptualized by the authors of the text as being evaluated on a continuum, all of the following would be true except:
* (A) research participants' exposure to the independent variable is fixed across studies
  (B) researchers rule out initial differences between treatment and control conditions with varying success
  (C) researchers can minimize the impact of extraneous variables with varying effectiveness
  (D) research participants' exposure to the active variable fluctuates across studies
  (E) cannot answer as more information is needed

5. Which of the following variables would be exempt from manipulation in a study?
  (A) communication skills, such as listening
  (B) content of Public Service Announcements (PSAs) focusing on practicing safe sex
* (C) chronological age of research participants
  (D) interaction duration with confederates of the researcher
  (E) all of the above would be exempt from manipulation

For item 6, consider the following.
During a study, two researchers observe the following.
(i) Ninety students first complete a questionnaire about seat belt use, relevant PSAs, and then describe key message strategies to encourage friends to wear their seat belts.
(ii) Thirty then watch a videotape which is part of a national seat belt use campaign.
(iii) Thirty others sit in an adjacent room watching a videotape about how to construct public health campaigns.
(iv) The remaining thirty participants sit in a third room quietly.
(v) Upon completion of the videotapes, all 90 students complete the initial questionnaire again.

6. Which of the above best describes the pretest?
* (A) i
  (B) ii
  (C) iii
  (D) iv
  (E) v

For item 7, consider the following.
(i) Throughout a study, research confederate Blue, always role plays a verbally aggressive teaching associate.
(ii) Throughout the same study, research confederate Rosie, always role plays a shy teaching associate.

7. According to the authors of the text, the results from such a study might be problematic because of _____ effects.
   - (A) threshold
   - (B) treatment
   - (C) spurious
   - *(D) experimenter
   - (E) double-blind

8. The authors of the text suggest that suppressor variables are <u>primarily</u> characterized as:
   - (A) identical to independent variables
   - (B) similar to dependent variables
   - (C) identical to reinforcer variables
   - *(D) similar to confounding variables
   - (E) typically found in blank experiments

9. Rank the following research designs in terms of highest-to-lowest degrees of control:
   - (A) preexperiments, qualitative designs, full experiments
   - *(B) full experiments, quasi-experiments, preexperiments
   - (C) quasi-experiments, qualitative designs, full experiments
   - (D) qualitative designs, preexperiments, full experiments
   - (E) preexperiments, quasi-experiments, qualitative designs

10. According to the authors of the text, random assignment <u>only</u> occurs in:
    - (A) preexperiments
    - (B) qualitative designs
    - *(C) full experiments
    - (D) quasi-experiments
    - (E) cannot answer as more information is needed

For items 11-12, consider the following observed during a study.
(i) Thirty students watch a videotape about the Challenger space shuttle disaster.
(ii) After watching the videotape, all 30 students complete a questionnaire.

11. Which of the following experimental designs <u>best</u> describes statements i and ii?
    - (A) one-group pretest-posttest design
    - (B) posttest-only nonequivalent groups design
    - (C) quasi-experimental design
    - *(D) one-group posttest-only design
    - (E) pretest-posttest quasi-equivalent groups design

150

12. Which of the following research designs employs nonrandom assignment of participants to treatment and control groups and administers a posttest?
    (A) one-group pretest-posttest design
    * (B) posttest-only nonequivalent groups design
    (C) quasi-experimental design
    (D) one-group posttest-only design
    (E) pretest-posttest quasi-equivalent groups design

13. A factorial experimental design can feature or be characterized by all of the following except:
    * (A) a single independent variable
    (B) a full experiment
    (C) multiple independent variables
    (D) a quasi-experiment
    (E) a preexperiment

14. In which experimental design are treatment carryover effects most likely to occur?
    (A) factorial design
    * (B) time series design
    (C) posttest-only nonequivalent groups design
    (D) one-group posttest-only design
    (E) pretest-posttest quasi-equivalent groups design

15. All things being equal, which type of research setting facilitates experimental researchers exercising the highest level of control?
    (A) field experiments
    * (B) laboratory experiments
    (C) preexperiments
    (D) quasi-experiments
    (E) cannot answer as more information is needed

True/False
F 16. According to the authors of the text, experimental research is concerned with establishing universal rather than statistical laws.
T 17. To establish causation in experimental studies, the independent and dependent variables must covary.
T 18. Many gambling schemes, such as pyramid games, are characterized by spurious relationships among the variables considered.
F 19. In experimental studies, the control group is typically exposed to the independent variable.
F 20. Natural experiments are ones in which a researcher manipulates a variable that

151

occurs naturally.

T   21.   In experimental studies, equivalent conditions are usually achieved through random assignment.

F   22.   A pretest measures research participants on relevant variables that need to be accounted for after exposing the treatment group(s) to the manipulation of the independent variable.

T   23.   The primary difference between full and quasi-experiments is that the former uses random assignment while the latter does not.

F   24.   Factorial designs are used only when researchers can conduct a full experiment.

T   25.   In general, experimental research typically is conducted in a laboratory rather than in the field.

Short-Answer/Essay Questions

1. Explain the importance of distinguishing between universal and statistical laws in communication research.
2. Compare a placebo group with a control group.
3. Define "reinforcer variable."
4. Describe the key features of a full experiment and how they differ from a preexperiment.
5. Describe and briefly evaluate a one-group posttest-only design.
6. Describe and briefly evaluate a pretest-posttest quasi-equivalent groups design.
7. Define second-order (also called higher order) interaction effects.
8. In a repeated-measures design, why should researchers be on guard against treatment carry-over effects?
9. Distinguish between laboratory and field experiments.

CHAPTER 8: SURVEY RESEARCH

I. Introduction
 A. Communication research concerns a wide range of situations, from intimate exchanges to mass appeals, from one-to-one interaction between members of a family to messages sent from one person to a large audience.
   1. Survey research is particularly relevant to the latter end of this continuum.
   2. Researchers use the **survey method** to ask questions about the beliefs, attitudes, and behaviors of respondents for the purpose of describing both the characteristics of those respondents and the population they were chosen to represent.
II. The Prevalence of Surveys
 A. Surveys have been used almost as long as people have gathered into social groups.
   1. The Romans used them as a census to tax people and the English, in 1086, conducted a survey to list all landowners.
   2. Surveys came of age in the twentieth century.
     (a) Survey research is particularly useful for gathering information about populations too large for every member to be studied.
     (b) The survey method also is a relatively straightforward research strategy: You ask people questions and analyze their answers.
III. Applied Uses of Survey Research
 A. Survey research has become a big business; survey research organizations grossed over 4.4 billion in worldwide revenues in 1994 (J. K. Stewart, 1994a).
   1. Surveys are most used as a tool in **public opinion research**, with three major applications.
     (a) **Political polls:** Results of political polls are presented to us routinely by the media, especially during election years.
       i. Decades ago, political polls were held in disrepute after highly publicized election predictions were shown to be inaccurate.
       ii. One reason today's pollsters do make more accurate predictions on election days is because of the use of **exit polls**, asking people how they voted just after they cast their ballot.
     (b) **Market research:** Seeks to determine current, and predict future, levels of consumption of products and services, evaluate consumer satisfaction with the performance of existing products, predict consumer preferences for new products, and identify persuasive strategies for product packaging, pricing, and advertising.
       i. **Advertising readership surveys:** Conducted regularly to identify differences in demographic characteristics between readers and nonreaders of a publication and to identify those who read advertisements for specific products.
       ii. **Editorial content readership surveys:** Conducted to determine which articles newspaper and magazine subscribers like and don't like and what topics they would like to see covered in the publication.
       iii. **Broadcast audience surveys:** Identify the size and composition of the audience

that television and radio stations and specific programs reach.
- (a) A variety of measurement services are used by rating services, such as A. C. Nielsen.
- iv. Market research is a dynamic field that is constantly developing new research techniques.
  - (a) **Usability testing:** Involves watching potential users interact with a new product under carefully controlled conditions, such as in a laboratory (See Chapter 7).
  - (b) **Contextual inquiry:** Involves studying customers' use of a product at their place of work.
- (c) **Evaluation research:** Surveys are used to evaluate the effectiveness of specific programs or products by inquiring about audience members' and customers' experiences and feelings.
  - i. **Formative evaluation:** Conducted while a program or product is in the process of being developed to identify ways to refine it.
  - ii. **Summative evaluation:** Conducted after a program or product is completed to learn its overall effectiveness, usually to determine whether to continue or discontinue it.
  - iii. **Need analysis:** Research to identify specific problems experienced by a target group, usually by identifying gaps between what exists and what is preferred, as well as to test reactions to potential solutions to those problems.
  - iv. **Organizational feedback surveys and audits:** Organizational members and representatives of groups those organizations serve are questioned about current or potential opportunities and constraints facing the organization.
  - v. **Network analysis**: Used to identify the patterns of interaction within a social system by gathering information about who system members communicate with and how often, either by surveying system members via questionnaires or interviews or by observing them.

IV. Use of Surveys in Communication Research
A. Many contributions to our understanding of people's communication behavior have been made by scholars who use the survey method.
  1. Figure 8.1 presents some recent examples of how researchers use the survey method to study communication.
  2. When studying relationships between variables, survey researchers rarely exercise the same amount of control as experimental researchers.
     (a) **Correlational design:** A questionnaire or interview is used to assess all the variables of interest at one point in time, and then analyze the relationships among them.
     (b) Survey research typically establishes noncausal relationships among variables.
  3. One survey can sometimes provide data for multiple studies.
     (a) Reanalysis by one scholar of data collected by someone else is called secondary data analysis, to distinguish it from primary research collected by the original researcher (See Chapter 3).

V. Survey Research Design
A. Designing an effective survey study involves a series of challenging decisions centering on the sample's selection; survey strategy such as phone or face-to-face; wording of the survey questions; and the amount of time for data collection.
B. Selecting Survey Respondents
   1. To select a sample, researchers first identify the population they want to describe.
      (a) **Sampling frame:** A list of the population from which they will sample.
      (b) It may not be possible to obtain a list of all the population.
      (c) In the case of large cities, for example, survey researchers often use telephone directories as the sampling frame.
         (i) **Random digit dialing:** Helps solve the problem of unlisted phone numbers by randomly generating via computer all the possible combination of telephone numbers in a given exchange.
   2. Sampling method is selected after the sampling frame is identified or created.
      (a) A random sample provides the best guarantee of generating an externally valid sample from a population (See Chapter 5).
      (b) Many large-scale surveys use *cluster sampling* to select respondents, and this procedure entails: Selecting states, counties within the state, cities within the counties, streets within the cities, houses on the streets, and finally, household members, all in a random manner.
      (c) *Stratified* samples help ensure that individuals with particular characteristics are selected, often in numbers proportional to their occurrence in the actual population.
   3. Obtaining random samples is fraught with problems.
      (a) In a recent study, for example, it was reported that in 1990, the **contact rate**--the percentage of phone calls that result in contact with an English-speaking interviewee--was only 56.4 percent.
      (b) The average **cooperation rate**---the percentage of phone calls in which the interviewees agree to participate---was only 53.2 percent and 26 percent of the respondents had been interviewed too frequently bu other researchers; referred to as the **surveyed rate**.
   4. Survey researchers usually obtain responses from individuals, but individuals are not always the unit of analysis in the survey.
      (a) Individuals are often asked questions about a larger unit of analysis, such as their family or work unit, and **cross-level inferences** are drawn about this larger unit.
      (b) There is some danger involved in such generalizing and if an **ecological fallacy** exists---where the data collected from one unit do not describe accurately the larger unit of analysis--- the study may have little value.
      (c) Researchers have to also be concerned with the **response rate**, that is, the number of usable responses divided by the total number of people sampled.
         i. The response rate is crucial for evaluating survey research, for if there are important differences between those who did and those who did not respond, the results of the study may not be valid.

  ii. There is no generally accepted minimum response rate, and researchers have to be concerned about *nonresponse bias*.
  iii. Researchers try very hard to maximize response rates and some strategies include: people are more likely to respond if the topic is important to them, or they believe they are contributing to an important cause; monetary rewards can also be used; and confidentiality or anonymity is assured when reporting results.
  iv. Despite such strategies, studies show that about 35 percent of adults refuse to cooperate with survey researchers (Looney, 1991).
  v. Two practices that discourage people from participating in surveys are *sugging and push-polling*: The former involves selling under the guise of a survey and the latter involves asking questions in a way to discredit a person or product.

VI. Cross-sectional versus Longitudinal Surveys
 A. Surveys that study respondents at one point in time are called **cross-sectional surveys,** and surveys that study respondents at several points in time are called **longitudinal surveys**.
 1. Cross-sectional surveys are easy to do, used most often, and very effective for studying the status quo.
 2. When evaluating the results from a cross-sectional survey, it is important to take into account the particular point in time when the survey was conducted.
  (a) The results of cross-sectional surveys can be misleading if done at unrepresentative point in time.
 3. Longitudinal surveys help to overcome the limitations of cross-sectional surveys.
  (a) By gathering data from respondents at several points in time, longitudinal surveys are much more effective at capturing the processual nature of communication.
 4. Three primary techniques are used to conduct longitudinal surveys.
  (a) A **trend study** measures people's beliefs, attitudes, and/or behaviors at two or more points in time to identify changes or trends.
  (b) A **cohort study** gathers responses from specific subgroups of a population, usually divided on the basis of age, and compares the responses over time.
  (c) A **panel study** (also called a **prospective study**) obtains responses from the same people over time to learn how beliefs, attitudes, and/or behaviors change.
   i. *Panel attrition*: This occurs when panel members cannot be replaced and fall out of the study, also known as mortality (See Chapter 5).
 5. Researchers can sometimes combine cross-sectional and longitudinal survey designs into an **accelerated longitudinal design** to study individuals over time.

VII. Survey Measurement Techniques
 A. Questionnaires and interviews are the primary measurement techniques employed by survey researchers; therefore it is essential to focus on question design and issues about using such self-report methods.
 B. The value of survey instruments rests on asking effective questions.
 1. Good questions elicit useful information; poor questions evoke useless information.
 C. Asking the "right" question is always important and evaluation criteria depend on the purpose(s) or objective(s) of the survey.

1. Many types of questions can be asked (See Figure 8.2) and these can be grouped into two category schemes (See Figure 8.2).
2. The type of question asked influences the accuracy of people's answers, especially when they call for recall of past events.
    (a) **Forward telescoping:** People tend to think that past events either occurred more recently then they did.
    (b) **Backward telescoping:** People tend to think that past events occurred longer ago than they actually did.
    (c) People also tend to report inaccurately incidents that are unpleasant or ego-threatening.
D. Phrasing Questions: The way a question is phrased influences the kind of responses received.
    1. *Closed questions*: Provide respondents with a limited number of predetermined responses from which to choose
    2. *Open questions:* Ask respondents to use their own words in answering questions.
    3. Whether closed or open, the wording of questions needs to be appropriate for the specific respondents being surveyed.
        (a) Researchers must take into account respondents' educational levels and cultural backgrounds and pose questions that use language with which they are familiar and thereby maximize the chances that the questions will be understood and answered.
        (b) Good survey questions are straightforward, to the point, and stated clearly.
        (c) To keep wording simple, or at least appropriate for the intended audience, researchers conduct a *readability analysis* to measure how easy or difficult it is to read a particular passage.
        (d) Good survey questions should ask about one and only one issue.
        (e) *Double barreled questions* ask about several issues at once and should be avoided.
        (f) The responses to closed questions should also be limited to a single referent.
        (g) Good survey questions are not *loaded questions,* that is, they don't lead people to respond in certain ways.
        (h) Good survey questions avoid using emotionally charged, inflammatory terms that can bias people's responses.
        (i) Good survey questions avoid using double negatives.
E. Questionnaires and interviews are structured in a variety of ways, depending on the type and arrangement of questions used.
    1. The *tunnel format* asks a series of similarly organized questions.
    2. The *funnel format* begins with broad, open questions followed by narrower, closed questions.
    3. The *inverted funnel format* begins with narrow, closed questions and builds to broader, open questions.
VIII. Questionnaire Survey Research
A. Questionnaires are commonly used in survey research to gather information from large

samples.
- B. There are two common types: self-administered questionnaires and mail surveys.
  1. Self-administered questionnaires (two types): Those completed by respondents in the presence of the researcher; and those completed by respondents without the presence of the researcher.
  2. Group administration of questionnaires is obviously more efficient than individual administration because a large number of respondents can be surveyed in a short amount of time.
- C. There are three types of paper-and-pencil self-administered questionnaires.
  1. *Traditional paper questionnaire* is the most common form.
  2. *Scannable questionnaires** ask respondents to mark their answers on a special form that is scanned by a computer. Provides a question sheet and a <u>separate</u> answer sheet.
  3. A *customized scannable questionnaire* provides the questions and answers on the <u>same</u> scannable sheet.

* A scannable questionnaire must rely on only closed questionnaires and limits the number of categories from which respondents can choose.

  4. *Mail surveys* provide an efficient and inexpensive way to reach representatives of large, geographically dispersed populations.
     (a) Must be self sufficient and user friendly.
     (b) Afford respondents more privacy and anonymity than questionnaires completed in the presence of a researcher.
     (c) Potentially jeopardizes the response rate and result in a much lower rate than other forms of questionnaires.

IX. Interview Survey Research
- A. Structured interviews are the only other major tool of survey research.
  1. Involves the interviewer (person conducting the interview) and the interviewee (person who is being interviewed).
  2. The degree to which the interviewer establishes rapport with interviewees influences somewhat how much and what kind of information interviewees offer in response to questions.
- B. Training interviewers is important as the quality of the data gathered in the interview is largely dependent on the skills of interviewers.
  1. Many researchers train interviewers before the actual case study because unskilled interviewers can destroy the validity of a well-designed interview, or can impugn the reputation of the research organization that sponsors the survey.
  2. All interviewers should be educated about goals and methods of the survey so that they can answer respondents' questions accurately.
  3. Interviewers should become familiar and comfortable with the interview schedule and be given opportunities to practice before the actual interview.
  4. *Directive interviews* use more closed questions and demand only that interviewers read questions to respondents clearly and accurately and record their answers.
  5. *Nondirective interviews*, in contrast, use more open questions and demand added sensitivity, flexibility, and communication skills.

C. There are relative advantages and disadvantages to face-to-face and telephone interviews.
   1. The advantages of face-to-face interviews follow:
      (a) Interviewers have more cues available for identifying when interviewees do not understand questions, are unsure about their answers, or even when they appear to provide misleading answers.
      (b) With the advent of portable computers, it is also possible to set up question sequences based on respondents' answers prior to the interview; see for example, **computer-assisted personal interviewing (CAPI)**.
   2. The disadvantages of face-to-face interviews follow:
      (a) These take more time to gather data.
      (b) These can decrease the privacy and anonymity of interviewees, making it more difficult to gather valid data about personal, risky, or embarrassing topics.
   3. The advantages of telephone interviews follow:
      (a) These can overcome some of the time, expense, and reactivity problems of face-to-face interviews.
      (b) These cost about 25 percent less than personal interviews.
      (c) These can reach interviewees over long distances and can increase respondents' privacy and anonymity.
      (d) **Computer-assisted telephone interviews (CATI)** selects and calls respondents automatically, cuing interviewers to the questions to be asked, and providing a simple mechanism for recording, coding, and processing responses.
      (e) Two new computer-assisted telephone interviewing techniques don't require a human interviewer: *Touchtone data entry (TDE)* and *voice recognition entry (VRE)* are both systems in which a "computer reads questions from a record and the respondent has to answer by use of the telephone" (Saris, 1991, p. 30).
   4. The disadvantages of telephone interviews follow:
      (a) Amount of nonverbal information available to the interviewer is limited to paralinguistic cues, and thus, may make it more difficult to assess honesty of answers.
      (b) Limits interviewer's ability to identify respondents' demographic characteristics.
      (c) Answering some closed questions can be difficult.
D. In considering whether to use individual versus group interviews, the purpose(s) of the study help researchers make an informed decision.
   1. Survey researchers usually interview respondents individually, unless their research purpose(s) call for respondents to be interviewed as a couple or group.
   2. *Focus group interviews*: A facilitator leads a small group of people (5-7) in a relatively open discussion about a specific product or program.
      (a) Focus group interviews encourages participation;
      (b) Make it easier for reluctant communicators to participate by encouraging people to "piggy-back" on others' ideas;
      (c) Are becoming increasingly popular for gathering data in communication survey research;
      (d) Are demonstrating effectiveness in developing survey questionnaires;

   (e) Can help generate information that can be used to design persuasive messages for communication campaigns.
 E. Beginning the interview
  1. How interviews are begun often determines whether, and how fully, respondents cooperate.
  2. In-depth interviews may require a great deal of rime and disclosure from respondents.
 F. Planning the interview questions
  1. Interviewers usually prepare the major questions they will ask in advance.
  2. List of questions that guide the interview is referred to as the *interview schedule* or *protocol*.
  3. Type of interview schedule depends on the purpose of the research.
   (a) *Structured interviews* require the interviewer to follow a preset list of questions the same way each time.
   (b) *Semi-structured interviews* require the interviewer to ask the specific primary questions but then allow for probing secondary questions.
   (c) *Unstructured interviews* provide interviewers with a set of questions, but allow them maximum freedom to decide what questions to ask and how to phrase them.
 G. Responding to answers
  1. Interviews are influenced as much by how researchers respond to the answers they receive as by how initial questions are posed.
  2. To obtain accurate and complete information, interviewers probe for more information when responses are too brief or general.
   (a) Probes often planned in advance, but can be improvised.
X. Using Multiple Methods in Survey Research
 A. Questionnaires and interviews often are used together in the same research study.
 B. Sometimes researchers conduct interviews after asking people to complete a questionnaire.
  1. This is done when researchers want to learn more about questionnaire answers.
 C. Survey research may help to verify findings that have been obtained using other methodologies.
 D. Researchers, especially those who conduct longitudinal research, sometimes design a study to include both survey and other methods.
XI. Conclusion
 A. What we learn from the survey method may be likened to what we see from the window of an airplane---an overview of a vast territory. We must be careful that we record and analyze accurately the terrain we are observing.
 B. Many scholars are employing new technologies and more ingenious methodologies to overcome traditional survey limitations. They will be measuring more elusive phenomena and getting more accurate results as social science evolves in the 21 century.

TEST ITEMS

1. According to the authors of the text, all of the following contributed to the popularity of surveys except:
   - (A) major government institutions
   - (B) newspaper polls
   - (C) market research
   - (D) university-sponsored surveys
   * (E) all of the above contributed

2. Advertising readership surveys target _____, whereas editorial content readership surveys target _____.
   * (A) demographic differences between readers and non-readers; subscriber evaluation of articles and desired coverage topics
   - (B) demographic differences between television ad viewers and non-viewers; subscriber evaluation of editorials and desired coverage topics
   - (C) attitudinal similarities between readers and non-readers; subscriber evaluation of magazine covers and newspaper first pages
   - (D) demographic differences between Internet users and non-users; subscriber evaluation of e-zines and other electronic publication vehicles
   - (E) cannot answer as more information is needed

3. Survey researchers often use correlational research designs, which are best characterized as establishing:
   - (A) cause-and-effect relationships among variables
   - (B) the impact of the independent variable's manipulation
   * (C) the strength of the relationship between examined variables
   - (D) whether certain relationships are spurious
   - (E) the impact of a manipulation of the dependent variable

For item 4, consider the following.
A Chamber of Commerce hires a consultant to assess the extent to which their communication skill training program was effective. The two-year pilot program ended last month. It is unknown whether it will be revived in the near future.

4. On the basis of the preceding information, which type of assessment or process will the consultant execute?
   - (A) formative evaluation
   - (B) organizational feedback survey
   - (C) need analysis
   * (D) summative evaluation
   - (E) call-out research

5. Ideally, the sampling frame in a survey research study will list _____; however, in practice, the sampling frame lists _____.
* (A) all members of the population; as many members of the population as possible
  (B) large numbers of registered voters; relatively low numbers of property holders
  (C) all members of the sample; as many key organizational informants as possible
  (D) small numbers of aberrant individuals; as many non-felons of the population as possible
  (E) all members of the sample; shrinking numbers of ethnic individuals

6. While prescreening possible research participants, your research team learns that 20 percent of the participant pool has completed 5 questionnaires already, and this situation primarily illustrates the:
  (A) cooperation rate
* (B) surveyed rate
  (C) contact rate
  (D) response rate
  (E) cannot answer as more information is needed

For item 7, consider the following.
(i) In 1995, a meta-analysis was conducted to help ascertain the efficacy of mammograms in preventing deaths among older U.S. women.
(ii) Studies that used the European one-view mammogram were compared to studies that used the U.S. two-view mammogram.
(iii) The results were then generalized to the larger U.S. population of older women.

7. On the basis of statements ii and iii, which of the following is most likely occurring?
  (A) cluster sampling
  (B) stratified sampling
* (C) ecological fallacy
  (D) cross-level inferences
  (E) nonresponse bias

8. According to the authors of the text, the alarming trend that plagues survey research today is that many individuals:
  (A) are very apprehensive about being surveyed
  (B) openly deceive investigators with erroneous replies
  (C) have trouble understanding college-level surveys
* (D) refuse to participate in part due to being over-surveyed
  (E) refuse to take surveys very seriously

9. Cross-sectional surveys can be characterized as:
   (A) occurring at two points in time
   (B) measuring enduring beliefs, attitudes, and values of participants
   (C) gauging patterns of attitudes across contexts
   (D) ideally suited for measuring cohort groups
 * (E) describing a sample at a fixed point in time

10. Longitudinal surveys are best suited for measuring:
    (A) generation effects
    (B) period effects
    (C) cohort effects
    (D) attitudes across contexts
 * (E) all of the above

For item 11, consider the following.
During a study, a survey item asks: "Please describe what you remember about your significant other when he or she became angry with you for the first time."

11. According to Patton (1980), the preceding question is best classified as a/an _____ question.
 * (A) sensory
   (B) feeling
   (C) opinion and value
   (D) experience and behavior
   (E) knowledge

For item 12, consider the following.
During a study, a survey item asks: "How well do you communicate with your significant other, your boss, and government officials?"

12. The preceding question primarily exemplifies a/an _____ question.
    (A) leading
 * (B) double-barreled
    (C) devil's advocate
    (D) opinion and value
    (E) experience and behavior

13. According to the authors of the text, all of the following are recommended suggestions for phrasing survey questions except:
    (A) using complete sentences
    (B) using short questions and simple wording
    * (C) using slang to create "down-to-earth" questions
    (D) using underlining or italics to garner others' attention
    (E) all of the above are recommendations

For item 14, consider the following.
A team of three researchers is about to conduct interviews with Native Americans living on reservations in the Southwest. The goal is to better understand how Native Americans' traditional stories inform their contemporary educational strategies.

14. Which of the following interview styles is best suited to this context?
    (A) highly directive type
    (B) one that employs many knowledge questions
    * (C) highly non-directive type
    (D) one that employs many devil's advocate questions
    (E) cannot answer as more information is needed

15. All of the following are disadvantages of face-to-face interviews except that they:
    (A) are time consuming
    (B) decrease research participants' privacy
    (C) usually increase the difficulty of gathering risky information
    * (D) decrease the opportunity for follow-up probes
    (E) all of the above are disadvantages

True/False

T   16. Survey research is particularly useful for gathering information about populations too large for every member to be studied.
F   17. Public opinion research has two primary applications: political polls and evaluation research.
F   18. When studying relationships between variables, survey researchers exercise the same amount of control as do experimental researchers.
T   19. Survey researchers typically use a correlational design; they assess all variables of interest at one point in time.
T   20. The ideal, although seldom practical, sampling frame is one that lists all population members.
T   21. Cluster sampling involves narrowing a large population down using such criteria as states, counties within the states, and cities within the counties.
F   22. In survey research, response rate refers to the number of usable responses divided by the total number of people who returned a questionnaire.

T	23.	Cross-sectional surveys describe the characteristics of a sample at one point in time, whereas longitudinal surveys gather data from respondents at several points in time.
F	24.	Generally speaking, it is preferable to use closed questions when conducting an interview.
F	25.	Non-directive type interviews usually require minimal interviewer communication skills.

Short-Answer/Essay Questions

1. Explain the fundamental purpose of the survey method.
2. Identify the three major applications of survey in public opinion research.
3. Many politicians claim that political polls are inaccurate, mainly on the basis of old polls that were faulty (such as the 1936 Literary Digest poll). Explain to them why political polls today are so much more accurate.
4. In lieu of having a complete list of the population from which to draw a sample for a survey, identify at least two sampling frames that are quite often used by survey researchers to try and acquire a representative sample.
5. Discuss the relative advantages and disadvantages of cross-sectional versus longitudinal surveys.
6. Give an example of (a) a double-barreled question and (b) a loaded question.
7. Drawing from your class research project, develop and explain an interview schedule "complete with a preview, body, and conclusion" that has the following characteristics: (a) four closed-ended demographic questions relevant to your class research project; (b) four open-ended and primary questions that introduce a topic; (c) four somewhat closed-ended secondary or follow-up questions that probe for additional information; and (d) one closing open-ended question designed to provide a synthesis of the interview experience. Be sure to explain the purpose of each section "preview, body, and conclusion" as well as each question type.
8. Describe and briefly evaluate the advantages of a directive versus non-directive interview schedule.
9. Explain how you might use multiple methods in survey research to see whether customers are satisfied with a new communication technology.

CHAPTER 9: TEXTUAL ANALYSIS

I. Introduction
 A. **Textual analysis** is the method communication researchers use to describe and interpret the characteristics of a recorded or visual message.
   1. The purpose of textual analysis is to describe the content, structure, and functions of the messages contained in texts.
   2. The important considerations in textual analysis include selecting the types of texts to be studied, acquiring appropriate texts, and determining which particular approach to employ in analyzing them.
   3. There are two general categories of texts:
     (a) Transcripts of communication (verbatim recordings);
     (b) Outputs of communication (messages produced by communicators)
   4. In terms of acquiring texts, outputs of communication are more readily available than transcripts.
     (a) **Archival communication research** involves examining the communication embedded in existing records of human behavior kept in archives.
     (b) Acquisition of texts is important as is the representativeness of the texts selected since sampling is typically used.
     (c) Another issue is determining how complete and accurate the texts are in order to conduct a sound analysis.
II. Approaches to Textual Analysis
 A. There are four major approaches to textual analysis: rhetorical criticism, content analysis, interaction analysis, and performance studies.
   1. The terms, *rhetoric* and *criticism*, conjure up interesting images.
     (a) Rhetoric often carries negative connotations, such as when it is applied to grand, eloquent, bombastic, or verbose discourse.
     (b) Andrews believes that criticism is typically associated with tearing down or denigrating comments; despite its function as constructive advice.
     (c) For scholars, the word rhetoric is associated with Aristotle's definition: "the available means of persuasion" and criticism is the "systematic process of illuminating and evaluating products of human activity" (Andrews, 1983, p. 4).
   2. **Rhetorical Criticism**, therefore, is a systematic method for describing, analyzing, interpreting, and evaluating the persuasive force of messages embedded within texts.
   3. The process serves five important functions (Andrews, 1983) including:
     (a) sheds light on the purposes of a persuasive message;
     (b) can aid in understanding historical, social, and cultural contexts;
     (c) can be used as a form of social criticism to evaluate society;
     (d) can contribute to theory building by showing how theories apply to persuasive discourse;
     (e) serves a pedagogical function by teaching people how persuasion works and what constitutes effective persuasion.

4. **Classical rhetoric** examined the characteristics and effect os persuasive public speaking during the Greek and Roman civilizations.
5. **Contemporary rhetoric** has expanded to incorporate a wide range of philosophical, theoretical, and methodological perspectives that are used to study the persuasive impact of many different types of texts and messages.

B. There are four steps to conducting rhetorical criticism
   1. Choosing a text(s) to study;
   2. Choosing a specific type of rhetorical criticism;
   3. Analyzing the text(s) according to the method chosen;
   4. Writing the critical essay.

C. There are several types of rhetorical criticism and they may be used to answer a wide range of questions including:
   1. What is the relationship between a text and its context?
   2. How does a text construct reality for an audience?
   3. What does a text suggest about the rhetor?
       (a) *Historical Criticism* examines how important past events shape and are shaped by rhetorical messages. Researchers go beyond merely describing and recreating past events from documents to evaluate the reasons why the past events occurred as they did.
       (b) *Oral Histories* investigate spoken, as opposed to written, accounts of personal experiences to understand more fully what happened in the past.
       (c) *Historical Case Studies* examine texts related to a single, salient historical event to understand the role played by communication.
       (d) *Biographical Studies* examine public and private texts of prominent, influential, or otherwise remarkable individuals. They analyze how the messages used by these individuals helped them to accomplish what they did.
       (e) *Social Movement Studies* examine persuasive strategies used to influence the historical development of specific campaigns and causes.
       (f) *Neo-Aristotelian Criticism* evaluated whether the most appropriate and effective means, as articulated in the specific set of criteria given in Aristotle's *Rhetoric*, were used to create the rhetorical text(s) intended to influence a particular audience.
       (g) *Genre Criticism* rejects using a single set of criteria to evaluate all persuasive messages, arguing instead, that standards vary according to the particular type, or *genre* of text being studied.
        (i) *Forensic* Rhetoric deals with the past and concerns issued involving legality and justice.
        (ii) *Epideictic* rhetoric concerns the present and is ceremonial.
        (iii) *Deliberative* rhetoric speaks to the future and involves political oratory.
       (h) *Dramatistic Criticism* primarily analyzes texts according to philosopher Kenneth Burke's view that all communication can be seen in terms of five essential elements that comprise a dramatic event.
        (i) Act: A particular message produced by a communicator.

(ii) Purpose: The reason for the message.
(iii) Agent: The person who communicated the message.
(iv) Agency: The medium used to express the message
(v) *Pentadic Analysis,* as it is called, uses these five elements to isolate essential characteristics of and differences between symbolic acts.
(i) *Metaphoric Criticism* assumes that we can never know reality directly.

(j) *Narrative Criticism* assumes that many (or all) persuasive messages function as narratives--storied, accounts, or tales.
(k) *Fantasy Theme Analysis,* based on the work of Ernest Bormann, examines the common images used to portray narrative elements of situations described in a text. Fantasy themes are mythic stories present in communication that involve characters with which people identify.
(l) *Feminist Criticism* analyzes how conceptions of gender are produced and maintained in persuasive messages.

B. **Content Analysis** is used to identify, enumerate, and analyze occurrences of specific messages and message characteristics embedded in texts.
   1. *Qualitative Content Analysis:* Researchers are more interested in the meanings associated with messages than with the number of times message variables occur.
   2. *Quantitative Content Analysis* is the systematic, step-by-step procedure used to answer research questions and test hypothesis.
   3. Considered an unobtrusive technique because researchers study texts that already exist rather than asking people to produce texts.
   4. Vast majority of content analyses employ quantitative procedures, which involve selecting texts, determining the units to be coded, developing content categories, training observers to code units, and analyzing the data.
      (a) Selecting texts: Choosing appropriate texts to study such as, newspapers, magazines, books, public service announcements, and Internet messages, etc.
      (b) Determining the unit of analysis: First identify the appropriate message unit to code (unitizing).
   5. There are five units including:
      (a) *Physical units* are the space and time devoted to content;
      (b) *Meaning units*, which the remaining four types reside within, involve symbolic meaning;
      (c) *Syntactical units* consist of discrete units of language, such as individual words, sentences, and paragraphs;
      (d) *Referential units*, also called *character units*, involve some physical or temporal unit referred to or alluded to within content;
      (e) *Thematic units* are topics contained within messages.
   6. Developing content categories into which units can be classified is done thru the use of nominal measurement procedures. This is a very creative process; there are an infinite number of categories into which units could potentially be classified.
   7. Analyzing the data, coding units into nominal categories, yields qualitative

data in that what is being communicated is determined by the type of category.
C. **Interaction Analysis**: Scholars view interaction as a complex accomplishment that requires much knowledge on the part of individual communicators and the ability to coordinate behavior with others.
  1. To describe interaction, researchers focus on a number of characteristics including:
     (a) Linguistic features: Studies range from the analysis of particular words and sentence components (verbs), to nonverbal features (eye contact & touch), to more interpretive aspects of language (powerful vs. powerless speech).
     (b) Types of topics that people talk about.
     (c) The purposes of specific actions and utterances in an interaction.
  2. Group decision making requires that group members satisfy four fundamental tasks, called functional requisites:
     (a) Thorough and accurate understanding of the choice-making situation;
     (b) Identification of a range of realistic alternative courses of action;
     (c) Thorough and accurate assessment of the positive qualities or consequences associated with alternative choices;
     (d) Thorough and accurate assessment of the negative qualities or consequences associated with alternative choices.
  3. Researchers interested in the functional nature of messages exchanged during interaction focus on the purpose of each communicator's moves.
  4. Others analyze the structure of interaction by studying the relationship between conversants' moves.
  5. Relating interaction to other variables: Most interaction analysts go beyond description to study the ways in which interaction is related to significant input and output variables.
     (a) How the characteristics of interactants influence their behavior during an interaction;
     (b) The effects of sociodemographic characteristics, such as gender or race;
     (c) Personality traits, such as affective orientation (the tendency to use one's emotions as guiding information);
     (d) Anxiety;
     (e) Attachment style (the type and quality of relationship one wants to share with another);
     (f) Attributional confidence (confidence in the ability to predict other people's feelings and behavior);
     (g) Cognitive complexity (the degree of differentiation, articulation, and integration within a cognitive system);
     (h) Defensiveness; depression; extroversion; empathic ability;
     (i) Locus of control (degree to which people versus the environment are held accountable for enacted behavior);
     (j) Loneliness; need for privacy;
     (k) Self-efficacy (degree of confidence people have in being able to attain their goals);

(l) Self-esteem;
   (m) Self-monitoring (the extent to which people pay attention to their verbal and nonverbal behaviors);
(n) Tolerance for disagreement.
6. Conducting Interaction Analysis: Conducting interaction analysis involves two general tasks: Obtaining a sample of interaction, and analyzing that sample.
   1. In gathering a *sample of interaction*, researchers make choices that affect both the type and the quality of the data obtained, including the type of interactional data required, the desired location of the interaction, and the appropriate means for gathering the data.
      (a) Type: Will it be any interaction or a specific interaction? natural and unstructured or structured? Real or hypothetical?
      (b) Location: Will it be in a laboratory, in interactants' homes or offices, or in some publicly accessible place.
      (c) Means for gathering data: Audio taping, videotaping, observational notes taken by researchers and questionnaires answered by respondents.
   2. Analyzing the *sample of interaction:* Specific analysis depends on whether the goal is to describe interaction or relate it to other variables. It also depends on the form the data take.

D. **Performance Studies**: Final approach to textual analysis; "the process of dialogic engagement with one's own and others' aesthetic communication through the means of performance." Researchers interpret texts as a method of inquiry that enables them and audiences of performances to interpret the aesthetic richness of those texts. There are six steps in generating and reporting insights in performance studies.
   1. Selecting: Identifying the communication act or text they wish to examine;
   2. Playing: Trying on different vocal and bodily behaviors;
   3. Testing: Establishes the range of legitimate understandings;
   4. Choosing: Question of selecting those valid interpretations to isolate one possible understanding to pursue.
      (a) Sets in motion a *performance vision*, a reading that the performance researcher attempts to enact.
   5. Repeating: Sets and refines the researchers chosen interpretation.
   6. Presenting: Report of what has been discovered through public performance. Puts on a display for others' consideration what the performance researcher has come to understand.

III. Conclusion
 A. A famous industrialist once said, "a person's language, as a rule, is an index of his or her mind." This suggests that examining word choices can provide insights into people's characters.
 B. The essence of this message is also a basic premise of textual analysts. Their mission is understanding how people think, and consequently act, by studying patterns displayed in their discourse, broadly defined.

TEST ITEMS

1. According to the authors of the text, all of the following characterize textual analysis except:
   - (A) content of major speeches, such as those in Vital Speeches of the Day, may be examined
   - (B) messages in music videos, from MTV, for example, may be examined
   - *(C) a universal paradigm guides this type of analysis
   - (D) personnel records may be examined
   - (E) all of the above characterize textual analysis

2. If a researcher examines graffiti, films, and refuse, he or she is studying in sequence:
   - (A) scripted transcripts, artifacts, and signs
   - *(B) written artifacts, works of art, and symbolic outputs
   - (C) public outputs, scripted transcripts, and signs
   - (D) symbolic outputs, signs, and artifacts
   - (E) private outputs, scripted transcripts, and signs

3. In their seminal work, Webb, Campbell, Schwartz, and Sechrest (1973) identified types of public records that are available in archives. Which of the following are examples of such public records?
   - (A) actuarial reports
   - (B) political and judicial records
   - (C) traffic accident reports
   - (D) newspaper articles
   - *(E) all of the above are examples

4. According to Foss (1989), all of the following are steps involved in rhetorical criticism except:
   - *(A) conducting the analysis using quantitative data-analytic techniques
   - (B) selecting a text to study
   - (C) analyzing the text in concert with the technique selected
   - (D) writing the critical essay
   - (E) all of the above are included

5. Oral histories can function to:
   - (A) corroborate historical inquiry
   - (B) enable a conversation
   - (C) correct historical inquiry
   - (D) transmit culture
   - *(E) all of the above

6. The Hacker and Hansen study (1974)---conducted among Japanese Americans who were imprisoned during World War II within the U.S.---is illustrative <u>primarily</u> since the researchers were able to interview the:
    (A) camp administrators
    (B) top military officials still living
    * (C) camp prisoners
    (D) surrounding populace
    (E) all of the above

<u>For item 7, consider the following</u>.
In the closing years of the twentieth century, several cults emerged and competed for public attention by emphasizing that Armageddon was imminent. One such cult was Heaven's Gate. In line with the arrival of a comet, over 20 cult members committed suicide so that they might be transported to the alleged "mother ship" trailing the comet.

7. If a scholar were to examine the <u>web site of Heaven's Gate</u> and the <u>persuasive appeals</u> used by the members, he or she would be engaging in which type of rhetorical criticism?
    (A) genre criticism
    (B) dramatistic criticism
    (C) oral studies
    * (D) social movement studies
    (E) metaphoric criticism

8. All of the following are key components of Burke's form of rhetorical analysis <u>except</u> the:
    (A) act
    * (B) jeremiad
    (C) purpose
    (D) agent
    (E) all of the above are components

9. Which of the following types of rhetorical criticism assumes that individuals can never know reality directly?
    (A) genre criticism
    (B) dramatistic criticism
    (C) oral histories
    (D) social movement studies
    * (E) metaphoric criticism

10. Another type of textual analysis, performance studies, is characterized by all of the following except that it:
* (A) is similar to content analysis and interaction analysis
  (B) combines elements of naturalistic research
  (C) allows researchers to use their own bodies and voices as tools of exploration
  (D) is a process of dialogic engagement
  (E) all of the above are characteristics

11. According to one of the leading scholars in the area, Pelias, performance studies is based on a simple, yet powerful premise, and it is that:
  (A) researchers work somatically to uncover communication nuances
  (B) performance should be viewed as both an event and process
* (C) embodying the communication acts of others is a profound way of coming to understand them
  (D) performance should be viewed as both an event and method
  (E) researchers give voice to many otherwise disenfranchised individuals through this process

12. All of the following research questions would be appropriate for content analysis except:
  (A) What messages do the media present about cancer, heart disease, and AIDS?
  (B) How many sexual words are used on television soap operas?
  (C) Do billboard advertisements differ depending on where they are located in a city?
* (D) To what extent have interpersonal relationships changed since the 1970s?
  (E) What types of messages are used when heinous crimes are portrayed on prime-time television shows?

13. The line of research conducted by Pollock and associates---called the community structure approach---is illustrative in that it primarily demonstrates:
  (A) deliberative rhetoric
  (B) qualitative content analysis
* (C) that input variables can shape message content
  (D) unstructured content analysis
  (E) cannot answer as more information is needed

14. When coders are used to classify units into categories, such as in content analysis and interaction analysis, the level of intercoder reliability should be at least:
  (A) .30
  (B) .40
  (C) .50
  (D) .60
* (E) .70

15. Interaction Analysis Schemes, such as Bales' (1950) Interaction Process Analysis (IPA), are designed <u>primarily</u> to examine the:
    (A) linguistic features of interaction
    (B) content features of interaction
    (C) unstructured aspects of interaction
*   (D) functions of interaction
    (E) cannot answer as more information is needed

True/False

F   16. Textual analysis is a method communication researchers use primarily to analyze nonverbal interaction among people.

T   17. Textual analysis is somewhat unique from other methodologies in that some textual analysts go beyond description and the study of relationships between variables to evaluate texts.

T   18. Outputs of communication include verbal utterances, written artifacts, works of arts, and other symbolic outputs, such as footprints.

T   19. Rhetorical criticism is a systematic method for describing, analyzing, interpreting, and evaluating the persuasive force of messages within texts.

F   20. Rhetorical criticism can be used to quantitatively determine how a text constructs reality for an audience.

T   21. Content analysis identifies, enumerates, and analyzes specific messages and message characteristics embedded in texts.

T   22. Content analysis can be done either qualitatively or quantitatively.

F   23. Generally speaking, interaction analysis examines messages exchanged between the media and various publics.

F   24. In performance studies, the step of testing, which establishes the range of legitimate understandings of a text, is similar to hypothesis testing in quantitative research studies.

F   25. In performance studies, researchers first report their findings in written form, such a scholarly article, and they then perform that report.

Short-Answer/Essay Questions
1. Explain what a "text" and the fundamental purpose of "textual analysis" mean.
2. In addition to describing communication and relating communication to other variables, some textual analysts also _____ texts by using a set of standards. (Note: Use a single word only.)
3. Identify which of the following four general types of textual analysis is represented by the following research examples:
    A) Flesch (1949) developed a formula to assess whether a person with an 8th-grade education could understand words and sentences in

- B) Moore (1922) eavesdropped on people in public on the streets of Manhattan and notes the topics they talked about in same-gender and mixed-gender dyads;
- C) Johannesen (1986) analyzed a jeremiad speech by President Ronald Reagan, a speech that castigates a specific group, blaming the group for current problems and urging the members to remedy their ways;
- D) Brouwer (1988) analyzed the politically precarious performative phenomenon of individuals who acquire tattoos that proclaim that they have HIV/AIDS.

4. Identify the three general interrelated research questions that are asked by rhetorical critics according to Foss (1989) and then identify one specific type of rhetorical criticism for each of these questions.

5. Suppose you wanted to conduct a quantitative content analysis of how children are portrayed in magazine ads. Explain what type of and where texts would be drawn, what is the unit of analysis, and identify at least three content coding categories that could be used to classify units.

6. Suppose you wanted to study whether satisfied couples communicate more effectively than dissatisfied couples. Explain how you could use interaction analysis to study this topic. Make sure to explain whom you would choose and what specific aspect of their conversation you would study and how you might classify it in at least two different ways.

7. Explain how interaction analysis that focuses on the communication functions of particular messages views communication as a one-way process whereas interaction analysis that focuses on the structure of interaction views communication as a two-way process.

8. Describe and briefly evaluate how a researcher in line with a performance studies

9. Explain the nature and goals of performance studies and provide a concrete research example of how it has been used.

CHAPTER 10: NATURALISTIC RESEARCH

I. Introduction
  A. The social context (situations where people usually interact) in which people communicate influences what occurs.
  B. **Naturalistic inquiry** is research that focuses on how people behave when absorbed in genuine life experiences in natural settings.

II. Common Assumptions Guiding Naturalistic Inquiry
  A. The goal of naturalistic research is to develop context-specific statements about the multiple, constructed realities of all the key participants.
  B. There are three general assumptions of naturalistic research.
    1. **Naturalism**: The belief that phenomena should be studied in context.
    2. **Phenomenology**: The belief that the object of interest be examined without any preconceived notions or expectations.
      (a) *Presupposition-less research*: The researcher makes his/ her own norms, values, and ideology apparent and does not assume they are shared.
    3. **Interpretive nature** of naturalistic research: The belief that the researcher, while trying to see the situation from the point of view of those studied, cannot escape his/her own view.

III. Types of Naturalistic Inquiry
  A. The focus on methodologies centers on various aspects of ethnography:
    1. From the Greek "ethos" meaning "race, tribe, nation."
    2. From the Greek "graphos" meaning "something written down."
  B. There exist 4 types:
    1. **Ethnography**: The use of direct observation and extended field research to produce a thick, naturalistic description of a people and their culture.
    2. **Ethnomethodology**: Empirical study of methods used to give sense to and accomplish daily actions; attempt to understand commonplace talk routines.
      (a) *Ethnomethodological indifference*: Used by ethnomethodologists to abstain from judging others' actions.
      (b) *Experimental breaching*: Deliberately upsetting patterned routines to reveal rules participants use to organize experiences.
      (c) There are two lines of ethnomethodological inquiry:
        i. *Conversation analysis*: Examines interaction using qualitative methods.
        ii. *Formal ethnomethodology*: Perspective used by the researcher to view taken-for-granted behavior.
    3. **Critical Ethnography**: Ethnography designed to promote emancipation and reduce oppression; gives voice to mistreated people and those struggling for social change.
    4. **Autoethnography**: Personal ethnography) researchers examine their own life experiences and fieldwork.
      (a) Autobiography: story of one's own life; exemplified in autoethnography.

IV. The Flow of Naturalistic Inquiry
  A. Characteristics of the naturalistic research process.
    1. *Site*: Studying phenomena in context, or *in situ*.

2. *Embodied practice*: Researchers place their bodies in a context and use themselves as the primary "instrument" to collect data.
   3. *Qualitative methods*: An array of interpretive techniques which seek to describe, decode, translate, and come to terms with the meaning of naturally occurring phenomena.
B. The flow of naturalistic research (see figure 10.1) demands a human instrument and builds on tacit knowledge using qualitative methods engaging in purposive sampling, the design that emerges, along with induction and grounded theory (which involves negotiated outcomes) leads to a case report which is idiographically interpreted and tentatively applied.
C. Naturalistic researchers usually employ multiple methodological procedures for the best way to elicit the various and divergent constructions of reality that exist within a context of study.
   1. Naturalistic researchers use *nonrandom, purposive sampling*.
   2. **Informants** can provide unique insight into a culture.
   3. An **emergent design** introduces or changes procedures during the research process.
   4. **Member checks** occur when researchers give a draft of their research report to participants or similar people for feedback.
D. Findings from naturalistic research are reported in the form of a **case study** (a detailed examination of a single subject, group, or phenomenon).

V. Collecting Data on Naturalistic Inquiry
  A. There are *two major investigative strategies* used by naturalistic researchers.
     1. *Direct Observation*
     2. *In-depth interviews*
  B. Naturalistic observational research entails going "into the field" to observe everyday activities.
     1. Fieldwork involves a number of important issues.
          (a) Deciding what to study: Observe as much as possible, focusing on one of three interrelated aspects.
             i. Understanding the communication behavior of a particular group of people.
             ii. Gaining access to the group.
             iii. Being associated with a group in another role.
          (b) Role of the observer: Naturalistic researchers must decide on the observational role to assume (four types).
             i. **Complete participant**: Fully involved in a social setting and does not let people know they are being studied; "going native;" (consider ethical dilemmas).
             ii. **Participant-observer**: Involved as fully as possible in a social situation where people know they are being studied; agenda is revealed.
             iii. **Observer-participant**: Primarily observes and participates only to a limited extent; marginal member of the group.
             iv. **Complete observer**: Does not interact with the group, strictly an observer; greatest objectivity.
             v. Figure 10.2 presents examples of various long-term naturalistic inquiry.
          (c) Length of Observations varies.
             i. Only a single or few observational period(s) is/are necessary for a fleeting

phenomenon.
   ii. Sustained observations, or longitudinal research, is preferred because it helps establish quality relationships between researcher and participants.
  (d) Observe impressionistically; look for clues to comprehend a setting's actions.
  (e) Recording observations
   i. **Field notes**: written or audiorecorded records of what occurred.
   ii. *Headnotes* which are: written examples of mental logs.
   iii. Use of *activity logs*, journals, or self-observational diaries.
   iv. *Notes* are crucial to describing and inferring patterns in people's communication.
   v. *Experience Sampling Method*
C. Interviewing in naturalistic inquiry
  1. Interviews are used to obtain information from a relatively small, representative sample so that generalizations can be made about the population of interest.
  2. **In-depth interviews**, in contrast to surveys, proceed inductively and use an unstructured format consisting of open questions; highly exploratory.
  3. There are several issues interviewers face including:
    (a) Whom to interview and sampling strategy:
      i. Purposive (nonrandom) sample?
      ii. Key informants?
      iii. **Theory-based sample**?
      iv. Network (snowball) sample?
      v. Convenience sample?
      vi. See Figure 10.3.
    (b) Interview logistics must also be addressed ranging from::
      i. Where?
      ii. One-on-one vs. team approach?
      iii. Alone or together?
      iv. Focus groups?
      v. When?
    (c) The interview format must also be ascertained prior to data-collection:
      i. Unstructured versus structured type?
      ii. Use a **long interview** that uses a questionnaire to create a sharply focused and intense series of messages?
      iii. Use a funnel format that proceeds from general to specific levels of inquiry?
    (d) There are also a variety of interview methods and philosophies:
      i. Phenomenology: Interviews are used to understand how people experience life processes without imposing preconceptions;
      ii. Feminist perspective: Speaks to the unique experiences of women;
      iii. Ethnomethodological interview;
      iv. **Life story interview** (oral history);
      v. Similarity between interviewer and interviewee;
      vi. **Critical Incident Technique**: Asks for most memorable positive and negative experiences within a specific, social context;

vii. **Episode analysis**: Reconstruction of a scene that represents a reoccurring pattern in a relationship;
viii. **Account analysis**: Asking people to account for observations;
ix. **Protocol analysis**: Verbalization of feelings, thoughts while engaged in an activity;
x. **Stimulated recall**, using a tape recording for example to help trigger participants' reflections of an exchange.
(e) When recording and transcribing interviews, the amount of detail depends on the purpose of the research and must be done accurately.

VI. Start Making Sense: Analyzing and Reporting Qualitative Data
A. A massive amount of detail must be made sense of and reported.
   1. Consider Levine's five general storage and retrieval processes.
B. **Analyzing qualitative data**: Analysis of data that indicates the meanings people have of something exemplified by:
   1. Should be viewed as an ongoing process;
   2. Collected data must be reduced;
   3. The goal is to explain the meaning of the data---
      (a) **First-order explanations**, that is, the research participants' explanations;
      (b) **Second-order explanations**, that is, the researcher(s)' explanations.
   4. Some naturalistic researchers analyze for the purpose of theory development.
   5. Testing theory and building grounded theory:
      (a) Some researchers analyze data deductively to see if data conforms to their expectations.
      (b) **Analytic induction**: To infer meanings from the data collected; look for emerging patterns.
      (c) **Grounded theory**: Generalizations are inferred from the collected data.
         i. See for example the constant comparative method.
      (d) Memoranda: Researcher's hunches and theoretical ideas about the structure underlying the studied phenomenon.
      (e) Eventually, categories become "saturated."
      (f) Research that seeks to develop theory from the ground up should meet four criteria:
         i. Believable; comprehensive; grounded; and applicable.
   6. Qualitative data-analytic techniques:
      (a) **Dialectical analysis**: Explores tensions produced from seemingly contradictory elements within a system (i.e., a stepfamily).
      (b) Metaphor analysis: Seeks participants' use of metaphors.
      (c) Fantasy theme analysis: Examines the stories shared among people;
         i. See Symbolic Convergence Theory.
C. Reporting findings from naturalistic research.
   1. Telling a tale: A story told by a member of one culture about another culture (or own) to the members of his/her own culture.
      (a) **Realist tale**: Story told from the point of view of the people studied.
      (b) **Confessional tale**: Focuses primarily on the researcher and his/her experiences during fieldwork.

- (c) **Impressionistic tale**: Blends realist and confessional tales to provide an account of the participants and the researcher as central characters.
- (d) **Critical tale**: Critiques problematic social structures through the perspective of those who are disadvantaged.
- (e) **Formal tale**: Follows the rules of a particular theory or analytic procedure.
- (f) **Literary tale**: Told using a novelist's sense of narration.
- (g) **Jointly told tales**: Researchers and participants work together.
2. Writing the report (several structures):
    - (a) Thematic;
    - (b) Chronological;
    - (c) Puzzle-Explication;
    - (d) Separate narration and analysis;
    - (e) Narrowing and expanding the focus;
    - (f) Exemplars: Quotes and descriptions that help illustrate and crystallize the concept.
3. Other forms of presentation:
    - (a) Performance;
    - (b) Film;
    - (c) Photography.

VII. Conclusion

A. Naturalistic researchers must identify and gain entry to the site they want to study, determine the role they will take, what and how they will observe, who they will interview and what they will ask. and how to record the information and present it.

TEST ITEMS

1. All of the following are appropriate for naturalistic communication research except studying:
    - (A) listening patterns of young teens and focusing on the influence of N'Sync lyrics
    - (B) viewing patterns of young adults and focusing on the influence of the Simpsons
    - (C) gossip among reporters covering an imminent press conference
    - (D) conversations between two close friends about to become lovers
    * (E) all of the above are appropriate

2. The _____ assumption encourages researcher introspection about his/her underlying values while attempting to assume the perspective of the research participants.
    - (A) axiological
    * (B) interpretive
    - (C) naturalism
    - (D) phenomenological
    - (E) epistemiological

3. If a group of researchers is about to study the ways in which newspaper stories demonize gang members, in line with the phenomenological assumption and prior to beginning the study, what must they address?
    - (A) how gangs are formed in urban communities
    * (B) their underlying attitudes as researchers
    - (C) understanding the role of gangs as surrogate families for members
    - (D) their prior training as researchers
    - (E) key features of the context

4. Which of the following types of research seeks to interpret everyday conversation and the methods used to make sense of talking behavior?
    - (A) critical ethnography
    - (B) experimental research
    * (C) ethnomethodology
    - (D) autoethnography
    - (E) ethnography

For item 5, consider the following.
(i) A researcher seeks to understand the conditions that give rise to the occurrence of sexually harassing messages among employees and supervisors at Ford Motor Company.
(ii) He or she then designs and administers a training program to lessen the intensity of these problems.

5. On the basis of the preceding information, this study best exemplifies:
* (A) critical ethnographic research
  (B) phenomenological research
  (C) autoethnographic research
  (D) ethnographical research
  (E) conversation analysis

For item 6, consider the following.
(i) Gina, Kristin, and Erin decide to study a newsroom one hour before deadline. They are investigating the suspected relationship among time constraints, word processing speed, and story depth. The research participants are college-educated and have been working at the newspaper for two-four years.

(ii) Todd, Josh, and Daryle decide to study the relationship among Internet use, communication apprehension, and relational satisfaction. The research participants are travelers at the local airport.

6. Situation i primarily represents a:
   (A) convenient sample
   (B) random sample
* (C) purposive sample
   (D) treatment sample
   (E) population

7. The need for grounded theory and an emergent design is reinforced by which of the following:
   (A) developing theoretical frameworks during data collection
   (B) social science research standards
   (C) an emphasis on operationalizations and conceptualizations
   (D) the changing nature of treatment and control groups
* (E) developing explanatory frameworks after collecting and analyzing data

For item 8, consider the following.
(i) A researcher attends a Gamblers' Anonymous Meeting, collects data <u>without</u> letting the people know he or she is a researcher, and <u>then</u> indicates to the group that he or she is studying them.

8. On the basis of the preceding information, this is an example of the researcher adopting a _____ role.
   (A) complete participant
   (B) participant-observer
   (C) observer-participant
 * (D) complete observer
   (E) cannot answer as more information is needed

9. According to the authors of the text, which of the following situations would be <u>best</u> suited for a minimum number of observations in naturalistic research?
   (A) monthly meetings of the local newspaper's editorial staff
 * (B) live coverage of the eulogy for a departed civic leader
   (C) weekly meetings of the public television channel's staff
   (D) daily coverage of the Kosovo conflict spanning several weeks
   (E) all of the above

For item 10, consider the following.
Five researchers have interviewed people about their emotional reactions to public service announcements encouraging them to register to vote. Each participant is asked to identify another person whom the researchers could interview.

10. According to the authors of the text, this type of sample is <u>best</u> defined as a _____ sample.
    (A) deviant
 * (B) snowball
    (C) maximum variation
    (D) disconfirming case
    (E) cannot answer as more information is needed

For item 11, consider the following.
While reading about a study of mentally-impaired children residing in group homes and the daily interaction with their parents, you notice that the researchers conducted in-depth interviews at the homes of the parents.

11. According to the authors of the text, the researchers' <u>primary</u> justification for conducting these home interviews is to:
    (A) develop an adversarial relationship with the parents being interviewed
    (B) create a highly stressful climate to better ascertain how the parents being interviewed communicate under such circumstances
  * (C) create an equal relationship between the researchers and the parents being interviewed
    (D) demonstrate that a focus group interviewing approach is ill-suited to home interviews
    (E) cannot answer as more information is needed

12. According to the authors of the text, in-depth interviews are characterized by all of the following <u>except</u>:
    (A) being inductive
    (B) relying on open-ended questions
    (C) being exploratory
    (D) being unstructured
  * (E) all of the above are characteristics

13. If a naturalistic researcher faces severe time constraints, he or she would be <u>less likely</u> to use a/an:
    (A) structured format
    (B) predominance of close-ended questions
  * (C) unstructured format
    (D) funnel format
    (E) cannot answer as more information is needed

14. According to the authors of the text, all of the following are characteristics of qualitative data analysis <u>except</u>:
    (A) the process should be viewed as ongoing
  * (B) collected data must be enlarged as much as possible
    (C) the goal is to explain the meaning of the data
    (D) building grounded theory
    (E) all of the above are characteristics

15. Which of the following tales would critique a federal agency, such as the Equal Employment Opportunity Commission, when it was slow to act on behalf of women employees who filed sexual harassment charges against Mitsuibishi Corporation?
    (A) realist
    (B) confessional
    (C) impressionistic
  * (D) critical
    (E) formal

True/False

F 16. Research that focuses on how people behave naturally in laboratory settings is called "naturalistic research."

T 17. Ethnography is derived from the Greek words ethnos (which means tribe, race, or nation) and graphos (which means something written down).

F 18. A critical ethnographer would be unlikely to study situations in which his or her research could lessen oppression and facilitate hearing the voices of previously "faceless" individuals, such as the homeless.

F 19. In naturalistic research, embodied practice means that researchers place research participants in comfortable environments and study their behavior.

T 20. When naturalistic researchers adopt the complete participant role, people do not know that they are being studied.

F 21. Naturalistic observation always involves longitudinal research.

F 22. Naturalistic in-depth interviews typically proceed deductively.

T 23. Naturalistic researchers typically rely on purposive, as opposed to random, samples when selecting people to interview.

F 24. First-order explanations are researchers' explanations of research participants' behavior; second-order explanations are research participant's explanations of their own behavior.

T 25. Grounded theory means that the generalizations researchers draw are inferred from the data collected.

Short-Answer/Essay Questions

1. Explain the three general assumptions that guide naturalistic inquiry according to Potter (1996).
2. Identify the specific type of naturalistic research for each of the examples below:
    A) Garfinkel's studies of breaching rules that typically are used in a context (such as staring at people on elevators);
    B) Jones's performances of a play in which she role-played people she had met during her fieldwork and another person role-played Jones for

the purpose of Jones getting perspective on the personal and subjective nature of her fieldwork experiences;
- C) Philipsen's studies of communication patterns in Teamsterville, a neighborhood on the south side of Chicago;
- D) Conquergood's studies of gang communication that offer an alternative voice to the demonization of gangs by mainstream media.

Answers: A = Ethnomethodology; B = Autoethnography; C = Ethnography; D = Critical Ethnography

3. Describe and briefly evaluate the utility of the four types of ethnographic research.
4. Describe what is meant by an "emergent design" in naturalistic inquiry and how that differs from experimental and most survey research.
5. Create a communication-based study that demonstrates the utility of the naturalistic paradigm. This example must illustrate and explain at least four key tenets of naturalistic research (see the flow chart). Close by arguing what information might be gained from this approach that could not be gained from positivist methods of inquiry.
6. Identify the ethnographic observational role (from Gold's four master roles) demonstrated in the following research examples:
   - A) An ethnographer who becomes a taxi driver for many months to study big-city drivers and does not tell the other taxi drivers that he/she is a researcher;
   - B) An ethnographer who undergoes police academy training him/herself (with the police recruits knowing that he/she is a researcher) to learn how police recruits are socialized into the culture of law enforcement
   - C) An ethnographer who sits in the back of a grade school classroom taking notes;
   - D) An ethnographer who studies interactions among Little League baseball teams by hanging around during practice and games and chatting with players and their families.

   Answers: A = Complete Participant; B = Participant-Observer; C = Complete Observer; D = Observer-Participant

7. Survey interviews typically proceed in a _____ manner, with as much as possible worked out ahead of time, and tend to be highly _____, with all respondents being asked the same _____ questions in the same order. In contrast, in-depth naturalistic interviews typically proceed in an _____ manner using an _____ format consisting of _____ questions.

   Answers: deductive, structured, closed, inductive, unstructured, open

8. Match the following types of interview methods with the definitions below: (A) account analysis; (B) critical incident technique; (C) episode analysis; (D) life story interview; (E) protocol analysis; (F) stimulated recall.
   1) First recording a conversation and then playing back the tape for

     participants and asking them to describe what they were thinking and feeling at points throughout the activity;
2) Asking people to construct in their own words their entire life as a story or narrative, starting from the time a person is born to the present day, as well as hopes and visions for the future;
3) Asking for actors' own statements about why they performed acts in questions and what social meanings they give to the actions of themselves and others;
4) Asking for people's most memorable positive and negative experiences within a specific, social context;
5) Asking people to reconstruct a scene, complete with lines of dialogue, that represents a recurring pattern in a relationship;
6) Asking people to verbalize their intentions, thoughts, and feelings as they engage in an activity.

Answers: A = 3; B = 4; C = 5; D = 2; E = 6; F = 1

9. Explain the process of building grounded theory in naturalistic inquiry and how it differs from the positivist practice of testing theory.

Chapter 11: DESCRIBING QUANTITATIVE DATA

I. Introduction
  A. We are constantly bombarded by information in the form of statistics, numbers people use to describe things; some are easy to understand, others are more complex.
  B. This chapter is designed to help explain various types of statistics used to analyze quantitative (numerical) data. The goal is to help you become a competent consumer of such information.
II. Making Sense of Numbers: Statistical Data Analysis
  A. A set of acquired data is not very useful in itself; it needs to be analyzed and interpreted.
  B. **Data Analysis**: The process of examining what data mean to researchers, transforming data into useful information that can be shared.
    1. **Statistical data analysis**: The process of examining what quantitative data mean to researchers.
  C. "Statistics" comes from the Latin "*status*" which implies that **statistics** are used to understand the status or state of quantitative data; statistics refers to any numerical indicator of a set of data.
    1. There are two broad levels of statistics: Descriptive and inferential statistics.
  D. Statistics are one of the most pervasive and persuasive forms of evidence used to make arguments; one should be wary of the fact that statistics are often used in a less that honest manner ("statiscalculation").
    1. The lack of knowledge about statistical information results either in the tendency to reject the information completely or to accept it at face value.
  E. The word statistics refers to two items:
    1. Products: Numerical descriptions and inferential statistics that characterize a set of quantitative data.
    2. Techniques: The application of procedures to produce numerical descriptions and statistical inferences.
  F. There exist two general purposes of description and inference as reflected in two types of statistical data analysis:
    1. **Descriptive statistical data analysis**: Used to construct simple descriptions about the characteristics of a set of quantitative data.
      (a) *Summary statistics*: Numerical indicators that summarize the data.
      (b) Conversion of raw scores into *standard scores*.
      (c) Constructing visual displays of data.
    2. **Inferential statistical data analysis** (two purposes)
      (a) *Estimation*: Estimating the characteristics of a population from data gathered on a sample.
      (b) *Significance testing*: Testing for significant statistical differences between groups and significant statistical relationships between variables.
III. Describing Data Through Summary Statistics
  A. The data that comprise a relatively large data set must be condensed in some way to make sense of them.

1. The data is condensed to a numerical indicator that best summarizes the data set, called a **summary statistic**, which is an efficient way to describe an entire set of quantitative data.
B. Researchers seek a summary statistic that provides the "typical" point in a data set, the best representation.
   1. **Measures of central tendency (representative values)**:
      (a) Each is a summary statistic that identifies the center point of an **array** of quantitative data.
      (b) **Mode**: The simplest measure of central tendency; indicates which score or value in a distribution occurs most frequently.
         i. Most appropriate for nominal data.
         ii. **Antimode**: Score or value that occurs the least frequently.
         iii. **Bimodal/unimodal distribution**, that is, two modes exist as opposed to one mode.
         iv. **Multimodal distribution**, that is, three or more modes are present.
      (c) **Median**: Divides a distribution of quantitative data exactly in half (locational, positional, or order measure).
         i. Very appropriate for describing the center point of a set of ordinal data and often is effective for describing the center point of interval/ratio data.
         ii. Takes into account the entire set of scores in a distribution.
         iii. Outliers: Extreme scores; median is not swayed.
         iv. The median is not sensitive to changes in the scores that comprise the data set.
      (d) **Mean**: The arithmetic average, computed by adding all the scores in a distribution of interval/ratio data and dividing by the total number of scores.
         i. Most appropriate and effective measure of central tendency of a set of interval/ratio data because it is sensitive to every change in the data; nonresistant to extreme scores.
         ii. **Trimmed means**: Removes the most extreme scores entirely.
         iii. **Winsorizing**: Changes the most extreme scores to the next less extreme scores.
         iv. **Geometric** and **harmonic means** are used for measuring relative change and averaging rates respectively.
         v. The mean most often results in a fractional value.
C. Measures of Dispersion: Simply giving the central tendency summary statistic itself by itself can be misleading.
   1. Measures of central tendency tell us nothing about how the scores in a distribution differ or vary from this representative score.
   2. **Measures of dispersion** (measures of variability) report how much scores vary from each other or how far they are spread around the center point of a data set and across that distribution (several types).
      (a) **Variation ratio**, used only for nominal data;
   3. **Range**: (Span); simplest measure of dispersion, reports the distance between the highest and lowest scores in a distribution.
      (a) Calculated by subtracting the lowest number from the highest number in a distribution (extreme values).

(b) Gives a general sense of how much the data spread out across a distribution (See Figure 11.2).
(c) Knowing the range can also provide a general understanding of how the scores of two groups of people vary.
(d) Nonresistant measure that is overly sensitive to extreme scores; hence, one or two extreme scores make a distribution look more dispersed than it actually is.
(e) To compensate, researchers can divide a distribution at the median and calculate the range of values between the median and the lowest score (lowspread) and the range of scores between the median and the highest score (highspread).
(f) **Interquartile range**: (Quartile deviation or midspread) dividing a distribution at the 25th and 75th percentiles. Dividing the interquartile range in half produces the semi-quartile range. The distribution can also be divided into 10 equal parts, or deciles.
(g) Range and its variations are the only measure of dispersion that can be applied meaningfully to ordinal data, but is limited in describing the amount of dispersion in a set of interval/ratio data.
4. **Variance**: The mathematical index of the average distance of scores in a distribution of interval/ratio data from the mean, in squared units.
   (a) Figure 11.3 shows how variance is calculated for this distribution, using both the definitional formula and an easier computational formula.
   (b) **Deviation score**: Amount that one score differs from the mean (deviate or error score).
   (c) Sum of squares: Adding the squared deviation scores cumulatively.
   (d) A variance score is confusing because it is expressed in units of squared deviations about the mean, which are not the same as the original unit of measurement.
   (e) **Standard Deviation (SD)**: A measure of dispersion that explains how much scores in a set of interval/ratio data vary from the mean, expressed in the original unit of measurement.
      i. SD is found by taking the square root of the variance; that is, the number that when multiplied by itself equals the variance.
      ii. The mean and standard deviation are the measures of central tendency and dispersion reported most frequently by researchers when analyzing interval/ratio data; they are often reported in a table, which is helpful when scores for different conditions or groups of people are compared (See Figure 11.4).

IV. Describing Data in Standard Scores
  A. **Standard score/standard normal deviates**: Researchers often report how many standard deviations a particular score is above or below the mean of its distribution.
  1. *Standard scores* provide a common unit of measurement that indicates how far any particular score is away from its mean.
     (a) **Z-score**: Standard score used frequently by researchers; the formula says that it can be computed for any score in a distribution by dividing its deviation score by the standard deviation for the distribution.
        i. Researchers can meaningfully interpret an individual score within a distribution by showing how many standard deviations it is away from the mean of that distribution.

(b) **Deviation-IQ scale**: One of the best known examples of using standard scores; used with many group-administered intelligence tests.
2. Another use of standard scores has to do with the fact that different people sometimes do not use the same measurement scale in the same way (See Figure 11.5).
3. Even though the same (valid and reliable) measurement scale may be used, relying on raw scores may not tell the whole story about the data; for this reason, some researchers first convert raw scores into standard scores, or even transformed standard scores.
   (a) **Raw/unstandardized scores**: Data kept in their original unit of measurement and not converted to standard scores.
4. Standard scores also allow comparisons between scores on different types of scales for the same individual or for different people.
5. Standard scores actually allow comparisons between different people's scores on different types of measurements (See Figure 11.6).
6. Converting scores on a measurement scale to standard scores that measure how far away they are from the mean of their distribution is an important tool for describing data.

V. Describing Data Through Visual Displays
  A. Researchers, educators, and other professionals often use tables, figures, graphs, and other forms to visually display distributions of data.
    1. These highlight important information in the data and/or make complex data more understandable.
    2. To construct visual displays of data and realize their benefits, one must know what types of visual displays are possible, how to construct them, and when to use them.
    3. The choice of which visual display to use is influenced by the type of data one seeks to portray.
  B. Frequency Tables
    1. In one way or another, all visual displays are attempts to describe **frequency distributions**, a tally of the number of times particular values on a measurement scale occur in a data set.
    2. The most basic way is to visually display the absolute frequency of the data obtained, the actual number of times each category or measurement point occurs in a distribution, in a frequency table -- a visual display in table form of the frequency of each category or measurement point on a scale for a distribution of data.
    3. **Relative frequency**: The proportion of times each category or measurement point occurs (found by dividing the number of cases for a particular category or measurement point by the total number of cases for the entire distribution).
    4. **Cumulative frequency (CF)**: The total frequency up to and including any particular category or measurement point (See Figure 11.7).
    6. **Frequency tables** are often used to describe the frequency of occurrence of categories, such as the number of times the categories associated with facilitative and inhibitive factors are mentioned; very effective for highlighting which categories are used most often, and can also be helpful for comparing at a glance the frequency of different

categories for two or more groups (See Figure 11.8).
  7. Frequency tables are also helpful for showing changes over short or long periods of time; however, they are fairly simple drawings and do not rely on such graphics as shaded areas or connected lines.
C. **Pie Charts**: Circles divided into segments proportional to the percentage of the circle that represents the frequency count for each category.
  1. A favorite way of visually presenting information in the popular media (TV, newspapers, and magazines);
  2. Although used infrequently in scholarly research reports, they have been used to provide descriptive information about a research data set (See Figure 11.9);
  3. Pie charts can also be very helpful for visually showing differences between groups (See Figure 11.10).
D. **Bar Charts**: A common and relatively simple visual depiction that use shaded "blocks" (rectangles and/or squares) to show the frequency counts for the groups that comprise a nominal independent variable.
  1. Typically are drawn using vertical blocks; the independent variable groups are presented on the abscissa, the horizontal (X) axis, and the frequency of occurrence on the dependent variable is presented on the ordinate, the vertical (Y) axis
  2. **Horizontal bar charts**: Contains blocks running horizontally from left to right; sometimes are used when the categories have long names or when there are many categories.
  3. Bar charts are especially helpful for visually depicting differences between groups on a variable (See Figure 11.11).
  4. **Grouped/segmented bar charts**: A very common use of bar charts; visually shows differences between the groups formed from the combination of two or more independent variables (See Figure 11.12).
E. **Line Graphs**: Use a single point to represent the frequency count on a dependent variable for each of the groups and then connect these points with a single line.
  1. The simplest type of line graph compares two groups with respect to a dependent variable (See Figure 11.13).
  2. Line graphs are particularly useful for showing changes in groups over two or more points in time (See Figure 11.14).
F. Frequency Histograms and Frequency Polygons
  1. **Frequency histograms**: Like bar graphs, uses blocks to show how frequently each point on an interval/ratio scale occurs; however, because an interval/ratio scale has equal distances between the points on a scale, the blocks touch (See Figure 11.15).
  2. **Frequency polygons**: Similar to line graphs, except that a line connects the points representing the frequency counts for each point on the interval/ratio scale used to measure the independent variable (rather than each group of a nominal independent variable, as in line graphs) (See Figure 11.16).
VI. Conclusion
A. The first step in analyzing a set of data is to understand its characteristics; once determined, it is then possible to go beyond description to infer conclusions about the data.

TEST ITEMS

1. When popular ads about some item only state that 3 out of 4 individuals surveyed endorse that particular product, the advertisers could be engaging in:
   - (A) inferential statistics
   - *(B) statiscalculation
   - (C) descriptive statistics
   - (D) estimation
   - (E) summary statistics

2. _____ statistics provide a synthesis of what the collected data look like in terms of central tendency and variability.
   - (A) inferential
   - (B) statiscalculation
   - (C) descriptive
   - (D) estimation
   - *(E) summary

3. The process of estimation would be most likely to occur in which of the following cases?
   - (A) to ascertain the influence of political debates on college voters, researchers survey 500 students at a Midwestern university
   - (B) to ascertain the effectiveness of a stop smoking campaign on adolescents, researchers interview 30 seventh graders
   - (C) to ascertain the frequency of surfing the Internet to locate research sources, researchers develop a program that tracks the online behavior of one computer programming class
   - (D) to ascertain the impact of hate speech, researchers survey an audience of 50 after a talk by a leader of the Klu Klux Klan
   - *(E) all of the above

4. The most elementary measure of central tendency is the _____ and it is appropriate for analyzing _____ data.
   - *(A) mode and nominal
   - (B) range and ordinal
   - (C) median and interval
   - (D) range and interval
   - (E) variance and ratio

For items 5-6, consider the following.

Sample 1	Sample 2	Sample 3
59	15	86
65	90	79
57	40	94
63	65	90
68	100	83

5. <u>In correct sequence</u>, which measure of central tendency should be used to analyze samples 1, 2, and 3 respectively?
   (A) mean, mode, median
   (B) mean, median, mode
   (C) median, mode, median
   * (D) mean, median, mean
   (E) median, mode, mode

6. Comparing the variances of the samples, we should <u>best</u> conclude that <u>proportionate</u> to the <u>mean's location</u> the variances will be:
   * (A) small, large, and small, respectively
   (B) large, small, and small, respectively
   (C) small, large, and large, respectively
   (D) large, small, and large, respectively
   (E) small, small, and large, respectively

For item 7, consider the following.
Bob has just found out that he scored a 64 on an exam. The total possible points was 100. The mean was 82. The variance was 81. The class distribution demonstrated a normal curve.

7. The standard deviation for this situation is:
   (A) 18
   (B) 14
   (C) 10
   * (D) 9
   (E) 1

8. According to the authors of the text, which measure of central tendency and measure of dispersion are reported most frequently when analyzing ratio/interval data?
   (A) mode and interquartile range
   * (B) mean and standard deviation
   (C) median and range
   (D) mode and standard deviation
   (E) variance and interquartile range

9. According to the authors of the text, standard scores, such as z-scores are useful because they help researchers <u>interpret an individual score</u> by showing the relationship to the _____ and in terms of _____.
   - (A) mode; standard deviation units
   - (B) median; variance units
   - (C) variance; standard deviation units
   - (D) resistant statistic; variance units
   - * (E) mean; standard deviation units

10. To compare Treva's score on the ACT to Norma's score on the SAT, an admission officer must employ:
    - * (A) standard scores
    - (B) ordinal data
    - (C) small medians
    - (D) nominal data
    - (E) large variances

11. All of the following are advantages of frequency tables <u>except</u> that they can be useful for:
    - (A) comparing frequency levels of some categories for multiple groups
    - (B) highlighting which categories are used more often
    - (C) providing a summary of the data collected
    - (D) showing trends over varying time periods
    - * (E) all of the above

12. In a distribution of data, the relative frequency of a category, such as a particular score, is calculated by dividing the number of:
    - * (A) cases residing within a particular category by the total number of cases in the distribution
    - (B) dependent variables by the total number of cases in the distribution
    - (C) nominal variables by the total number of cases in the distribution
    - (D) independent variables by the total number of cases in the distribution
    - (E) cannot answer as more information is needed

13. _____ charts are a popular means by which the media and those in the business world often visually display differences between groups on some variable or category.
    - (A) horizontal bar
    - * (B) pie
    - (C) bar
    - (D) line graph
    - (E) group/segmented bar

14. A _____ chart displays frequency counts for the groups that comprise a nominal independent variable?
* (A) horizontal bar
  (B) pie
  (C) bar
  (D) line graph
  (E) group/segmented bar

15. Histograms are appropriately used when the collected data are:
    (A) nominal and ordinal measurements
    (B) ratio and nominal measurements
    (C) ordinal measurements and uses independent variables
*   (D) ratio and interval measurements
    (E) nominal measurements and use independent variable

True/False

F 16. The word, statistics, comes from the Latin root, staticus, which means that symbols are used to understand the qualitative nature of collected data.
F 17. Inferential statistics are used to construct descriptions about the characteristics of a data set.
T 18. Measures of central tendency describe the center point of a distribution of quantitative data.
T 19. Three measures of central tendency are the mean, median, and mode.
T 20. The mode is the appropriate measure of central tendency for a set of nominal (categorical) data.
F 21. The median is sensitive to extreme scores, or outliers, and, therefore, will be a poor reflection of a data set.
T 22. Measures of dispersion are typically applied to ordinal, interval, and ratio data.
T 23. Standard deviation explains how much scores in a set of interval/ratio data vary from the mean, expressed in the original unit of measurement.
F 24. It is impossible to compare two scores from different distributions through the use of standard scores.
T 25. A frequency distribution reports the number of times particular values on a measurement scale occur in a data set.

Short-Answer/Essay Questions
1. Give five examples of everyday statistics to which people are exposed.
2. Drawing from a current event article that reported a study, support or reject the claim that statistics are inherently intimidating,

misleading, and not worthy of much confidence unless one is a mathematical genius.
3. Explain the difference between descriptive statistical data analysis and inferential statistical data analysis.
4. Define the term "summary statistic."
5. Explain the difference between measures of central tendency and measures of dispersion.
6. Explain the difference between the mode, median, and mean, pointing out when each is the appropriate measure of central tendency.
7. Some people have claimed that "one can't compare apples and oranges." Explain what standard scores are and how they can be used to compare different distributions of data.
8. Describe and briefly evaluate the utility of frequency tables, bar charts, pie charts, and line graphs.
9. Explain when researchers would want to use pie charts, bar charts, and line graphs versus frequency histograms and frequency polygons.

CHAPTER 12: INFERRING FROM DATA: ESTIMATION AND SIGNIFICANCE TESTING

I. Introduction
  A. Often one needs to go beyond the usual descriptions of data acquired from particular people to infer conclusions about a much larger group of people.
  B. **Inferential statistics/inductive statistics**: The set of statistical procedures that allows a researcher to go beyond the group that has been measured, and make statements about the characteristics of a much larger group (two purposes).
    1. **Estimation**: Used to generalize the results obtained from a sample to its parent population.
    2. **Significance testing**: Examines how likely differences between groups and relationships between variables occur by chance.
  C. In this chapter, we first explore estimation and then focus on principles of significance testing that apply to both difference and relationship analysis.
II. Estimation
  A. The size of most populations usually makes it too difficult or impossible to conduct a census, so researchers must study a sample(s) drawn from a targeted population and use the results from that sample to describe the population.
  B. The ultimate purpose for many researchers is to generalize the results found for a sample back to its parent population.
  C. Researchers, therefore, often estimate population characteristics (called **parameters**) on the basis of characteristics found in a sample (called **statistics**).
    1. Estimation procedures are often referred to as parametric statistics. The statistics computed are called estimates and the formulas used to compute estimates are called estimators.
    2. Estimates of population parameters from sample statistics are possible as long as two assumptions are met:
      (a) The variables(s) of interest is assumed to be distributed "normally" in the population being studied.
      (b) A random sample has been selected from that population.
  D. Estimation procedures start with the assumption that scores on the variable(s) of interest in the population being studied are distributed in the shape of a symmetrical bell (Figure 12.1). This type of distribution is called a **normal distribution, normal curve,** or, because of its symmetrical geometric shape, a **bell-shaped curve**.
    1. In a normal distribution, the center point is in the exact middle of the distribution and is the highest point of the curve.
      (a) The center point is the mean, median, and mode of the distribution.
    2. Because of the symmetrical shape of a normal distribution, researchers know the proportion of scores that falls within any particular area of the curve.
    3. In a normal distribution, 34.13% of scores fall in the area between the center point and +1SD (standard deviation), and 34.13% of scores fall between the center point and -1SD. Together, these two areas account for 68.26% of all the scores in a normal distribution.
    4. The curve continues to run on theoretically forever, a curve that runs on, getting ever closer to the line but never touching it is called asymptotic.

5. The normal distribution, thus, tells researchers the relative probability of a score falling in any given area of the curve.
6. Distributions not in the shape of a normal curve can be described using two characteristics.
   (a) **Kurtosis** refers to how pointed or flat is the shape of a distribution of scores.
      i. **Mesokurtic**: The shape of the normal curve, with the center point being the highest peak and the two tails leveling off in a similar way.
      ii. **Leptokurtic/peaked**: A curve that is tall and sharply pointed, with scores clustered around the middle.
      iii. **Platykurtic/flat**: A curve that is flat and more spread out because scores do not cluster around the middle but are dispersed rather evenly across the distribution.
   (b) **Skewness**: The majority of scores are toward one end of a distribution and the curve tails off (becomes pointy, like a skewer) across the rest of the distribution, which creates an asymmetrical distribution
      i. **Positively skewed distribution** occurs when the tail runs to the right side of the curve (Figure 12.2).
      ii. **Negatively skewed distribution** occurs when the tail runs to the left side of the curve.
E. Use of random sampling: The second assumption that informs estimation procedures is the selection of a random sample from the population being studied.
   1. The best assurance of a representative sample is random selection of population members, such that each population member has an equal chance of being selected for the sample.
   2. The reason a random sample is representative of a population is that is probable that if a population is normally distributed on a variable, then a random sample drawn from that population will also be normally distributed on that variable.
   3. **Central Limit Theorem**: "For samples of a sufficiently large size, the real distribution of means is almost always approximately normal. The original variable can have any distribution. It doesn't have to be bell-shaped in the least."
      (a) Larger samples give more accurate results than do smaller samples.
   4. Random samples are where it is at as far as inference is concerned; if researchers ever have to choose between a random and a nonrandom sample, they go with the random sample, even if they have to use a somewhat smaller sample size.
F. Inferring from a random sample to a population
   1. **Sampling Distribution**: Occurs when treating the random sample means as a distribution of data; can also be formed of other values, such as percentages or median scores.
   2. **Standard Error of the Mean (SEm)**: Tells researchers how much these random sample means are likely to differ from the grand mean of the sampling distribution.
   3. Researchers assume that any characteristic normally distributed in a population will also be normally distributed in a random sample selected from that population.
   4. **Confidence Level/Coefficient**: The range of scores needed to cover a given percentage of random sample means; the degree of assurance that an actual mean in a sampling distribution accurately represents the true population mean.
      (a) **Confidence Interval (CI)**: The range of scores of the random sample means (or other statistics) associated with a confidence level.
   5. How confident a researcher is when estimating population parameters from a sampling

distribution depends on the purpose of any particular estimation and the potential consequences of being wrong.
  - (a) The 95% confidence level is an arbitrary level accepted by those in the social sciences.
6. Most researchers use a single random sample to stand for the large number of random samples that should have been selected. That is, they select a random sample, calculate the mean and the standard error of the mean (or other appropriate statistics), and use the mean from that one sample to represent the sampling distribution mean and the standard error of the mean for that one sample to represent the sampling distribution's standard error of the mean.
  - (a) Researchers select a random sample, calculate the mean and SD (or other statistics), move out -1.96SD (standard deviation) and +1.96SD away from the mean so that they are 95% confident, and use that range of scores as the confidence interval or "margin of error."
    - i. **Confidence Limits**: The actual values of the upper and lower limits of a confidence interval.
7. The size of the confidence interval is influenced by three features:
  - (a) The variability that exists on the topic in the population being studied;
  - (b) The confidence level employed;
  - (c) The size of the random sample.
8. There isn't much that can be done about the variability that exists in a population; reducing the size of the confidence interval can be accomplished by decreasing the confidence level.
  - (a) The best way to reduce the size of the confidence interval is to increase the size of the random sample selected.
    - i. **Law of Large Numbers**: The smaller the size of a random sample, the less accurately it approximates a true population parameter.
  - (b) Most researchers rely on much smaller samples and accept larger confidence intervals (or errors) in their population estimates (Figure 12.3).

III. *Significance Testing*: "Significant" meaning "important; momentous."
  A. Significance testing seeks to answer the question, "How is communication variable 'X' related to other variables?" by inferring relationships between variables within a population on the basis of relationships found in a sample selected from that population.
  B. Unlike estimation, not all significance tests assume that the variable(s) being studied is normally distributed in the population of interest.
    1. Significance tests that do assume this are called parametric statistics; significance tests that do not assume this are called **nonparametric statistics** (or **distribution-free statistics**).
  C. Researchers often use a small, nonrandom sample, proceed to test for significant differences and relationships in that sample, and, then, in the discussion section of a journal article, generalize the results to the population
  D. The Logic of Significance Testing
    1. A one-tailed hypothesis about a relationship between variables predicts the direction of the suspected relationship as being either positive (as scores increase on one variable, so

does the other variable) or negative (as scores increase on one variable, the other variable's score decreases).
2. Testing a null hypothesis: Researchers cannot prove a prediction by testing all possible instances in which it might apply--there might be millions; however, if researchers find a situation in which the idea does not work, they know the hypothesis is incorrect.
   (a) **Null hypothesis** (Ho): An implicit statement that underlies every hypothesis and predicts that there is no difference between the groups or no relationship between the variables being studied; represents chance occurrence--that the difference or relationship occurred simply by chance.
   (b) **Significance/hypothesis testing**: The process of analyzing quantitative data for the purpose of testing whether a null hypothesis is probably either correct or false.
      i. On rare occasions, researchers may actually predict no significant difference or relationship, in which case the null hypothesis serves as a research hypothesis.
3. Rejecting a null hypothesis: The point at which the evidence suggests that a researcher can reject a null hypothesis of no difference or no relationship as being false and accept the most likely alternative explanation, the research hypothesis that predicts a difference or relationship.
   (a) The null hypothesis might be false because of one of the threats posed by researchers, the way the study was conducted, or because of the research participants studied.
   (b) If a researcher conducts a study in such a way as to confidently rule out or sufficiently minimize these validity threats, then the most likely explanation for the null hypothesis being false is the suspected difference between the groups or the relationship between the variables predicted by the research hypothesis.
   (c) Conditional probability: Where a preceding occurrence influences a subsequent occurrence.
   (d) Gambler's fallacy: Mistakenly thinking that independent events are conditional.
4. Deciding on the probability level:
   (a) **Significance level**: The probability level (p value) researchers set for rejecting a null hypothesis; establishes a point at which a researcher is confident enough of a statistical difference or relationship to reject a null hypothesis.
   (b) **Decision rule**: The specific significance level set by a researcher for rejecting a null hypothesis prior to conducting a study and analyzing the data.
   (c) In significance testing, the 95% confidence level is referred to as the .05 significance level, which references the probability of the difference or relationship being significant. Researchers set the significance level quite high to minimize reporting a significant difference or relationship that occurs due to chance.
   (d) Medical researchers typically make it much more difficult to reject the null hypothesis by setting the significance level much higher, such as .0001 (see additive error).
   (e) Occasionally, social science researchers use a less stringent significance level, such as .10, which means they are 90% confident of rejecting the null hypothesis; (between .10 and .05 is sometimes considered a trend, or, if very close to .05, marginally significant).

E. The Practice of Significance Testing (three steps):
 1. **Posing a research question or hypothesis and a null hypothesis**: A hypothesis is posed when a researcher has enough evidence from theory, relevant literature, or sometimes logic and/or observations from everyday life to make a prediction.
 2. **Conducting the study**: To investigate the suspected difference between groups or relationship between variables. the population is identified and a random sample size is selected from it.
 3. **Testing the null hypothesis** (entails three items):
    (a) **Setting the significance level**: Most often set at .05;
    (b) **Computing the calculated value**: There are many types of significance-testing procedures, each resulting in a final number, a numerical value called the calculated value. This calculated value is then assessed in terms of the probability of its occurrence.
    (c) **Comparing the calculated value to the critical value** needed to reject the null hypothesis: if the calculated value has a 5% or less probability of occurrence by chance, the researcher can reject the null hypothesis; if more that 5%, must accept.
      i. Researchers can assess the probability of obtaining the calculated value they found for the data analyzed from any particular study by constructing a table for each statistical significance test.
      ii. This is done by first locating the critical value that corresponds to the .05 significance level needed to reject the hypothesis.
      iii. Running down the side of the table are what are called **degrees of freedom**, the number of scores that are "free to vary."
      iv. If the calculated value does not reach the critical value it falls into the **region of acceptance** and the null hypothesis of no difference or no relationship is accepted; if the calculated value reaches or exceeds the critical value, it falls into the **region of rejection/critical region**.
      v. When degrees of freedom are tied to sample size, the larger the degrees of freedom, the smaller the critical value needed for rejecting the null hypothesis.
      vi. The critical value needed for accepting/rejecting a null hypothesis also depends on whether a *one-tailed hypothesis*, *two-tailed hypothesis*, or *research question* is posed (Figure 12.4).
      vii. **NS** is often used to signify a result that is not [statistically] significant.
F. Type I and Type II Error
 1. There are two kinds of decision errors researchers might make when employing significance testing:
    (a) **Type I error (alpha error)** occurs when researchers reject a null hypothesis and accept a research hypothesis when, in fact, the null hypothesis is probably true and should have been accepted.
    (b) **Type II error (beta error)** is exactly the opposite, and occurs when researchers accept a null hypothesis when, in fact, it is probably false and thereby, reject a sound research hypothesis.
    (c) As Figure 12.5 reveals, there are two correct and two incorrect decisions that can

be made concerning significance testing.
- (d) The chance of committing a Type I error is easy to calculate; it is equal to the significance level employed.
    - i. If multiple tests are made, sum the significance levels (e.g., .05 + .05 + .05 = .15); and these are called **familywise error** or **experimenter error**.
- (e) Type II error is far too complex to be explained here as there are numerous factors that affect its calculation.

G. Statistical Power
1. This factor affects the strength of inferences about significant differences and relationships.
    - (a) **Statistical power** estimates the probability of rejecting a null hypothesis that is, in fact, probably false and should be rejected.
    - (b) Statistical power calculates, before conducting a study, the number of participants needed to have a reasonable chance of rejecting the null hypothesis.
    - (c) Statistical power is equal to 1 minus the probability of committing a Type II error (failing to reject a false null hypothesis).
        - i. The range of statistical power, then, is from a minimum of 0 to a maximum of 1.0
        - ii. Authorities generally agree that statistical power should be set at .80.

IV. Conclusion

A. We explored how researchers infer from a relatively small sample to its parent population. Inferring in this way certainly is not limited to research; it's a common feature of everyday life.

TEST ITEMS

1. Which statistical process allows researchers to extend their findings from a sample to the population.
   - (A) difference analysis
   - (B) parameter identification
   - * (C) estimation
   - (D) relationship analysis
   - (E) significance testing

2. Rank order the following terms from <u>largest to smallest</u>.
   - (A) sample, census, population
   - (B) census, sample, population
   - (C) population, census, sample
   - * (D) census, population, sample
   - (E) sample, population, census

For item 3, consider the following.
(i) Edward has just learned that he scored 81 on an examination out of a possible total of 100 points.
(ii) The distribution of the class scores was normal with a mean of 72 and a variance of 81.

3. Using the standard deviation, Edward should know that he scored similar to _____ of the class.
   - (A) 2.14%
   - (B) 13.59%
   - * (C) 68.26%
   - (D) 88.44%
   - (E) 98.72%

4. According to the Central Limits Theorem, and assuming a normal distribution of data, we should expect the mean, median, and mode to be:
   - * (A) identical
   - (B) negatively skewed
   - (C) relatively small
   - (D) positively skewed
   - (E) relatively large

5. If a distribution of data is normally distributed, its shape should be _____.
    (A)   negatively skewed
*   (B)   mesokurtic
    (C)   leptokurtic
    (D)   positively skewed
    (E)   platykurtic

For item 6, consider the following.
(i) A group of five researchers obtains the <u>complete list</u> of enrolled seniors from the registrar at a local community college.
(ii) They then use a <u>computer-generated numbers table</u> to <u>arbitrarily assign</u> them identification numbers.
(iii) Participants are then selected for the study based on their <u>otherwise meaningless identification number</u> and every senior has <u>an equal chance of being chosen</u> to take part in the study.

6. According to the authors of the text, the preceding techniques, i-iii, <u>best</u> assure obtaining a:
    (A)   large sample
    (B)   sample with unclear parameters
    (C)   sample ideally suited for applying descriptive statistics
*   (D)   representative sample
    (E)   cannot answer as more information is needed

7. Which of the following reports the degree of assurance that a sample mean accurately represents the true population mean from which the sample was selected?
    (A)   coefficient level
    (B)   skewness level
*   (C)   confidence level
    (D)   kurtosis level
    (E)   standard error of the mean level

8. According to the authors of the text, which of the following confidence levels is accepted as "the standard" by many researchers in the social sciences?
    (A)   100%
*   (B)   95%
    (C)   90%
    (D)   85%
    (E)   80%

9. When calculating the size of a confidence interval for a particular study, all of the following should be considered except:
   (A) sample size
   (B) confidence level used
   (C) topic variability level among the population
   * (D) the sample's standard deviation
   (E) all of the above should be considered

10. In concert with the Law of Large Numbers, which of the following is true?
    (A) as sample size decreases, measurement accuracy of population parameters increases
    (B) sample sizes of 10-35 are ideal for most statistical tests
    (C) sample sizes of 40-65 are ideal for most statistical tests
    (D) as population size decreases, measurement of sample parameters increases
    * (E) as sample size increases, measurement accuracy of population parameters increases

For item 11, consider the following.
Prior to conducting a study examining television viewing frequency and receptivity to certain advertisements, two researchers conclude that the variables to be studied will reflect an abnormal distribution.

11. For the purpose of significance testing, according to the authors of the text, these researchers should primarily use:
    (A) descriptive statistics
    (B) parametric statistics
    (C) summary statistics
    * (D) nonparametric statistics
    (E) cannot answer as more information is needed

For items 12-13, consider the following.

The International Brotherhood Of Electrical Workers has commissioned you to do a study. The details follow.

i. You will be examining the roles of in-service training, productivity, and job burnout among 750 electricians from four different countries.
ii. You will conduct in-depth interviews and administer questionnaires.
iii. You are exploring the idea that the amount of in-service training (INST) is related to productivity (PRO) level and job burnout (JBURN).
iv. You also believe that monthly INST is associated with a low amount of JBURN.

12. According to statement iii, the relationship between INST and PRO is best described as:
    - (A) hypothetical
    * (B) nondirectional
    - (C) decreasing in complexity
    - (D) directional
    - (E) increasing in complexity

13. According to statement iv, the relationship between INST and JBURN is best described as:
    - (A) hypothetical
    - (B) nondirectional
    - (C) decreasing in complexity
    * (D) directional
    - (E) increasing in complexity

14. When a research team agrees to establish the significance level at .10, they are stating that:
    - (A) they are ten percent confident of rejecting the null hypothesis
    - (B) they are ten percent confident of failing to reject the null hypothesis
    * (C) they are 90 percent confident of rejecting the null hypothesis
    - (D) they are 90 percent confident of failing to reject the null hypothesis
    - (E) cannot answer as more information is needed

For item 15, consider the following.
After computing the calculated value for a significance test (equals 4.58), a researcher compares it to the critical value (equals 2.68) needed.

15. On the basis of this comparison, the best conclusion is to:
    - (A) fail to reject the null hypothesis
    * (B) reject the null hypothesis
    - (C) repeat the study
    - (D) gather more data
    - (E) none of the above

True/False

T 16. Significance testing examines how likely differences between groups and relationships between variables occur by chance.

T 17. On the basis of statistical theory, assuming a normal distribution of the data, we should expect that 68.26% of the collected scores will reside within +/- 1 standard deviation of the mean.

F 18. If a person's score on some variable, such as IQ, is +2.75 standard deviations from the mean, he or she would be considered an average student.

F 19. The extent to which a data set exemplifies skewness and kurtosis is irrelevant

T	20.	to the confidence researchers place in the results from a study. The confidence level is the degree of assurance that an actual mean accurately represents population mean.
T	21.	The confidence limits is also known as the "margin of error" or "sampling error."
F	22.	Researchers typically seek to prove the research hypothesis.
F	23.	After statistically analyzing the data, if a researcher obtains a calculated value of 4.56 and compares it the critical value of 6.50, he or she should fail to reject the null hypothesis.
T	24.	Type I error occurs when researchers reject a null hypothesis and accept a research hypothesis when, in fact, the null hypothesis is probably true and should have been accepted.
F	25.	If an effect size is small, the findings are not important.

Short-Answer/Essay Questions
1. Identify and explain the two purposes of inferential statistics.
2. One assumption underlying estimation procedures is that scores on the variable of interest in the population being studied are distributed in the shape of a normal curve. Explain this principle and discuss whether you believe that this assumption is valid.
3. Discuss why random selection of population members is the best assurance of obtaining a representative sample.
4. Define the terms "confidence level," and "confidence limits," and explain how they are related.
5. Define the term "statistically significant."
6. Explain how the logic of testing a null hypothesis is similar to the way a defendant (the accused) is treated in a criminal trial.
7. Explain under what research conditions the .05 significance level might need to be lowered or raised.
8. Walk through the significance testing processes, explaining the various steps in which researchers must engage to reject a null hypothesis.
9. Explain the difference between Type I Error and Type II Error, and identify one way in which each type of error may be lowered.

CHAPTER 13: ANALYZING DIFFERENCES BETWEEN GROUPS

I. Introduction
   A. While we don't always celebrate differences, we certainly seem fascinated by them.
   B. There are many important differences in types of data that can be analyzed; in each case, we would want to ask whether the difference is statistically significant; that is, whether the difference occurs by chance so rarely that the results are probably due to the real difference that exists.
   C. In this chapter, we focus on statistical procedures used in communication research to analyze such differences.

II. Types of Difference Analysis
   A. Difference analysis examines differences between the categories of an independent variable that has been measured using discrete categories as on a nominal scale.
      1. For example, difference analysis is used to see whether there are differences between or among groups of people or types of texts.
      2. In each case, the independent variable is measured using a nominal scale and the research question or hypothesis is about the differences between the nominal categories with respect to some other variable; the dependent variable may be measured using a nominal, ordinal, interval, or ratio scale.
         (a) The particular type of procedure used to determine whether the differences between the categories of the nominal independent variable are statistically significant depend on how the dependent variable is measured (See Figure 13.1).
   B. The Nature of Nominal Data
      1. The **Chi-square (χ^2) test** examines differences between the categories of an independent variable with respect to a dependent variable measured on a nominal scale; there are two types of chi-square tests.
         (a) A **one-variable chi-square test** (also known as a **one-way/single-sample chi-square test**): assesses the statistical significance of differences in the distribution of the categories of a single nominal independent or dependent variable.
            i. This statistical test begins by noting the frequencies of occurrence for each category, called the **observed frequencies**; researchers then calculate the **expected frequencies** (also called the **theoretical frequencies**) for each category (See Figure 13.2).
            ii. When both the observed and expected frequencies have been noted, the chi-square calculated value is found by subtracting the expected frequency for each category/cell from the observed frequency, squaring this figure, and dividing by the expected frequency. The resulting figures for each category/cell are then added together to obtain the calculated value.
            iii. The degrees of freedom are equal to the number of categories minus one.
         (b) A **two-variable chi-square test** (also called **contingency table analysis, cross tabulation, multiple-sample chi-square test, two-way chi-square test**) examines differences in the distributions of the categories created from two or more nominal independent variables or a nominal independent and dependent

variable.
2. It can be used to compare differences among the categories created from two nominal independent variables with regard to a nominal dependent variable, or to compare differences among the categories of a nominal independent variable with regard to the categories of a nominal dependent variable.
   i. Researchers are interested in assessing differences among the distributions of the categories of two nominal variables of interest (See Figure 13.3)..
   ii. The two-variable chi-square test is also used to assess differences between the categories of one nominal independent variable that constitute different groups of people and the categories of a nominal dependent variable.

C. The Nature of Ordinal Data
1. Ordinal measurements not only categorize variables but also rank them along a dimension.
2. Most analyses of data acquired from groups measured on an ordinal dependent variable use relationship analysis to see whether two sets of ordinal measurements are related to one another.
3. Sometimes researchers examine whether there are significant differences between two groups of people with respect to how they rank a particular variable.
   (a) The **median test** (See Figure 13.4) is a statistical procedure used to analyze these data; the raw scores for all respondents are listed together, and the median is then calculated.
      i. The total number of scores in each of the two groups that fall above and below the median are determined and these are placed in a table that has the two groups as rows and the ratings above the grand median and below the grand median as the columns.
   (b) The **Mann-Whitney U-test** is used to analyze differences between two groups especially when the data are badly skewed.
   (c) The **Kruskal-Wallis test** is used to analyze differences between three or more groups.
   (d) The **Wilcoxon signed-rank test** is employed in the case of related scores, and can be used to examine differences between the rank scores.

D. The Nature of Interval/Ratio Data
1. When the dependent variable is measured on an interval or ratio scale, the statistical procedures assess differences between group means and variances (See Chapter 11).
2. A significant difference tends to exist when there is both a large difference between the groups and comparatively little variation among the research participants within each group.
3. There are two types of difference analysis employed to assess differences between groups with respect to an interval/ratio dependent variable.
4. t Test: used by researchers to examine differences between two groups measured on an interval/ratio dependent variable. Only two groups can be studied at a single time (Two types):
   (a) Independent-Sample t test: examines differences between two independent (different) groups; may be natural ones or ones created by researchers (Figure 13.5).

(b) Related-Measures t Test (matched-sample or paired t test): examines differences between two sets of related measurements; most frequently used to examine whether there is a difference in two measurements.
5. Analysis of Variance (ANOVA or F test): used when three or more groups or related measurements are compared (avoids additive error)
   (a) One-variable analysis of variance (one-way analysis of variance): examines differences between two or more groups on a dependent interval/ratio variable.
   (b) Repeated-measures of analysis of variance: examines whether there are differences between the measurement time periods.
   (c) Figure 13.6
   (d) Formula for one-variable ANOVA says that an F value is a ratio of the variance among groups (MSb), also called systematic variance, to the variance within groups (MSw), also called random variance.
   (e) ANOVA tells researchers if the difference among the groups is sufficiently greater than the differences within the groups to warrant a claim of a statistically significant difference among the groups.
   (f) ANOVA is an omnibus test, an overall statistical test that tells researchers whether there is any significant difference(s) that exist among the groups of related measurements.
   (g) Researchers use a multiple comparison test as a follow-up procedure to pinpoint the significant difference(s) that exists:
      i. Scheffe Test
      ii. Tukey Test
      iii. Least Significant Difference
      iv. Bonferroni technique
   (h) Factorial analysis of variance: used when researchers examine differences between the conditions created by two or more nominal independence variables with regard to a single interval/ratio dependent variable; all factorial ANOVAs yield two types of F values.
      i. Main effects: refers to the overall effects of each independent variable.
      ii. Interaction effects: refers to the unique combination of the independent variables.
      iii. When there are two independent variables, a factorial analysis of variance yields three F values; when there are three independent variables, a factorial analysis yields seven F values.
      iv. It is possible that a factorial ANOVA may reveal a significant main effect but no significant interaction effect (the reverse is also possible)
      v. Ordinal interaction: an interaction that, when plotted on a graph, the lines representing the two variables do not intersect.
      vi. Disordinal interaction: an interaction in which the lines cross.
III. Advanced Difference Analysis
A. There exist many additional and more complex significance tests for analyzing differences between groups.
   1. Multivariate analysis: statistical procedures, which examine three or more independent

      variables and/or two or more dependent variables at the same time.
    2. Figure 13.7 explains the purpose of some of these advanced difference analyses and illustrates how each has been used to study communication behavior.
IV. Conclusion
 A. To know whether groups of people or texts are significantly different, researchers use the statistical procedures discussed in this chapter. All of these procedures result in a numerical value(s) that indicates how often the observed difference is likely to occur by chance or error.
 B. A finding that is very unlikely to occur by chance is assumed to be due to the actual difference that exists.

TEST ITEMS

<u>For items 1-2, consider the following.</u>
Three researchers seek to ascertain if the 1999 *Vital Speeches of the Day* focused more on campaign reform strategies than those appearing in the 1998 issues. They count up the number of times campaign reforms strategies were mentioned in each year.

1. The variable, campaign reform strategies, is <u>best</u> operationalized as a/an _____ variable.
   - (A) ratio
   - (B) ordinal
   - (C) interval
   - (D) confounding
   - * (E) nominal

2. Given the way the variable(s) were measured, which of the following would be the correct statistical test to use to analyze the data?
   - (A) two-variable Chi-Square test
   - (B) median test
   - * (C) one-variable Chi-Square test
   - (D) t-test
   - (E) Mann Whitney U-test

<u>For item 3, consider the following.</u>
Bruess and Pearson (1997), in their study of the types of rituals performed in marital and adult friendship dyads, identified four idiosyncratic/symbolic rituals: favorites, private codes, play rituals, and celebration rituals. They reported that 129 of these were observed during the study.

3. In line with the null hypothesis, the number of expected frequencies for each category of the Chi-Square test is _____; the degrees of freedom for this test are ____.
   - (A) 125 and 4
   - (B) 43.25 and 3
   - * (C) 32.25 and 3
   - (D) 29 and 3
   - (E) 29.25 and 4

For item 4, consider the following.
A public health researcher wants to know if there is a statistically significant difference between individuals who smoke and those who do not with respect to the perceived effectiveness of a smoking cessation promotion campaign that uses Public Service Announcements (PSAs). Smokers and non-smokers review the various PSAs and then report a score from 0-100. After compiling the data, the researcher notices that there is a high number of scores toward the lower end, or close to zero.

4. To best analyze this data, the researcher should use a:
    (A) two-variable Chi-Square test
*   (B) median test
    (C) one-variable Chi-Square test
    (D) t-test
    (E) Mann Whitney U-test

For items 5-7, consider the following
(i) A corporation is very concerned about the devastating impacts of sexual harassment. The management team hires an outside consultant to design and implement workshops to address the problem. The consultant decides to first pilot test a workshop used by other companies with a sample of 20 males and 20 females. After completing the trial workshop, participants fill out a questionnaire measuring their understanding of and sensitivity to sexual harassment. Scores can range from 1-100. (ii) After computing the calculated value for the appropriate significance test (equals 14.77), a researcher compares it to the critical value (equals 1.68), with accompanying degrees of freedom for the statistical test.

5. To best analyze this data, the consultant should use a:
    (A) two-variable Chi-Square test
    (B) median test
    (C) one-variable Chi-Square test
*   (D) t-test
    (E) Mann Whitney U-test

6. For this situation, the degrees of freedom would be:
    (A) 140
    (B) 100
    (C) 40
    (D) 39
*   (E) 38

7. After comparing the calculated value to the critical value (see statement ii), the best conclusion is to:
   (A) fail to reject the null hypothesis
   * (B) reject the null hypothesis
   (C) repeat the study
   (D) gather more data
   (E) none of the above

For items 8-10, consider the following.
(i) A group of researchers seeks to ascertain if first-born, middle-born, and last-born children in North America will report varying levels of verbal aggressiveness (VAG); sample one.
(ii) In a later study, using different individuals across the three categories above, they examine VAG and interaction involvement (IAINV); sample two.
(iii) Both samples are comprised of 150 individuals, with 50 in each group. The questionnaire scores, drawn from five-point Likert scales, are compared.
(iv) After computing the calculated value for the appropriate significance test (equals 3.00), the researchers compare it to the critical value (equals 3.00), with accompanying degrees of freedom for the statistical test.

8. To best analyze the data obtained in sample one (statement i), the researchers should use a:
   * (A) one-way analysis of variance
   (B) two-variable Chi-Square test
   (C) factorial analysis of variance
   (D) t-test
   (E) Mann Whitney U-test

9. The "between groups degrees of freedom" are ___ and the "within groups degrees of freedom" are ___.
   (A) 3, 150
   (B) 2, 149
   (C) 3, 149
   * (D) 2, 147
   (E) 2, 150

10. After comparing calculated value to the critical value (see statement ii), the best conclusion is to:
    (A) fail to reject the null hypothesis
    * (B) reject the null hypothesis
    (C) repeat the study
    (D) gather more data
    (E) none of the above

11. The variance among different groups is also called _____ ; the variance within groups is also called _____.
   (A) random and systematic
   (B) sum of squares and random
   * (C) systematic and random
   (D) random and sum of squares
   (E) cannot answer as more information is needed

For item 12, consider the following.
You decide to study the effects of computer-assisted learning on student achievement. Over a six-month period, at two-month intervals, you have the students evaluate the <u>effectiveness of the instruction</u> and report their <u>level of satisfaction</u> with assignment grades. These dependent variables are measured with Likert-type scales.

12. To <u>best</u> analyze the data obtained in the study, you should use a:
   (A) one-way analysis of variance
   (B) two-variable Chi-Square test
   (C) factorial analysis of variance
   (D) t-test
   * (E) repeated-measures analysis of variance

13. According to the authors of the text, the <u>primary</u> purpose of a post hoc comparison when conducting difference analysis is to:
   (A) reconsider failing to reject the null hypothesis
   (B) revisit the composition of the different research participant groups
   (C) reexamine the size of the mean square compared to the grand mean
   * (D) pinpoint the specific, statistically significant difference that exists between/among groups
   (E) reconsider the nature of the research design

14. In factorial analysis of variance, the overall effect of the independent variables is called _____ effects; the combined effect of independent variables is called _____ effects.
   (A) interaction; main
   (B) omnibus; interaction
   * (C) main; interaction
   (D) multiple-variable F; main
   (E) cannot answer as more information is needed

15. Within a study using a factorial analysis of variance, which of the following is true?
* (A) statistical significance may be obtained for a main effect, but not for an interaction effect
  (B) statistical significance may not be obtained for a main effect, but it may be obtained for an interaction effect
  (C) the null hypothesis may fail to be rejected for a main effect, but it may be rejected for an interaction effect
  (D) Tukey's Honestly Significant Difference Test may be used for a main effect, but not for an interaction effect
  (E) cannot answer as more information is needed

True/False

T 16. Difference analysis examines statistical distinctions between the categories of an independent variable that has been measured using discrete categories.
T 17. The specific difference analysis test employed depends on how the dependent variable is measured.
T 18. The one-variable chi-square test examines differences in the distribution of the categories of a single nominal independent or dependent variable.
F 19. After analyzing collected data using the chi-square procedures, if a researcher obtains a calculated value of 19.56 and compares it the critical value of 12.550, he or she should fail to reject the null hypothesis.
F 20. A t-test is used to measure differences between two groups measured on an ordinal dependent variable.
T 21. If a researcher examines suspected differences between two groups of students, with each group having 50 members, the degrees of freedom are 98.
T 22. Researchers most often use a related-measures t-test to examine whether there is a difference between a pretest and posttest.
F 23. One-way analysis of variance examines the differences between two or more groups on a dependent variable measured via a nominal or ordinal scale.
F 24. "Bad" variance means could be thought of as the differences within groups that increase the possibility of alternate causality.
F 25. Multiple comparison tests, such as the Bonferroni technique, lessen the chance of observing a statistically significant difference between groups.

Short-Answer/Essay Questions

1. Explain when a researcher would use a one-variable chi-square test versus a two-variable chi-square test.
2. Explicate the procedures for conducting a two-variable chi-square test. Be sure to discuss how to obtain observed and expected frequencies, row and column totals, how the calculated value is derived, and the degrees of freedom.

3. Explain the difference between an independent-sample t test and a related-measures t test and give an example of a study where an independent-sample t test would be used and an example of a study where a related-measures t test would be used.
4. Explain when a researcher would want to use an analysis of variance procedure as opposed to a t test.
5. Discuss the logic that underlies a one-variable analysis of variance with respect to the variance between groups versus the variance within groups. Make sure to explain what these variance need to be (e.g., low or high) to find significant differences between groups.
6. Explain the purpose of a "multiple comparison test" as a follow-up to an analysis of variance procedure.
7. Explain how it is possible that a factorial analysis of variance (ANOVA) may reveal a significant interaction effect, but no significant main effects, and give a hypothetical example to illustrate this possibility.
8. Match the examples given below with the following significance test that would be most appropriate to use: (A) One-variable chi-square; (B) two-variable chi-square; (C) t test; (D) one-variable analysis of variance; (E) Factorial analysis of variance.
   1) Examining the differences between U.S. Americans, Asians, and Europeans with regard to the number of hours of television watched per week;
   2) Examining the differences between male and female U.S. Americans, Asians, and Europeans with regard to the number of hours of television watched per week;
   3) Examining the differences between males and females with regard to the number of hours of television watched per week.
   4) Examining the differences between males' and females' choice of comedy or drama television programs
   5) Examining the differences between people's choice of comedy or drama television programs.
   Answers: 1 = D 2 = E 3 = C 4 = B 5 = A
9. Identify one advanced difference analysis and explain why it would be used.

CHAPTER 14: ANALYZING RELATIONSHIPS BETWEEN VARIABLES

I. Introduction
   A. This chapter examines how two or more variables may be related: It starts by considering the relationship between two variables (**bivariate association**) and then expands to consider more variables.
   B. The chapter examines the types of possible relationships between variables, explains how relationships are analyzed statistically, shows how relationship analysis is used to make predictions, and introduces some advanced statistical relationship analyses used in communication research.

II. Types of Relationships
   A. A **scatter plot (scattergram** or **scatter diagram)** is a visual image of the ways in which variables may or may not be related.
   B. Two variables can be associated in one of three ways: unrelated, linear, or nonlinear.
      1. **Unrelated variables** have no systematic relationship; changes in one variable simply are not related to the changes in the other variable.
      2. **Linear relationships** between variables can generally be represented and explained by a straight line on a scatter plot.
         (a) There are two types of linear relationships: positive and negative
            i. **Positive relationship**: Two variables move, or change, in the *same* direction.
            ii. **Negative relationship**: Two variables move in opposite directions.
      3. **Nonlinear relationships** between variables can be represented and explained by a line on a scatter plot that is not straight, but curved in some way.
         (a) A **curvilinear relationship** is described by a polynomial equation, which means that it takes at least one curve, or turn, to represent the data on a scatter plot.
            i. A **quadratic relationship** is a curvilinear relationship that has only one curve in it, while cubic, quartic, and quintic relationships describe even more complex relationships between variables.
               a. A **U-shaped curvilinear relationship** means that two variables are related negatively until a certain point and then are related positively.
               b. An **inverted U-shaped curvilinear relationship** means that two variables are related positively to a certain point and then are related negatively.

III. Correlations: Statistical relationships between variables
   A. A statistical relationship between variables is referred to as a **correlation**
      1. A correlation between two variables is sometimes called a **simple correlation**.
      2. The term **measure of association** is sometimes used to refer to any statistic that expresses the degree of relationship between variables.
      3. The term **correlation ratio (eta)** is sometimes used to refer to a correlation between variables that have a curvilinear relationship.
   B. To determine the statistical correlation between two variables, researchers calculate a *correlation coefficient* and a *coefficient of determination*.
      1. Correlation coefficient: A **correlation coefficient** is a numerical summary of the type and strength of a relationship between variables.

(a) A correlation coefficient takes the form: rab = +/-x, where r stands for the correlation coefficient, a and b represent the two variables being correlated, the plus or minus sign indicates the direction of the relationship between the variables (positive and negative, respectively), and x stands for some numerical value.
  i. The first part is the sign (+ or -), which indicates the *direction* (positive or negative) of the relationship between the variables of interest.
  ii. The second part is a numerical value that indicates the *strength* of the relationship between the variable; this number is expressed as a decimal value that ranges from +1.00 (a perfect positive relationship) to -1.00 (a perfect negative relationship). A correlation coefficient of 0.00 means two variables are unrelated, at least in a linear manner.
(b) Interpreting correlation coefficients: interpreting the importance of or strength of a correlation coefficient depends on many things, including the purpose and use of the research and sample size.
(c) Calculating correlation coefficients: Researchers use a variety of statistical procedures to calculate correlation coefficients between two variables, depending on how the two variables are measured.
  i. Relationships between ratio/interval variables can be assessed in the following ways.
    a. The **Pearson product moment correlation** calculates a correlation coefficient for two variables that are measured on a ratio or interval scale.
    b. The **point biserial correlation (rpb)** is used when researchers measure one variable using a ratio/interval scale and the other variable using a nominal scale.
  ii. Relationships between ordinal variables can be assessed in the following ways.
    a. The **Spearman rho correlation** can be used to compare two sets of ranked scores for the same group of research participants, or the ranked scores of various items by two different groups might be compared.
    b. **Kendall's correlation (tau)**, which refers to three measures of association and is used in lieu of a Spearman rho correlation coefficient, typically when a researcher has a pair of ranks for each of several individuals.
  iii. The procedures for computing a correlation coefficient between nominal variables, such as **Cramer's V**, are based on the chi-square value associated with the two-variable chi-square test (see Chapter 13).
(d) Correlation matrices: A **correlation matrix** lists all the relevant variables across the top and down the left side of a matrix where the respective rows and columns meet, researchers indicate the **bivariate correlation coefficient** for those two variables and whether it is significant by using stars (such as one star for significance at the .05 level) or in a note that accompanies the matrix.
(e) Causation and correlation: Correlation is one of the criteria used to determine causation, but causation cannot necessarily be inferred from a correlation coefficient.
  i. Researchers can sometimes use the sequencing of events in time to infer causation.
  ii. Two variables may also be correlated, but their relationship is not necessarily meaningful.
2. Coefficient of Determination: A **coefficient of determination** (r-squared) is a numerical

indicator that tells how much of the variance in one variable is associated, explained, or determined by another variable.
   i. A coefficient of determination rages from 0.00 to 1.00 and is found by squaring the correlation coefficient.
   ii. Researchers must pay careful attention to the correlation of determination when interpreting the results of the correlation coefficients found in their studies.
3. Multiple correlation: A **multiple correlation** is computed when researchers want to assess the relationship between the variable they wish to explain, the **criterion variable**, and two or more other independent variables working together; and the procedure yields two types of statistics:
   (a) A **multiple correlation coefficient (R)** is just like a correlation coefficient, except that it tells researchers how two or more variables *working together* are related to the criterion variable of interest.
      i. A multiple correlation coefficient indicates both the direction and the strength of the relationship between a criterion variable and the other variables.
      ii. Takes the form Ra.b.x = +/-x, read "The multiple correlation of variables b and c with variable a (the criterion variable is . . . ."
   (b) A **coefficient of multiple determination (R-squared**, R2) expresses the amount of variance in the criterion variable that can be explained by the other variables acting together; it is computed by squaring the multiple correlation coefficient.
      i. The **coefficient of nondetermination** is that part of the variance in the criterion variable that is left unexplained by the independent variables, symbolized and calculated as 1-R2.
4. Partial Correlation: A **partial correlation** explains the relationship between two variables while statistically controlling for the influence of one or more other variables (sometimes called **effects analysis** or **elaboration**).
   (a) A partial correlation coefficient takes the form rab.c = +/-x, read, "The partial correlation coefficient between variable a and variable b with variable c controlled for is . . . . ."
   (b) A **First-order partial correlation** controls for one other variable; **higher-order partial correlation** controls for two or more variables; **zero-order correlation** is a correlation between two variables with no variable being controlled.
   (c) A **semi-partial correlation** partials out a variable from one of the other variables being correlated.
      i. A semi-partial correlation coefficient takes the form ra(b.c) = +/-x, read, "The semipartial correlation coefficient of variables a and b after variable c has been partialed out from variable b is . . . . "
IV. Regression Analysis
A. Used to *predict or explain* how people are likely to score on a criterion, or outcome variable on the basis of their scores on another variable, called a **predictor variable** (also called a **regression**).
B. Statistical procedures used to make such predictions are referred to as **regression analysis**.
C. **Linear regression (simple regression)**: used to predict or explain scores on a criterion

variable on the basis of obtained scores on a predictor variable and knowledge of the relationship between the two variables.
1. The **regression line (line of best fit)** is denoted by a straight line through the data on a scatter plot.
2. Regression analysis is accomplished by constructing a **regression equation** (also called a **prediction equation** or **regression model**), which is an algebraic equation expressing the relationship between variables.
   (a) The typical regression equation for two variables is: y = a + bc, where y is the criterion variable, a is the intercept, b is the slope, and x is the predictor variable.
      i. The **intercept** is how far up the y-axis the regression line crosses it.
      ii. The **slope** denotes how many units the variable Y is increasing for every unit increase in X; it depends on the correlation between the two variables.
   (b) A **regression coefficient**, which is part of a regression equation, is a statistical measure of the relationship between the variables (a **bivariate regression coefficient** references two variables).
   (c) Significance tests are applied to a regression equation to determine whether the predicted variance is significant.
   (d) The extent to which any model or equation, such as a regression line, summarizes or "fits" the data is referred to as the **goodness of fit**.
C. Multiple linear regression: allows researchers to predict or explain scores on a criterion variable on the basis of obtained scores on two or more predictor variables and knowledge of the relationships among all the variables.
1. There are different ways to do multiple linear regression with respect to how the predictor variables are entered into the regression analysis to see how much variance they explain in the criterion variable.
   (a) **Hierarchical regression analysis**: the researcher determines, on the basis of previous theory and research, the order of the variables entered into the regression equation.
   (b) **Stepwise regression**: the computer is instructed to enter the predictor variables in various combinations and orders until a "best" equation is found.
2.. Multiple linear regression provides researchers with at least three important pieces of information:
   (a) A *multiple correlation coefficient* (R) that tells researchers the relationship between the criterion variable and all the predictor variables.
   (b) A *coefficient of multiple determination* (R2) that expresses the amount of variance in the criterion variable that can be explained by the predictor variables acting together.
      i. An **adjusted R2 (*R2)** takes into account the number of independent variables studied.
   (c) How much each of the predictor variables contributes toward explaining the criterion variable by providing a *regression coefficient*, a **beta coefficient** (often called a **beta weight**, **regression weight**, or sometimes standardized regression coefficient), that indicates the extent to which, or relative weight

that, each predictor variable contributes to explaining the scores on the criterion variable, while controlling for the other predictor variable.
3. Researchers must be aware of the potential problem of **collinearity (or multicollinearity)**, the extent to which the predictor variables are correlated with one another.
   (a) A correlation between independent/predictor variables is called an **intercorrelation**, as compared to a correlation between an independent/predictor and dependent/criterion variable.
4. Because multiple linear regression assesses the relationships between numerous predictor variables and a criterion variable, researchers frequently use this procedure to capture the complexity of events, including communication processes, called **polynomial regression analysis** (or **curvilinear regression**).

V. Advanced Relationship Analysis
  A. There are more complex multivariate analytic procedures that assess relationships among three or more variables (see Figure 14.8).
   1. **Canonical correlation analysis (Rc)** is a form of regression analysis used to examine the relationship between multiple independent and dependent variables.
   2. **Path analysis** examines hypothesized relationships among multiple variables (usually independent, mediating, and dependent) for the purpose of helping to establish causal connections and inferences by showing the "paths" the causal influences take.
   3. **Discriminant analysis** is a form of regression analysis that classifies, or discriminates, individuals on the basis of their scores on two or more ratio/interval independent variables into the categories of a nominal dependent variable.
   4. **Factor analysis** examines whether a large number of variables can be reduced to a smaller number of factors (a set of variables).
   5. **Cluster analysis** explains whether multiple variables or elements are similar enough to be placed together into meaningful groups or clusters that have not been predetermined by the researcher.
   6. **Multidimensional scaling (MDS)** plots variables or elements in two or more dimensions to see the statistical similarities and differences between and among them

VI. Conclusion
  A. Like the relationships that exist between people, relationships between variables range from positive to neutral to negative.
  B. Relationships among variables quickly become numerous and complex, especially when the goal is to make a prediction about something.
  C. Caution must be exercised about the difference between correlation and causation; researchers and readers of research must be careful interpreting statistical relationships between variables.

TEST ITEMS

1. Spano and Zimmerman (1995) finding that communication competence did not make a statistically significant difference during simulated hiring interviews, with regard to intent to hire, indicates these variables have a/an _____ relationship.
    - (A) negative
    - *(B) unrelated
    - (C) related
    - (D) linear
    - (E) positive

2. After analyzing some data that you have collected, you find that as Internet use increases, face-to-face communication eagerness decreases, which means there is a/an _____ relationship between these variables.
    - *(A) negative
    - (B) unrelated
    - (C) related
    - (D) linear
    - (E) positive

For item 3, consider the following.
(i) A study investigates the relationship among political campaign volunteerism, willingness to work in public service organizations, and the narratives individuals use to describe their interaction with potential voters.
(ii) The results reveal that individuals who <u>volunteered many hours</u> told <u>positive stories</u> about their experiences with prospective supporters.
(iii) The results reveal that individuals who <u>volunteered few hours</u> told <u>positive stories</u> about their experiences with prospective supporters.
(iv) The results reveal that individuals who <u>volunteered a moderate amount of hours</u> told <u>negative stories</u> about their experiences with prospective supporters.

3. Statements ii-iv demonstrate a/an _____ relationship between the variables studied.
    - (A) inverted U-shaped curvilinear
    - *(B) U-shaped curvilinear
    - (C) negative
    - (D) linear
    - (E) positive

4. When evaluating the intensity of a correlation coefficient, its range can be from:
   (A) +5.0 to -5.0
   (B) +4.0 to -4.0
   (C) +3.0 to -3.0
   (D) +2.0 to -2.0
 * (E) +1.0 to -1.0

5. According to Guilford's (1956) guidelines, when interpreting a statistically significant correlation coefficient, a level of .56 reveals a:
   (A) slight, almost negligible relationship
   (B) definite but small relationship
 * (C) substantial relationship
   (D) marked relationship
   (E) very dependable relationship

6. According to the authors of the text, it is appropriate to use a point biserial correlation when the two variables are measured using a/an:
 * (A) ratio/interval scale and nominal scale, respectively
   (B) ordinal scale and nominal scale, respectively
   (C) two nominal scales and ratio scales, respectively
   (D) nominal scale and ordinal scale, respectively
   (E) cannot answer as more information is needed

For items 7-9, consider the following.
(i) A researcher believes there is a positive relationship between communication style and relationship satisfaction among young adults. A questionnaire is administered using Likert-type scales. The scores can range from 36-180 for both variables (with 36 representing the "high" level). One hundred and twenty individuals participate in the study with 60 being males and 60 females.
(ii) After performing the necessary calculations, the analysis yields a .68 bivariate correlation/relationship, and .890 for the calculated value. The researcher compares the calculated value to the critical value (equals .514), with accompanying degrees of freedom for that statistical test.

7. To best analyze this data, the researcher should use a:
   (A) biserial point correlation
   (B) one-way analysis of variance
   (C) Spearman rho correlation
   (D) factorial analysis of variance
 * (E) Pearson product moment correlation

225

8. For this situation, the degrees of freedom would be:
   (A) 180
   (B) 178
   (C) 120
   * (D) 118
   (E) 98

9. Based on the comparison between the calculated and critical values, the best conclusion is to:
   (A) fail to reject the null hypothesis
   * (B) reject the null hypothesis
   (C) repeat the study
   (D) gather more data
   (E) none of the above

For items 10-12, consider the following.
(i) A group of researchers seeks to ascertain whether South Africans and New Zealanders use similar strategies to terminate romantic relationships. One hundred individuals from each country are sampled. They are presented with a series of scenarios and then asked to write how they would communicate in that situation to end the relationship.
(ii) The data analysis categorizes the responses and then ranks them in terms of highest to lowest occurring.
(iii) After performing the necessary statistical analysis, the researcher finds a .42 for the bivariate relationship, and .765 for the calculated value. The researcher compares the calculated value to critical value, .802, with accompanying degrees of freedom for that statistical test.

10. To best analyze this data, the researcher should use a:
    (A) biserial point correlation
    (B) one-way analysis of variance
    * (C) Spearman rho correlation
    (D) factorial analysis of variance
    (E) Pearson product moment correlation

11. For this situation, the degrees of freedom would be:
    (A) 200
    (B) 199
    * (C) 198
    (D) 100
    (E) 98

226

12. After comparing the calculated value to the critical value, the best conclusion is to:
* (A) fail to reject the null hypothesis
  (B) reject the null hypothesis
  (C) repeat the study
  (D) gather more data
  (E) none of the above

13. Which of the following should be calculated and used to ascertain the extent to which the change in one variable influences the change in another variable?
* (A) coefficient of determination
  (B) coefficient of reliability
  (C) biserial point correlation coefficient
  (D) Pearson product moment correlation coefficient
  (E) path coefficient

14. Which of the following best describes linear regression?
  (A) four or more predictor variables are used to explain the scores on a criterion variable
  (B) two predictor variables are used to explain the scores on a criterion variable
* (C) one predictor variable is used to explain the scores on a criterion variable
  (D) slopes represent the correlation among multiple predictor variables
  (E) y-intercepts represent the correlation among multiple criterion variables

15. All of the following are examples of advanced relationship analysis except:
  (A) canonical correlation analysis
  (B) path analysis
  (C) discriminant analysis
  (D) factor analysis
* (E) all of the above are examples

True/False
F 16. There are three types of statistical relationships between variables: linear, nonlinear, and monlinear.
F 17. If two variables change in opposite directions, their relationship is deemed linear and positive.
T 18. A curvilinear relationship means that there is at least one curve, or turn, in the data when they are viewed on a scatterplot.
T 19. A correlation coefficient is a numerical summary of the type and strength of a relationship between variables.

F. 20. A coefficient of determination indicates how much knowledge of one variable can be used to predict another variable.
F   21. The Pearson product moment correlation tests the strength of a relationship between two variables that are measured on a nominal or ordinal scale.
F   22. Correlation equals causation.
T   23. Multiple correlations assess relationships between a criterion variable and two or more independent variables working together.
F   24. A zero-order correlation is an association between two variables with no variable being controlled.
T   25. Regression analysis is used to predict or explain how people are likely to score on a criterion, or outcome, variable on the basis of their scores on a predictor variable.

Short-Answer/Essay Questions
1. Explain the difference between unrelated, linear, and nonlinear relationships. In your answer, show how each relationship would look on a scatter plot.
2. Explain the difference between a positive and a negative relationship and give a common, everyday example for each type of relationship.
3. The statistical analysis of a relationship between variables is called a _____; its range is from _____ to _____
   Answers: Correlation, +1.00, -1.00
4. A +.80 relationship between communication competence and relational satisfaction means that there is a _____ relationship between these variables, such that as communication competence _____, relational satisfaction _____.
   Answers: positive, increases, increases
5. Explain and give an example of when it would be best to use the Pearson product moment correlation.
6. Support or refute the statement that correlation does not necessarily equal causation.
7. Explain what squaring the correlation coefficient tells researchers.
8. Identify the basic purpose of regression analysis and explain what researchers need to know in order to conduct effect regression analysis.
9. Identify one advanced relationship analysis and explain when it would be used.

CHAPTER 15 EPILOGUE: CONCLUDING RESEARCH

I Introduction
   A. Research studies are cyclical: Each ends by returning to the issues introduced at the start, ideally with greater understanding.
      1. Reports of research thus follow an "Hourglass" shape.
   B. This chapter focuses on the expansive phase that completes the research process; in particular, when researchers return to broader issues that are at the heart of the concluding the "so what?" portion of a research project.
   C. This chapter is concerned with the reconceptualization that occurs when researchers rethink the topic of inquiry as a result of the systematic processes associated with conceptualization, planning and designing research, using methodologies to gather data, analyzing the data, and, finally, interpreting research findings.

II. Discussing Research Findings
   A. In the final section of a research article ("Discussion" or Conclusion"), researchers expound on the findings and place what they found in a larger context.
   B. Interpreting the meaning of research findings
      1. **Substantive significance** describes the theoretical and/or practical significance of the findings.
         (a) Figure 15.1 illustrates the case of statistical vs. practical significance, the question of whether a research finding can be put to good use.
      2. Relating findings to theory: To describe the larger meaning of the results, researchers often relate findings to theory, previous research, and expectations, and explain how the findings may be applied in relevant contexts.
         (a) Many research studies are theory-based; attempts to disprove a concise statement that purports to explain a wide range of human behavior.
         (b) If the findings from the theory-based study are consistent with the theory, the validity of that theory is strengthened.
         (c) Some researchers conduct research with the expressed purpose of revising a theory so that it accounts for a wider range of phenomena.
         (d) Sometimes researchers compare two theories that appear to be contradictory or mutually exclusive, and their findings are used to lend support to one theory or the other.
         (e) Finally, some communication research is oriented toward the development of new theories.
      3. Relating findings to previous research: research is a cooperative enterprise; researchers attempt to interrelate their study with what others have done and, thereby, build on others' work.
         (a) If the results of two or more studies are consistent, the strength of both studies is bolstered.
         (b) Comparisons to findings from other studies can also help researchers to explain their own findings.
         (c) When researchers' results are inconsistent with the studies of others, the discrepancy

must be explained.
4. Relating findings to expectations: after analyzing the data collected for a study, researchers occasionally obtain results that are *surprising or contradict their expectations*. When that happens, they attempt to offer an explanation or a rationale that takes these unanticipated findings into account.
   (a) In still other cases, the findings actually run counter to researchers' expectations and necessitate some explanation.
   (b) In the most extreme case, the results are so startling that they force researchers to completely reconsider their original expectations.
   (c) Finally, even if the findings of a study are as expected and consistent with prior research, more than one conclusion may be drawn from them; legitimately, the same research findings can be interpreted differently.
   (d) Researchers must consider alternative explanations for their results.
5. Applying findings: Researchers tend to suggest *practical uses* for their findings in the discussion section, and, thereby, explore the implications that their results may have for how others can operate more effectively.
   (a) Ideally, the findings would be beneficial to all.
   (b) Ideally, the findings would be specific to setting, issue, and people.
   (c) Perhaps the group that benefits the most from practical suggestions that researchers offer are practitioners, those who apply the knowledge researchers produce.
   (d) Much communication research is directed toward studying the media, and the findings from such research often lead scholars to make recommendations to those who work in the media.
   (e) Many communication practitioners are involved in various types of communication campaigns, such as health promotion campaigns, and researchers will assess the relative effectiveness of these campaigns and suggest modifications in the intervention programs.
   (f) Finally, communication researchers sometimes point out important implications their findings have for public policy.
6. Identifying limitations of the research: Researcher discuss the limitations or flaws in their studies (sometimes a separate subsection, entitled, "Limitations").
   (a) Limitations due to internal validity threats: When research is plagued by the internal validity threats, little confidence in the conclusions is warranted.
   (b) Researchers assess the internal validity of their findings in a number of ways:
      i. reporting any limitations or flaws in the study's design;
      ii. revealing problems or limitations with the methodological procedures researchers used;
      iii. pointing out shortcomings in the measurement techniques used to gather data for their study and how these might potentially limit or jeopardize the findings;
      iv. explaining the shortcomings of self-report methods;
      v. speculating whether any unobserved or intervening variables may have confounded the results.
7. Limitations due to external validity threats: Most research is externally limited in some way,

so conscientious researchers identify the context-bound limitations of their results (people, texts, events).
   (a) Many internally valid conclusions drawn from communication studies are not necessarily generalizable.
      i. Sampling procedures involve the way in which the subset of the population is studied and selected.
   (b) Many communication researchers do sample from "real-world" populations, but this does not necessarily solve the problem of acquiring representative samples.
   (c) Some samples are better than others.
   (d) Similar types of problems occur in the sampling of texts for textual analysis; the representativeness of the texts selected may be called into question.
      i. Analysts work with relatively unidentified texts in terms of who produced them, which raises concerns about their representativeness.
   (e) Sometimes research is externally limited because of the particular event or point in time studied.
   (f) Ecological validity is the extent to which the procedures mirror real-life situations.
      i. Ecologically invalid procedures may lead people to distort their behavior, overemphasizing things they typically would not do, or suppressing their normal ways of behaving.
   (g) Replication is based on researcher awareness that a single study does not "prove" anything; indeed, many studies need to be conducted before a conclusion can be fully accepted. Thus, researchers urge that the findings from their study be replicated.
 B. In suggesting directions for further research and that more research needs to be done, researchers often seek to:
   1. advance follow-up research questions or hypotheses;
   2. explain new or refined methodological procedures;
   3. transfer findings from laboratory experiments to the "real world;"
   4. extend the explanatory range of the findings;
   5. propose new topics;
 C. The mission of research is fulfilled in three essential steps by:
   (a) making a contribution to the reservoir of communication knowledge that scholars, professionals, and the general public can call on to explain, understand, and potentially influence communication events;
   (b) identifying important limitations that need to be kept in mind about the research findings;
   (c) raising meaningful new questions for future communication researchers to pursue; serves a heuristic function of encouraging future investigation.

III. Conclusion
 A. Doing research is a challenging endeavor.
 B. Knowledge is power.
 C. Through your own research efforts, you can discover, and pass along to the generation of students that will follow you, new information about what now is unknown about communication. In doing so, you will enrich their lives as countless researchers have enriched your life.

TEST ITEMS

1. According to the authors of the text, researchers usually begin the Discussion section of an article by explaining the _____ significance of the results.
   * (A) substantive
   (B) statistical
   (C) underlying
   (D) numerical
   (E) cannot answer as more information is needed

2. Observing that the findings from a study for a hypothesis <u>are statistically significant, but lacking in practical significance,</u> you should <u>primarily</u> conclude that the finding is:
   (A) reliable and important
   (B) potentially important but not reliable
   * (C) reliable but not important
   (D) neither reliable or important
   (E) so tentative that more data should be collected

3. On the basis of conducting a study that confirmed two hypotheses testing Uncertainty Reduction Theory among Japanese and American cultures, the researchers conclude that the theory should be:
   (A) elevated to the status of a universal law
   * (B) deemed as having merit, awaiting further confirmation
   (C) rejected by the scientific community
   (D) seen as true since its propositions had been proven to be true
   (E) deemed as having mixed merit since the results lacked definitiveness

4. According to the authors of the text, and in the absence of other information, when a theory is disconfirmed, a chief implication is that the:
   (A) hypotheses were vague
   (B) operationalizations were faulty
   (C) conceptualizations were overly broad
   * (D) reconceptualization of the theory might be necessary
   (E) research questions were overly narrow

5. According to the authors of the text, in the area of theory building and testing, some research seeks to:
   * (A) expand the explanatory scope of a theory
   (B) limit the explanatory scope of a theory through triangulation
   (C) emphasize practical instead of statistical significance
   (D) expand operationalizations of concepts to test a theory
   (E) emphasize statistical instead of practical significance

6. According to the conventions of scientific research, if unexpected findings are obtained within a study, the researcher(s) should:
   (A) wait a brief period and then conduct the study again with the same sample
   * (B) advance tentative explanations and draw from past research to support these explanations
   (C) wait a lengthy period and then conduct the study with the same sample
   (D) advocate others to join in a scientific revolution to help discard the examined theory
   (E) cannot answer as more information is needed

7. A research team discussing whether a study that was plagued by several internal validity threats be included in the literature review should <u>best</u> conclude that the findings are:
   (A) important and reliable
   * (B) suspect and warrant little serious consideration
   (C) theoretically-rich
   (D) indicative of a sound research design
   (E) generalizable

For item 8, consider the following.
(i) Three researchers conduct a content analysis of articles published by two national periodicals, *Time* and *Newsweek*, from January 1, 1998 to January 1, 1999. These periodicals were chosen as they were readily available to the researchers.
(ii) Twenty articles or short features, ten from each source, examine the ways in which the Japanese culture is portrayed and then linked to U.S. American corporate practices.
(iii) The researchers then report that their findings are not statistically significant.

8. These researchers should acknowledge sample size and methodological procedures used to select the texts as limitations <u>primarily</u> because:
   (A) internal validity has been lowered to some extent
   (B) some ability to detect significant findings may have been lost
   (C) representativeness appears to be an issue since the examined periodicals were chosen on the basis of ease of access
   (D) external validity has been lowered to some extent
   * (E) all of the above

9. Although it is impossible to anticipate every pitfall that a study could confront, care must still be exercised since <u>unobserved variables</u> can:
   (A) increase the external validity of the study's findings
   (B) increase the accuracy of the study's measurement techniques
   * (C) confound the results and their significance
   (D) increase the likely success of recommended action steps
   (E) cannot answer as more information is needed

10. When researchers issue a call for additional research to confirm their findings prior to full acceptance, they are primarily concerned about:
*
    (A) replication and external validity
    (B) securing additional funding sources and internal validity
    (C) quantitative research being preferred over qualitative research
    (D) self-report data-collection instruments confounding the results and their significance
    (E) none of the above

11. In reviewing a large body of published literature, the authors of the text concluded that one of the following types of sample occurred at alarming rates:
    (A) convenience samples of blue-collar workers
    (B) network samples of breast cancer survivors
*
    (C) convenience samples of college sophomores
    (D) network samples of white-collar employees
    (E) purposive samples of college faculty

12. If researchers select the *New York Times, Washington Post, Los Angeles Times,* and the *San Francisco Chronicle* to content analyze stories about new religious movements, the results will most likely be:
*
    (A) low in external validity due to poor representativeness
    (B) generalizable to the East and West coasts only
    (C) high in external validity due to excellent representativeness
    (D) generalizable to television news shows such as *20-20*
    (E) cannot answer as more information is needed

For item 13, consider the following.
(i) A researcher seeks to ascertain whether a videotape about stress reduction and teamwork is effective with middle-aged executives.
(ii) One hundred and ten executives view the videotape in a plush theater with stadium seating (large expansive chairs).
(iii) One hundred and ten executives view a videotape about the city in which the study takes place (control group).
(iv) The findings reveal that the executives in ii reported statistically significant, lowered stress levels and a heightened willingness to participate in work teams.

13. Despite the statistical significance reported in iv, item ii suggests these results may be misleading in that _____ is at issue here.
    (A) internal validity
*
    (B) ecological validity
    (C) sample size
    (D) measurement accuracy
    (E) cannot answer as more information is needed

234

14. When researchers address directions for future research, all of the following could be included except:
    (A) follow-up research questions
    (B) follow-up hypotheses
    (C) refined methodological procedures
    (D) extending the explanatory range of the findings
* (E) all of the above

15. The heuristic function of research primarily seeks to promote:
    (A) dissemination of findings to scholars
    (B) dissemination of findings to the general public
* (C) additional research
    (D) dissemination of findings to professional groups, such as physicians
    (E) none of the above

True/False

T 16. In many ways, the discussion section of a research article is the most important part of the written study, for it gives researchers the opportunity to discuss, and readers the chance to learn about, the larger meaning of the study in terms of the conclusions that can be drawn.

F 17. Researchers typically address three things in the discussion section of a research article: (a) interpret the meaning or significance of the research findings, (b) identify limitations of the study, and (c) critique other researchers' suggestions for future research.

F 18. If a study's findings lack statistical and practical significance, such results are considered important but unreliable.

T 19. Researchers can legitimately interpret the same results differently.

F 20. Researchers should never attempt to suggest practical uses for their findings; that should be left to practitioners.

T 21. It is incumbent on researchers to identify the limitations of their own study, rather than waiting for other researchers to identify them.

T 22. Virtually every sample employed by researchers is limited in terms of generalizability.

F 23. Discussing the ecological validity of a research study is very important for identifying the internal validity threats to a study.

F 24. The principle of replication reinforces the view that a single study proves an underlying theory.

T 25. One of the most important outcome of research is the generation of more research questions.

Short-Answer/Essay Questions
1. Explain the importance of the reconceptualization phase of a research study.
2. Identify the three things that researchers typically examine in the discussion section of a research article.
   ANSWERS: (a) interpret the meaning or significance of the research findings; (b) identify limitations of the study; and (c) suggest directions for future research
3. Explain the implications for the reliability and importance of research findings when one does and does not have practical significance and/or statistical significance.
4. Explain some of the choices researchers have when they discover that the findings obtained from a study do not support the theory being used.
5. Using the findings from your class project, suggest one or two practical uses to which these findings could be put.
6. Using your class research project, describe some of its limitations with regard to the potential internal and external validity threats that may have affected it.
7. Define the acronym "**MRNTBD**."
8. Using your class research project, suggest one concrete direction for future research in that area.
9. Support or refute the statement that perhaps the most important outcome of research is the generation of more research questions.

NOTES

NOTES

NOTES

NOTES

NOTES

NOTES

NOTES

NOTES

NOTES

NOTES

NOTES

NOTES